THE TEN-RUPEE
JEZAIL

By the same authors

Patrick Macrory
BORDERLINE
SIGNAL CATASTROPHE
(reprinted as KABUL CATASTROPHE)
LADY SALE
THE SIEGE OF DERRY
DAYS THAT ARE GONE

George Pottinger
THE WINNING COUNTER
MUIRFIELD AND THE HONOURABLE COMPANY
ST MORITZ; AN ALPINE CAPRICE
THE COURT OF THE MEDICI
THE SECRETARIES OF STATE FOR SCOTLAND, 1926–76
WHISKY SOUR
THE AFGHAN CONNECTION
MAYO, DISRAELI'S VICEROY

THE TEN-RUPEE JEZAIL

Figures in the First Afghan War
1838–1842

GEORGE POTTINGER AND
PATRICK MACRORY

> A scrimmage in a Border Station –
> A canter down some dark defile –
> Two thousand pounds of education
> Drops to a ten-rupee *jezail* –
> The Crammer's boast, the Squadron's pride,
> Shot like a rabbit in a ride!
>
> RUDYARD KIPLING
> 'Arithmetic on the Fronter'

MICHAEL RUSSELL

© George Pottinger, Patrick Macrory 1993

First published in Great Britain 1993
by Michael Russell (Publishing) Ltd
Wilby Hall, Wilby, Norwich NR16 2JP

Typeset at The Spartan Press Ltd,
Lymington, Hampshire
Printed and bound in Great Britain
by Biddles Ltd, Guildford and King's Lynn

All rights reserved
ISBN 0 85955 185 7

Contents

	Introduction	7
1	The Grand Military Promenade	11
2	Sikundar Barnes	17
3	The Other Eden	61
4	*Châteaux en Espagne*	82
5	He Rode upon a Razor	100
6	Fighting Bob and the Petticoat Grenadier	121
7	Through the Khyber	155
8	The Unpatronised Soldier	188
9	'Our Lord Palmerston'	214
	Sources	233
	Index	235

Introduction

In the autumn of 1839 London society danced to a galop called 'The Storming of Ghuznee' written to celebrate the capture of the Afghan fortress which was hailed as the first military success of the new Queen's reign. Five years later the audience at Astley's Circus was still being treated to a spectacular version of the campaign. But there was a heated public debate about the justification for, and the conduct of, the First Afghan War.

The Whigs supported the invasion across the Indus; the Tories opposed it. Palmerston was convinced that the expedition was essential; Wellington thought the whole business was a monstrous blunder. D'Israeli made political capital out of the Whigs' discomfiture. Pamphleteers were active on both sides.

Today the Afghan War is remembered as an appalling defeat for British arms, the worst by an Asian enemy until Singapore fell to the Japanese a hundred years later. In Sir John Kaye's words, 'the awful completeness, the sublime unity' of the Afghan debacle was on a scale to dwarf individual activities. The inexorable progress from triumph to catastrophe, followed by retribution, has all the elements of Greek, or at least Jacobean, tragedy, but the temptation to dramatise has been resisted. It is sufficient to let events speak for themselves.

For no wars are made up of unrelieved disaster, and the incursion into Afghanistan is more easily understood when seen through the eyes of those who took part. There is no substitute for the letters and despatches of the officers who penned their activities and reactions from their tents, or even from camel panniers.

The principal characters identified in this book have two things in common. They were marked for life by their participation in the campaign, and at many stages they had an influential effect on it. Although they belonged to a hierarchy, their personal qualities make them stand out in high relief. Many demonstrated military skill and courage, but contemporary opinion often appeared to dwell at more length on their shortcomings, and for the most part they did not get the recognition they deserved. They have been selected because they exemplify different aspects, in sequence, of the war.

Sir Alexander Burnes, earlier acclaimed as an explorer, made the initial reconnaissance, but he was murdered in Kabul before receiving the preferment he wanted. The romantic Major D'Arcy Todd, sent on an impossible mission, was demoted and dismissed from the political service before he died in action. Captain Colin Mackenzie was greeted as a hero for his perilous embassies from the enemy camp, but his later years were marked by monotonous frustration. Conversely, General Sale, sword always in hand, blundered his way to acquire more prestige than he deserved. General Pollock, the real hero, made history by forcing the Khyber, but was at odds with his superiors. Pollock's opposite number, the irascible General Nott, held Kandahar at a crucial time, but was thought too vehement for his own, or anyone else's, good. Sir William Macnaghten, scholarly, brave but refusing to recognise the impending disaster, the architect of the march to Kabul, provides an epilogue.

The two ladies who appear offer a complete contrast to the military men, and to each other. Emily Eden, Lord Auckland's sister, was his most intimate confidante. Emily is still known as an artist and novelist, but her letters, which show how reports of the hostilities were received within the Governor-General's close circle, also reveal how little she understood the real import of the Afghan affray.

Florentia, the wife of General Sale, is of a different stamp. The diary which she kept during the Kabul siege, the retreat, and her captivity, provides a vivid, at times almost unbearable, picture of the privations the *memsahibs* endured. She also displays a keener sense of the significance of what was happening than most of the men around her.

Within the kaleidoscope, careers before, and after, the campaign are touched upon to set the figures in the round, to indicate how their characters had developed before they were sucked into the Afghan maelstrom, and to indicate how they were affected.

Exploits in Afghanistan produced letters, journals and

memoirs in surprising profusion, surprising in that they survived. The Governor-Generals' private and official papers have been indexed. Public demand and rows in Parliament led to the printing of records in more detail than was the normal practice at the time. Sir John Kaye's *History of the War*, in two volumes and over 1,300 pages, appeared in 1851, and in recent years there have been Macrory's *Signal Catastrophe* (later republished as *Kabul Catastrophe*) and J. A. Norris's admirable and scholarly *The First Afghan War*. Anyone who writes about this 'insane enterprise' has a rich quarry of material.

In addition to those sources, Major Charles W. de L. fforde has generously made available the unpublished memoirs of Captain Charles Wilbraham Ford, who served at Kandahar. Major D'Arcy Todd's account of his journey from Herat to Simla, from which extracts are quoted, has been published only in the *Journal of the Asiatic Society of Bengal* (Calcutta, 1844).

We are grateful to Angus I. Macnaghten, Catherine Macnaghten, Sir Patrick Macnaghten, Dr Brian Trainor of the Ulster Historical Foundation, the staff of the Linenhall Library, Belfast, Cambridge University Library, the India Office Library, the London Library, and the other institutions where we have undertaken research. Lastly, it is a pleasure to acknowledge the assistance of many friends who have helped with their criticism and forbearance.

Retreat from Kabul to Jalalabad

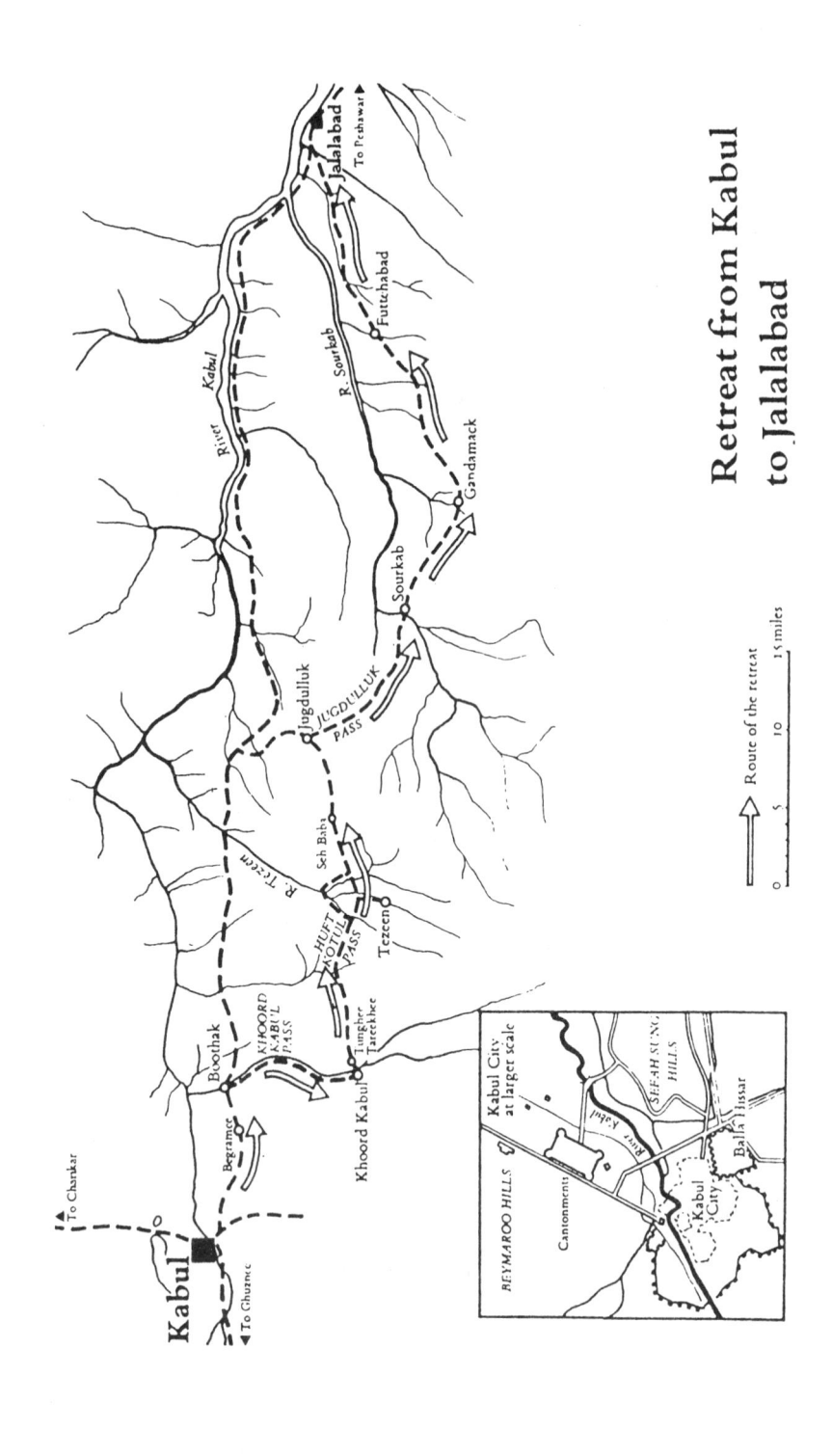

I
The Grand Military Promenade

The First Afghan War began in the autumn of 1838, when the Governor-General of India launched the Army of the Indus on its march into Afghanistan. After successes more superficial than lasting, Kabul was occupied. But the promenade, which started with pennants unfurled and bands playing, was not the jaunt that had been expected. Arid deserts, treacherous mountain passes that afforded cover to the tribesmen with their long jezails, and a dreadful commissariat system, all took their toll before the army encamped in Kabul in August 1839. Two years later the Afghans rebelled and forced the British to retreat from the capital. Apart from a handful of prisoners and hostages, the entire army was massacred in the course of a week, and only one European reached the safety of Jalalabad.

British prestige had to be restored. In 1842 the Army of Retribution – in two divisions, one starting from Peshawar, and the other breaking out from Kandahar – retook Kabul. The Afghans were routed. The British carried out some ritual destruction and withdrew across the Indus, leaving Afghanistan as it had been. The odd thing was that the real enemy, the Russians, had never been met.

In England there were many who thought that the war was incredible in its origins, inept in its execution, and disastrous in its consequences. Lord Auckland, the Governor-General when the expedition was mounted, was denounced for his bad judgement. Ironically, he was not by nature an expansionist. He went out to India in 1835 full of ideas for peaceful, liberal reforms. Before sailing for India he had declared that he 'looked with exultation to the new prospects opening out before him, affording him an opportunity of doing good to his fellow-creatures, of promoting education and knowledge, of improving the administration of justice in India, of extending the blessings of good government and happiness to millions of Indians', and we need not doubt his sincerity. But such advice as he took from his closest advisers – his secretary, the Ulsterman and oriental scholar William Macnaghten, two ambitious young civilians, John Colvin and Henry Torrens, and his sister Emily who was always at his side – proved singularly unfortunate. On 1 October 1838 he issued the notorious Simla Manifesto setting out his justification for the war that followed. A former Governor-General, Lord William Bentinck, could not believe it. 'What? Lord Auckland and Macnaghten gone to war? The very last men I would have expected of such folly.'

Lord Ellenborough succeeded as Governor-General in February 1842. By then Pollock's Army of Retribution, authorised by Auckland, had started on its way. The garrison at Jalalabad was relieved in April, and eventually, after much swithering on the new Governor-General's part, the Afghans were defeated and Kabul reoccupied before the final British withdrawal. Ellenborough in turn was heavily criticised for his indecision, his pomposity, and his lack of concern for the British prisoners. Auckland had behaved very differently. 'You will consider it *one of the first objects of your solicitude*', he had told Pollock, 'to procure the release of British officers and soldiers, and their families, private soldiers and followers.' There were (unsuccessful) attempts in Parliament to oppose the vote of thanks to Ellenborough for his services.

It would not, however, be altogether fair to make these two 'suns of glory', the Governors-General, the scapegoats. In the light of events in Europe in the early years of the nineteenth century the Afghan War, or at least a war fought in Afghanistan, was probably inevitable. The British had long suspected the French of having designs on India, but these fears had receded after the defeat of Napoleon. Then Russia was cast as the potential aggressor in the minds of Her Majesty's ministers at Westminster and of the Supreme Government of India. The British and Russians had for some time been edging towards each other. By the 1830s the British knew that some day they would have to establish a permanent presence in the Punjab and Sind, while the Russians, who had defeated Turkey and Persia, were looking in the direction of Khiva and Bokhara. Between the Indus and the Oxus lay Afghanistan. It was accordingly thought essential that, if the Persians were amenable to the Russians, they must be balanced by an Afghan régime friendly to the British. Given this theory, very prevalent in Calcutta, and Lord Palmerston's long-term machinations to contain the Russians in Europe, Auckland found ready support in England, extending at times to pressure, for a move into Afghanistan.

The question was which, if any, Afghan ruler would be willing to welcome the British. The two principal descendants of the Afghan royal line, the Suddozyes and the Barukszyes, had been feuding merrily with each other for the last fifty years. Shah Soojah, the Suddozye chief, had been evicted from the throne of Kabul by the Barukzye, Dost Mahomed, and had for years languished on a modest British pension at Ludhiana. But the important province of Herat was still ruled by Soojah's nephew, the Suddozye Shah Kamran, who was under threat from Persia. To add to the confusion, in 1834 the Maharajah Runjeet Singh, the ruler of the Sikhs, had seized Peshawar, which had long been an Afghan city and which Dost Mahomed believed was his. The Sikhs were the object of the Dost's special hatred, but they had a treaty with the British dating from 1809. It was all very complicated.

In November 1836 Auckland sent a promising young Company's officer, Alexander Burnes, on a mission to the court of Dost Mahomed. Ostensibly his task was commercial, but his real business was to spy out the land and report on the disposition of the Dost. Burnes consistently recommended an alliance with the Dost, and the Afghan ruler showed him signs of friendship. Others in Auckland's counsels thought differently, and the Governor-General came down in favour of replacing the Dost by Soojah. Auckland was aware that any expedition would have to be mounted through Runjeet Singh's territory, and that ruled out any understanding with Runjeet's enemy Dost Mahomed. The Maharajah obligingly agreed to take a token part in the campaign; a tripartite treaty was signed by him, Soojah, and the British; and Auckland was ready for war.

Meanwhile the Persians, with Russian encouragement, appeared outside Herat. Largely due to the fortuitous presence of Eldred Pottinger, a subaltern in the Bombay Artillery, the defence held out. The siege was lifted on 9 September 1838, but the news did not reach Auckland till October. The threat to Herat had featured prominently in the Simla Manifesto, but Auckland was not to be deterred. Following a grand durbar at Ferozepore the troops were on the move.

The promenade was marked by squabbles between the soldiers and the civilians, and between those who held the Queen's commission and the Company officers. Macnaghten, appointed Envoy to the Court of Shah Soojah, complained about military inefficiency and the huge, unwieldy column struggled on. The Commander-in-Chief's exhortation to the army to take the minimum of baggage and his appeal to all officers to travel light had been ignored to the extent that one brigadier needed fifty camels to carry his personal kit, and junior officers followed his example. At Quetta, after a bitter row, General Nott, the senior Company officer present, was left behind while the rest of the British force advanced to Kabul.

The Afghans, whom Soojah had uncompromisingly described to Macnaghten as 'a pack of dogs, one and all', showed no desire to welcome back their former monarch to his capital and watched his entry 'with the most complete indifference'. He had not seen his palace in the Bala Hissar for thirty years and now ran eagerly from room to room before bursting into tears and exclaiming pathetically that 'everything appeared to him shrunk, small and miserable'. Meanwhile the new régime was settling down and, despite the assurance in the Simla Manifesto that the British Army would be withdrawn when Soojah had been restored 'and the independence and integrity of Afghanistan established', it soon began to have a very permanent look. The British erected all the usual totems of garrison life, band concerts, gymkhanas, amateur theatricals, horse races and even cricket. The officers brought their wives up from India, a move inevitably interpreted by the Afghans and resented as betokening a long stay. Macnaghten refused to recognise the sporadic outbreaks over the next two years for what they were – the sure signs of incipient rebellion. 'All is quiet', he wrote, 'from Dan to Beersheba,' and by the autumn of 1841 he was looking forward to returning to India as Governor-Designate of Bombay. The Army Commander, the gout-ridden, impotent

General Elphinstone, hoped to go with him, retiring on health grounds.

In October, after Macnaghten as an economy measure had halved the subsidies paid to them to safeguard the route back to India, the Ghilzye chiefs rose in revolt and blocked the vital passes between Kabul and Hindostan. General Sale, whose brigade had been ordered back to India as a further economy, was instructed to clear the pass *en route*, became engaged in heavy fighting, and, unable to get back to Kabul, headed for Jalalabad. On 2 November Burnes, the Resident, was butchered by a mob of Afghans and from then on the British were under siege. They had plenty of troops, but they were short of rations, they lacked leadership, and they seemed mesmerised by the Afghans under Dost Mahomed's son, Akbar Khan. On 23 December Macnaghten, who had tried to outwit Akbar in the negotiations for withdrawal and had himself been outwitted, was treacherously slain by Akbar. Eldred Pottinger, who had escaped from Charekar in the Kohistan, reluctantly completed the surrender agreement, and on 6 January 1842 Elphinstone's army of 4,600 troops and 12,000 camp-followers straggled out into the snow and freezing cold to attempt a march of ninety-odd miles to Jalalabad.

Akbar Khan, who had promised to protect the retreating troops, cynically watched as they were either frozen to death or slaughtered by the tribesmen during the next few days. The destruction was complete, though the Afghan chief did take a few hostages who had to endure captivity till the following September.

In the spring of 1842 all that was left of the Raj's presence in Afghanistan was garrisons at Jalalabad and Kandahar, and outposts at Ghuznee and Khelat-i-Ghilzye – all surrounded by hostile country. General Pollock prudently waited at Peshawar till he had assembled an adequate force and then fought his way through the Khyber Pass to relieve Sale at Jalalabad in April. Ellenborough hesitated till July before sending highly ambivalent orders to Pollock, and Nott at Kandahar, leaving it to them to decide whether to come straight back to India, or to retire (*sic*) by way of Kabul. The two generals did not hesitate. Pollock reached Kabul on 15 September, after inflicting a heavy defeat on Akbar

Khan, and Nott arrived two days later. Vengeance was exacted, and the army, having recovered the hostages, withdrew by the now familiar route through the passes. Ellenborough met them at Ferozepore as though to celebrate a great victory, but the memory of the preceding disaster could not easily be erased. More significantly for the future, the sepoys had seen that the British were not invincible. All but one of the Bengal Native Infantry and Cavalry regiments which served in Afghanistan either rebelled or were disbanded in the Mutiny of 1857–8.

The First Afghan War was a monstrous debacle. A report by the East India Company, written before the final act, did not shirk the consequences:

Effects on India. – The exhaustion of her flourishing treasury; complete stop to internal improvement; loss of lives of fifteen thousand men (loss of camp-followers not known); destruction of fifty thousand camels; ... loss of at least £13,000,000; permanent increase of the charges on India of £5,500,000; paralyzation of commerce; diminution of the means of culture, of transport and of revenue; chilling the affections of the native army, and the disposition to enlist; loss of England's character for fair-dealing; loss of her character of success; the Mussulman population is rendered hostile; causes of rebellion developed by the pressure of taxes and the withdrawal of troops ...

2
Sikundar Burnes

I

Alexander Burnes is the most interesting, the most controversial, and in the end the most enigmatic of the British officers who were sucked into the maelstrom of the First Afghan War. In the 1830s his contemporaries, who never got the measure of him, were content to settle for an arid cliché – 'vaulting ambition', 'unstable', 'too clever for his own good'. Sir John Kaye, trying hard to reach an impartial verdict, could do no better than say that Burnes was overrated at the outset and underrated at the close of his career. No surprise need be evinced that, in the competitive hierarchy of the Honourable East India Company, his achievements should have attracted envy. Before he was murdered in Kabul on 2 November 1841 he had been the first European to navigate the course of the Indus; had made the hazardous journey to Bokhara; gained the respect of oriental rulers, including the Maharajah Runjeet Singh of the Punjab and Dost Mahomed at Kabul; been lionised on his return to England and congratulated by his Sovereign; and had been knighted at an exceptionally early age. His colleagues were jealous of his apparently inexorable progress. But there were defects to set against the virtues.

Alexander was born on 16 May 1805 in Montrose on the east coast of Scotland. He was the third surviving son of James Burnes, the Provost of the burgh. (The grandfather of Scotland's national poet and the grandfather of James Burnes were brothers, though they spelled their names differently.) Educated locally, Alexander wrote, 'I was very dull at school, and reckoned a *dolt*.' This may have been an excess of modesty – not one of his common failings – but there were no early signs that his abilities would develop in such a highly individual mould. His father was friendly with Joseph Hume, who had made a fortune in India before returning to become Member of Parliament for the Montrose constituency, and through Hume's influence a cadetship in the East India Company was obtained for young Alexander. In June 1821 he sailed for India on the *Sarah* along with his elder brother who had been appointed an assistant surgeon in the Bombay Presidency.

He was posted to the 1st Bombay Native Infantry at Surat. As the battalion was not engaged on active operations and the requirements of routine drill, usually finished by midday, made little demand on his time, Alexander applied himself to learning Hindustani, both from textbooks and by ordering his servants to address him only in their native tongue. Within a year, before he was transferred to the 11th Native Infantry at Poona, he had passed the interpreter's examination. He was something of an oddity among his fellows. Slight of build, he wrote in his journal how much he hated all gymnastic and athletic exercises. 'I like *argument* much – a *jolly* party only now and then; much study, and am very partial to history, but dislike novels extremely, even Scott's.' The normal subaltern in a native infantry regiment was, to put it mildly, a bit of a Philistine with few cerebral interests, and one might have expected the studious Burnes to be ragged by his mess-mates, or to be critical of their behaviour. Instead, he wrote, 'In point of officers there was never perhaps a more gentlemanly and pleasant set of men assembled together in an Indian Native Corps – in a word, I have got a regiment that delights me, and naturally makes my time pass delightfully.'

Either because he had a gift for learning foreign tongues, or because he knew that fluency in Persian – used for most diplomatic business with oriental princes – would help his own prospects, Burnes rapidly acquired a good knowledge of that language as well as of Hindustani and was soon employed on translation work. Promotion was quick in coming, and before his nineteenth birthday he wrote exultantly to his parents, 'Behold your son Alexander, the most fortunate man on earth for his years! Behold him Lieutenant and Adjutant Burnes of the 21st Regiment, on an allowance of from five hundred to six hundred rupees a month!' (Today's equivalent would be £50–60.)

He continued his Persian studies. 'I reckon three years more will make me a Persian scholar, and five more will give me a tolerable knowledge of Arabic.' He had already formed an ambition to visit these countries, since otherwise he would remain 'amongst the inferior class of linguists'. But he was in no sense a pedant. He had the most necessary of all gifts for a true explorer: he was indefatigably curious, whether it was conversing with the natives at Surat, or reconnoitring the area round his station. He had already been recommended for two papers on local geography when in 1829 he volunteered to explore the deserts, then largely unknown, between India and the Indus and follow the river down to the sea. Sir John Malcolm, the Governor of Bombay, was sympathetic and transferred him to the political branch of the Company's service, observing that he would thereby have 'influence with the rulers, through whose country he travelled, that would tend greatly to allay that jealousy and alarm, which might impede, if they did not arrest, the progress of his enquiries'. In the peculiar way in which careers in India were organised this was a decisive step for Burnes. There was a great deal of rivalry between regimental officers and the 'politicals', but in general only the brightest were selected for the political branch, in which the more glittering prizes were to be won.

At Calcutta the Governor-General approved the expedition, no doubt influenced by a report from Henry Pottinger,* the Resident in Cutch, who had written that 'there was no officer, of whatever rank or standing in the army, who was so particularly well qualified as Lieut. Burnes to give full effect to the plan'.

It was a mark of the Establishment's esteem that, despite his lack of experience, he should be given an assignment that called for considerable ingenuity. But Burnes had got no further than Jeysulmeer when an express letter arrived calling him back, since 'it was deemed inexpedient to incur the hazard of exciting the alarm and jealousy of the rulers of Sinde, and other foreign states, by the prosecution of the design'. The Governor-General, if he had not lost his nerve, had at least changed his mind. Advised by the sage Sir Charles Metcalfe, he did not wish to frighten the local Amirs who were suspicious of British intentions and wanted very much to be left alone. A disconsolate Burnes returned.

He may have been, for the moment, frustrated; but he had

*Sir Henry Pottinger, Bt (1789–1856): first Governor of Hong Kong, 1843; later Governor of Cape of Good Hope and ultimately of Madras.

reason to be satisfied with his progress. He had earned a good reputation as a geographer (explorer being, as yet, scarcely justified); and he had attracted the favourable notice of his superiors. There were no complaints of the arrogance of which he was later accused. At this stage all that could be said in criticism was that he did not seem to care for the social pursuits of his fellow officers. He was not attracted by the pleasures of the table or the zenana (both alleged to be subsequent frailties) and he gambled only once. Playing at hazard, in one evening he lost six months' pay; he recouped his losses; but he did not visit the card table again. The theological ramblings of young officers are seldom of interest, but Burnes, who was still only twenty-four, has left one reflection which is significant. Most of his colleagues affected an adherence to the Christian, usually Anglican, religion, and for some of them it was a matter of genuine belief. Burnes, though brought up in a stern Presbyterian household, had no such faith.

I entertain different ideas of religion daily, and am afraid they will end in my having no religion at all. A fatalist I am, but no atheist. No, nor even a deist. No – what shall I call it? – a sceptical blockhead whose head, filled with its own vanities, imagines itself more capable than it is.

It was this outlook that enabled him to understand, and record with exemplary lack of bias, the creeds of the different sects he met on his travels.

The first of his memorable journeys was to start very soon. He had already written to a friend that his interests were purely literary, and confined to investigating the antiquities of Asia and the wonders of her people.

I have been tracing the magnanimous Alexander on his Quixotic journey to these lands; and I shall set out at the end of 1830 to traverse further regions, which have been untrodden since the Greeks of Macedon followed their leader.

From an early age Burnes was fascinated by his namesake Alexander the Great, and like him was always referred to by non-Europeans as 'Sikundar', the Persian equivalent of his Christian name, 'and a magnanimous name it is,' he wrote. But though he lost no opportunity to visit and record traces of the

Macedonian, his next assignment took a different direction from that which he had in mind.

2

Lord Amherst, on returning to England after his five-year stint as Governor-General, had brought back some Kashmir shawls as a gift from the Maharajah Runjeet Singh to the British Monarch. Protocol demanded reciprocity, and it is easy to imagine the scene at the East India Company's London office in Leadenhall Street as brains were scoured to think of a suitable present. The exchange of gifts between Heads of State always tends to produce something absurd, and this occasion ran true to form. Runjeet Singh's proclivities were known to be both vinous and venereal, scarcely appropriate for a gesture from His Britannic Majesty. Then Amherst, recollecting the Maharajah's passion for horses, suggested that he should be sent a few peculiarly English animals – five dray horses, as it turned out, a stallion and four mares – which would impress the Sikh ruler with their size. This bizarre proposal was approved and the hardy beasts, having been six months at sea, reached Bombay at the end of 1830.

The Government of India now had to get them to Lahore, a thousand miles away. An overland journey was beyond the horses' capacity, and it was clear that they would have to be sent by boat up the Indus, leaving only a short march to Runjeet Singh's court. This solution had some incidental tactical advantages. It would afford an opportunity to test the navigability of the river, on which there was no information except for the seventy miles from Tatta to Hyderabad, and there was a good commercial argument that the Indus should eventually be the channel for ferrying British exports to Central Asia. Moreover, Sind lay adjacent to the Bombay Presidency and it was expedient to learn more of the disposition of its rulers. The snag was that the Amirs of Sind were still extremely distrustful of British motives; they also feared the ambitions of the Sikhs; and they were unlikely to view a British mission, even an ostensibly peaceful one, with any great enthusiasm. It was accordingly apparent that the equine embassy required a conductor possessed of both tact and resolution. Malcolm had no doubt that Burnes was the man, and the Governor-General agreed.

So Burnes and his small flotilla of five native boats sailed from Mandivee in Cutch on 21 January 1831. He was allowed to choose his entourage and was accompanied by Ensign Leckie of the 22nd Native Infantry, Mahomed Ali a surveyor, and an Indian doctor. His remit was wide; in effect he was to find out all he could. In order to allay suspicion there was no prestige escort, but he was cumbered by the addition of a large, unwieldy carriage which was to be a gift to Runjeet Singh from the Governor of Bombay. This had been suggested by Henry Pottinger at Cutch, 'since the size and bulk of it would render it obvious that the mission could only proceed by water', and therefore mollify the Amirs. It did not make Burnes's task any easier.

Progress was slow. 'We could advance, I found, by tracking or being pulled by men, at one mile and a half an hour; by gentle and favourable breezes at two miles, and by violent winds at three miles an hour.'* He was meticulous in his survey, taking twenty bearings a day. The Sindis, however, proved as intractable as had been feared. Burnes and his party were searched, threatened, and refused admittance to their territory. It was no help to Burnes that, three years before, his brother had visited Sind to give medical treatment to one of the Amirs. (His stock of quinine was promptly seized for use by the Amir's dependants.) To add to Burnes's discomfiture, two of his boats were dismasted in a gale. Then, on 18 April, after Henry Pottinger had sent the Hyderabad Amir a stern warning, Burnes was allowed to moor opposite the city. The Amir, who had given permission with a bad grace, did not disguise his cupidity at the presents offered to him, but Burnes persuaded him to make his state barge available. This strange vessel had three masts and two cabins, one of a 'peculiar shape, covered with scarlet cloth and the eyes of intruders were excluded on all sides by silken screens'. Making the most of the Amir's reluctant generosity, Burnes sailed again on 23 April.

There were incidental diversions. A Baluchi chief came to meet them with his followers.

A set of dancing girls were among his suite; and in the evening we were compelled, against our inclination, to hear these ladies squall for a couple of hours, and, what added to the disgusto of the scene, they

---

*Burnes, *Travels into Bokhara, etc*, 1834.

drank at intervals, to *clear their voices*, as they said, until nearly intoxicated.

At Khairpur the Amir received them under a canopy of silk, seated on a cushion of cloth of gold and surrounded by his forty sons. The watching crowd was greatly amused by the feathers in the ceremonial hat which Burnes wore to recognise the solemnity of the occasion. '"Such cocks" was literally the expression.'

On 21 May he started again upstream from the fortress of Bukkur (which he was to revisit in different circumstances), having exchanged the 'doondees' of Sind for another type of boat, the 'zohruk', eighty feet long and twenty feet broad, still flat-bottomed, but quicker in passage. Burnes's self-confidence grew when the Nawab of the buffer state of Bahawalpur greeted his unusual visitor with an eighty-gun salute. The most perilous part of the journey was over when they reached the Sikh frontier on 8 June.

Runjeet Singh sent one of his sirdars (generals) to meet them. It was Burnes's first encounter with the Sikhs, 'tall, bony men, with a very martial carriage'. The Sikhs for their part were astonished at the size of the dray horses — little elephants, they said — and even more at their enormous hooves. When a horseshoe was found to weigh 100 rupees, the same weight as four Sikh horseshoes, it was sent in advance to Runjeet Singh as an indication of what was to come. The Maharajah, anxious to emphasise his own status, had ordered great liberality in attending to Burnes's needs on the rest of the journey to Lahore, and even gave him permission to inspect fortresses *en route*. Burnes changed boats for the last time to travel in one which Runjeet had prepared for him with two wooden bungalows on deck. To the surprise of his escort, Burnes insisted on making a detour to see the 'fabulous Hydaspes' river and to reflect on the spot where the fleet of Alexander the Great met disaster in the rapids.

On 18 June he made his public entrance into Lahore. Both Runjeet and Burnes knew that the mission was a formality to give continued expression to the treaty which the Maharajah had signed with the British in 1809, and there was no shortage of official celebration. When Burnes handed over the letter from Lord Ellenborough, the President of the Board of Control, which accompanied the horses 'of the gigantic breed that is peculiar to England', Runjeet delightedly ordered a peal of artillery from sixty guns, each firing twenty-one times. Against this noisy background there were indigenous oriental entertainments, drinking orgies at which the Maharajah was concerned for their effect on Burnes's bowels, and military reviews – five regiments of infantry and fifty-one brass six-pounders taking part. In his two months at the capital Burnes was given freedom to wander at will round Lahore. He did not find it attractive, apart from the garden of Shah Jehan, the Shalimar or 'house of joy', where he admired the terraces and the 450 fountains in this magnificent remnant of Mogul grandeur. Runjeet displayed the Koh-i-Noor (which he had obtained by trickery from the Afghan Shah Soojah), and loaded Burnes with presents, emeralds and pearls, a ceremonial sword, a richly caparisoned horse, a robe of honour and 'many other manufactures of Cashmere'. In his fulsome reply to Ellenborough, Runjeet referred to 'that nightingale of the garden of eloquence, that bird of the winged words of sweet discourse, Mr Burnes'.

These were the outward signs of a successful mission. What was more surprising was the genuine empathy that developed between the pock-marked, one-eyed potentate showing all the signs of debauchery, and the young subaltern. Runjeet treated Burnes without condescension; Burnes had a high opinion of the Maharajah's humanity, as it appeared to him. 'He has never been known to punish a criminal with death since his accession to power; he does not hesitate to mutilate a malefactor, but usually banishes him to the hills.' In his account of the mission Burnes regretted that the Sikh ruler was probably near the end of his career, and doubted whether he could long survive a nightly dose of spirits 'more ardent than the strongest brandy'. (His favourite potion was said to be compounded of emeralds, grape spirit and oranges, a Sikh version of a kind of Grand Marnier which was improbably said to be good for the digestion.) Burnes was mistaken, for Runjeet lived for eight more years, before he died at a time singularly inconvenient for the execution of British policy.

Burnes was also wrong in another assessment. He mentions his gratifying reception by Captain Claude Wade, the British Agent at Ludhiana, who had been sent to Lahore for the ceremonies. He did not appreciate that Wade, who was later to have a baleful effect on Burnes's credibility with the Governor-General, regarded him as an upstart. Meanwhile he took his leave on 18th August and journeyed by way of Ludhiana to Simla. At Ludhiana coming events again cast their shadow before when he met two exiled Afghan rulers, the brothers Shah Zemaun and Shah Soojah. Zemaun, by the order of yet another brother, Mahmoud, had been deprived of his eyes many years before, a favourite Afghan ploy to render a man incapable of ruling. As for the corpulent, melancholy Soojah, fretting as a British pensioner since Dost Mahomed had driven him from power, Burnes thought that he still retained the same demeanour as when he had been king. He added an acute comment.

I do not believe the Shah possesses sufficient dignity to seat himself on the throne of Cabool; and that if he did regain it, he has not the tact to discharge the duties of so difficult a situation.

Later, as we will see, Burnes was to change this opinion against his better judgement, and to earn obloquy for so doing.

For the present, however, all was set fair. At Simla, Lord Bentinck, the Governor-General, congratulated him on what he had achieved, and in December he received formal acknowledgement of his map of the Indus and the mass of information he had collected. The Governor-General's secretary wrote that he was directed to commend the 'extreme prudence and discretion' of Burnes's conduct with the chiefs and sirdars, and the 'zeal, diligence, and intelligence' displayed in carrying out his duties. The narrative of his voyage on the Indus, which was published in 1834 along with that of his later travels, still makes good reading. It is a young man's account. He rejoices in his discoveries and in obtaining the goodwill of the different tribesmen. He points to the problems in carrying merchandise up the Indus. It could only be done with flat-bottomed boats. 'Steamboats could ply, if constructed after the manner of the country, but no vessel with a keel could be safely navigated.' His writing is objective. There is no sign of Jack Horner smugness, no sign of self-aggrandisement.

While at Simla Burnes suggested to Bentinck that he might undertake another expedition. In his own words, the success of the Lahore mission 'and the sight of so many tribes hitherto unknown, gave fresh strength to a desire I had always felt to see new countries, and visit the conquests of Alexander'. He proposed to travel to Afghanistan and then to the Caspian by way of Balkh, Bokhara and Samarkand, a route as perilous as it was unprecedented. He was riding his luck in making this request, but Bentinck liked the young man's enthusiasm and was impressed by his proven capacity. He was also influenced by growing fears entertained in both London and Calcutta about Russian intentions in these areas. The Great Game was about to enter a new phase and Burnes's offer was opportune. Bentinck gave his permission.

3

Burnes was provided with passports 'as a Captain in the British Army, returning to Europe', drawn out in French, English and Persian. He was again allowed to select his own companions. They were Surgeon James Gerard, who had a reputation as a Himalayan explorer; Mahomed Ali, the surveyor who had been with him on the Indus; Mohun Lal, a young Kashmiri educated at the English Institution at Delhi, who became Burnes's *moonshee* (secretary) and close friend; and one Indian servant Ghoolam Hoosain. If the party was to escape plundering, pillage, or worse, it must be as unobtrusive as possible, and Burnes decided that his style of travel would be simple, without a military presence. He determined, however, to retain the character of a European, accommodating himself 'in dress, habits, and customs' to those whom he met.

The early stages of the journey were for him a party of pleasure. At Lahore once more he was greeted with affection by Runjeet Singh and given some useful advice by the Maharajah's French officers, Allard and Court, on the best methods of dealing with the tribes beyond the Sikh border. Runjeet took him on a wild pig hunt. He also unbent to cross-examine Burnes about the system of paying British soldiers. (His own troops were, for disciplinary reasons, always kept in arrears.) Understandably, he wanted to know what Burnes was up to in coming so soon to his court for a second time. Burnes, aware of the Sikhs' hostility towards the Afghans, did not disclose his full purpose, merely saying that his journey would take him to Britain. In his journal he referred again to the Sikh ruler's moderation and sagacity, and looked back on the time he spent at Lahore as some of the happiest days of his life.

As soon as they left Runjeet's capital, where standards had to be maintained, Burnes's party threw away their European clothes, assumed native turbans, robes and cummerbunds, and shaved their heads. But his journal was not neglected. He lost no opportunity of recording native customs, whether they were religious observances, saltmining, or the sight of fishermen on the Indus washing the sand for gold. Coins were itemised as a matter of great interest, as was anything connected with his hero, Alexander the Great.

The Indus was forded at Attock, and the Sikhs escorted him to the limits of their territory, three miles beyond the river. 'Here we met the Afghans. Neither side would approach, and we drew up a distance of about 300 yards from each other.' Despite these uneasy frontier formalities, a friendly Afghan chief told them to consider themselves as secure as eggs under a hen, 'a homely enough simile, the truth of which we had no reason to doubt'. Burnes was mastering the art of making himself agreeable to all kinds of hosts, but he was more impressed than he should have been by the 'urbanity' of the governor of Peshawar, Sultan Mahomed. This chief was somewhat lacking in affection for his younger brother Dost Mahomed, the ruler of Kabul, and two years later betrayed him when the Sikhs seized the Peshawar province. Burnes spent a pleasant month in Sultan Mahomed's company, and as a mark of friendship received from him 'six blank sheets bearing his seal' for use in emergencies. He was also advised to stop giving medicine to the natives. Surgeon Gerard had been in the habit of treating ailments, but Burnes now agreed that to continue this humane practice would 'sound the tocsin of our approach'.

Burnes had been warned to avoid the predatory tribesmen in the Khyber Pass, 'no one trusts a Khyberee', but he still had to pay a toll before the avaricious Ghilzyes, after much haggling, would let him cross the mountains. He noted the Afghans' way of looking after their horses.

They never remove the saddle during the day, which they believe gives the horse a better rest at night. They never walk a horse up and down, but either mount him, or make him go round in a circle till he is cool . . . They always tie a knot on the tail.

(Colin Mackenzie records that the Afghans believed that the knot strengthened the animal's backbone.)*

Burnes pushed on through Gandamack, Neemla and Jugdulluk, the route that was later covered with the bones of British and Indian soldiers in the disastrous retreat from Kabul, when he had already been murdered in the city where he now received a warm welcome.

On entering Kabul he went first to the house of Dost Mahomed's brother, the amiable patriarch Nawab Jubbar Khan. The Nawab, who proved a good host, was easily distinguishable from the rest of his warlike family by his mild and pleasing manners. Burnes was not the only eccentric to reach Kabul, as he soon discovered from his first encounter with 'Mr Wolff, the missionary of the Jews'. Wolff is sufficiently *sui generis* to merit a mention. A Bavarian, the son of a Rabbi, he had been successively a Jew, a Lutheran, and a Roman Catholic. No matter what his current creed he would argue doctrinal issues to the exhaustion of his audience. He had travelled in Europe, Egypt and Persia, and on a visit to England in 1826 he married the whimsical Lady Georgiana Walpole, who accompanied him on some of his wanderings, though not to Afghanistan. His adventures, which lost nothing in the telling, included being shipwrecked, bastinadoed in Kurdistan, and stripped and left naked by the Afghans. He had argued with Pope Pius VII in Rome and with the Governor-General of India. He now claimed to be searching for the lost tribes of Israel, but Burnes noted that he made only a few enquiries of the Afghans in Kabul, 'though they claim themselves to be their descendants'. Burnes also concluded that Wolff's most recent misfortunes arose from calling himself 'a Hajee, which implies a Mahomeddan pilgrim, and for which he had been plundered and beaten'.

On 4 May Wolff and Burnes went to pay their respects to Dost Mahomed. Burnes acted as interpreter for the missionary in a long dispute with the Dost's Mahomedan doctors. As might be expected, neither side made any religious concessions, and Wolff,

*Mackenzie, *Storms and Sunshine of a Soldier's Life*, 1884.

who soon after left Kabul, disappears from this story. He reappears in 1844, when with great courage he made his way alone to Bokhara to ascertain the fate of Colonel Stoddart and Captain Arthur Conolly, and narrowly escaped with his own life.*

Of more significance was Burnes's own conversation with the Dost. The Afghan questioned him closely on the terms on which European kings lived in adjacent countries without destroying each other, and how English revenues were raised – both of them questions in which the Dost had a keen personal interest. He wanted to know about China. 'The mention of Chinese manufactures led to a notice of those in England; he enquired about our machinery and steam engines, and then expressed his wonder at the cheapness of our goods.' Next the Dost turned to more political topics. He evinced a 'cordial hatred' for Runjeet Singh, and asked if the British would 'accept his services as an auxiliary to root him out'. Burnes replied as tactfully as he could that Runjeet was a friend of the British. Then the Dost offered Burnes the command of his army. 'Twelve thousand horse and twenty guns shall be at your disposal.' When Burnes declined, 'He requested me to send some friend to be his generalissimo.'

This may have been a genuine offer, for there were precedents for British officers accepting service in the courts of Indian princes. It may have been an attempt by the Dost to inveigle the British on to his side, but at least it seems certain that, just as he had done with Runjeet, Burnes had gained the Dost's confidence. He had an instinct for getting on the right terms with everyone he met, no matter what the circumstances, and the relationship he forged with Dost Mahomed was to have an important bearing on both their futures. But if Burnes was right in regarding the Dost's natural air of authority, his 'accomplished address and manner', with respect, one of his other conclusions was a serious misjudgement.

In his fortnight in the city Burnes was enchanted with the whole ambience of Kabul. He was impressed by the Great Bazaar, its enormous variety of merchandise, the 'falodah', a white jelly strained from wheat and drunk with sherbet or snow, the Kabul

*Fitzroy MacLean, *A Person from England*, Jonathan Cape, 1958.

wine which tasted like Madeira, and the famous rhubarb. 'Rhuwash was the dainty of the May season in Cabool. It is merely blanched rhubarb which is reared under a careful protection from the sun . . . Its flavour is delicious.' He admired the fruit trees in full bloom and listened to the nightingales. He was deferred to by the Dost's entourage, and in his enthusiasm he wrote,

The Afghans are a nation of children . . . They cannot conceal their feelings from one another, and a person with any discrimination may at all times pierce their designs . . . No people are more incapable of managing an intrigue.

This is a major defect in Burnes's appreciation of the Afghan scene. Nine years later two treacherous Afghan chiefs intrigued to murder him in his Residency within the city walls, and the Shah's garden, which he had described in such eulogistic terms, was to see bitter fighting as the insurgents attacked the British cantonment. It is hard to see why Burnes was so ingenuous, because his reaction to the other tribes he met was invariably cool and objective. Anyone, it can be argued, may be allowed a single mistake, but in this case it was fatal. Colin Mackenzie was nearer the mark when he noted that Afghans 'can sneak, lie, cheat and practise any other of the smaller virtues to attain an object'.

4

On 18 May Burnes left Kabul and turned his face towards the Hindu Kush, with the most dangerous part of his journey still lying ahead. It was one thing to win the friendship of the Afghans and Dost Mahomed; it was very different to pass through the lands of the Uzbegs and the Toorkomans, or to escape the clutches of the slaver Moorad Beg, the chieftain of Koondooz. Burnes had taken Jubbar Khan's advice to employ a *cafila-bashee* (caravan conductor) to facilitate dealings with the suspicious tribesmen he was bound to meet, and this proved to be a wise step. On 21 May he reached the Hajeeguk pass where he was almost blinded by the reflection from the snow. The local Hazaras, however, were friendly, and 'one good matron' who had sheltered him in her dwelling dug into the ground prescribed the use of antimony, 'which I applied with a pencil, much to the improvement of my appearance, as she informed me'. At Bameean he made careful note of the two colossal idols Silsal and Shahmama, 120 and 60 feet high respectively, but he could make nothing of the native traditions regarding their origin.

His caravan now crossed the Afghan border into Tartary. 'We were already in a different country; the mosques were spread with felts, which indicated greater attention to matters of religion, and they were also much better buildings.' As a precaution, Burnes cut the central part of his moustache, since otherwise he would have been identified as 'a Shiah, and consequently an infidel'. He still had ninety-five miles to go before clearing the mountains, but he was in good spirits. He found their normal pattern of riding about twenty-five miles till two or three in the afternoon, breakfasting in the saddle and sleeping on the ground, perfectly acceptable. 'We were quite happy in such scenes, and the novelty of everything . . . our society, too, was amusing; and I took every favourable occasion of mingling with the travellers whom we met by the way, and at the halting places.' On 30 May they debouched into the plains of Kooloom and alighted at a caravanserai – a walled square surrounded by individual cells.

It was the practice for travellers to keep to themselves. At first Burnes and his team escaped notice, but the next morning they were stopped and ordered to report to the dreaded Moorag Beg at Koondooz, some seventy miles away. Burnes thought of making a run for it, but was dissuaded by his party. On arrival at Koondooz they were brought before the chief. Burnes gave a spirited performance, which he had rehearsed with his companions, as an Armenian watchmaker, but Moorag Beg was still doubtful. At the critical moment he again enquired whether it was certain that he was an Armenian. 'A second assurance carried conviction, and he issued an order for our safe conduct beyond the frontier . . . I could have embraced him when he pronounced it finished.' It had been a near thing, and Burnes was very conscious of the fate of an earlier English traveller, Moorcroft, who had been imprisoned at Koondooz in 1824 and had died in unexplained circumstances at Balkh. But he still found time to record his impressions of the Uzbegs, particularly their interminable tea-drinking – the tea being taken with salt, and sometimes mixed with fat.

On the way to Balkh – the ancient Greeks' Bactria – they saw a magnificent mirage, which Burnes described as a snaky line of vapour, as large as the Oxus itself. 'It mocked our parched tongues, for we had expended the contents of the leather bottles we always carried.' There was little to detain them at Balkh. The apricots were luscious, but the climate was unhealthy. He visited Moorcroft's grave, impossible to view without 'many melancholy reflections' and some apprehension about his own prospects. It was time to change the horses for camels, beasts more suited to the conditions that lay ahead. Camels, he observed, moved best at night or in the cool of the morning, but began to flag after about twenty-five miles. The party had to travel in 'kujawas', panniers thrown across each camel, a passenger on one side balancing his companion on the other. The panniers were no more than four feet long and two and a half wide, and suppleness and ingenuity were required 'to stow a body of five feet nine inches in such a space'. The one compensation was that he could still read, and even make notes without being seen.

The march to the river Oxus and then to Bokhara was so hot that travel was only possible by night. This was desert country and the party covered eighty-five miles without seeing a tree. They had to halt, stricken with fever, at the oasis of Koorsee. From the symptoms Burnes describes it was probably malaria. He dosed himself with quinine, but Gerard obstinately took calomel, and 'did not shake off the disease till long after we left the country'. Rumours reached them that they would not be allowed to enter Bokhara, and Burnes took the initiative of despatching a letter 'with all the forms of eastern etiquette and eloquence' to the principal Bokhara Minister, saying that he had been well received elsewhere and seeking the protection of the Commander of the Faithful, as the King of Bokhara was called. Surprisingly it worked, and they were informed that they would be welcome. On 27 June they reached the city gates.

5

Burnes stayed at Bokhara till 21 July. His party discarded their turbans for sheepskin caps with the fur inside and modified their dress to attract as little attention as possible. Since none but

Moslems were allowed to ride through the city they invariably proceeded on foot. Burnes struck up a rapport with the Koosh Begee, the Chief Minister. He gave him a compass and was amused by the childish way in which the Vizier seized the gift. They had long discussions on European customs, on astronomy, and inevitably on religion. Burnes had to swear that Christians did not worship idols before the Vizier condescended to agree that they were 'people of the book, better than the Russians'. Burnes was slyly asked if the Christians ate pork and what was its flavour, but he was wise to the trap and said he had heard it was like beef. 'God forgive me!' he had written earlier, 'for I am very fond of bacon and my mouth waters as I write the words.'

When he was given a musket and asked to perform platoon drill the Vizier looked at Burnes's slight physique and observed that foreigners were undersized and could not fight the Uzbegs. Burnes had two disappointments. He thought it unwise to ask for permission to visit Samarkand, and he was denied an audience with Nasrullah Bahadur Khan, the Bokhara ruler. 'What have travellers to do with courts?' he was asked.

Instead, he stationed himself outside the Kalyan Mosque to watch the potentate emerging from his devotions. He was not alarmed as he might have been by Nasrullah, merely recording that, with small eyes and a pale visage, he did not have a prepossessing countenance. 'The life of this king was less enviable than that of most private men, since all his food had first to be tasted by his acolytes lest it be poisoned.' As a result, the good king of the Uzbegs never enjoyed a hot meal or a freshly cooked dinner. Though Nasrullah did not see Burnes he consented to the Koosh Begee giving him a *firman* which amounted to a safe conduct. It may be assumed that Nasrullah, the most savage of contemporary rulers, had not yet gone off his head, but before he died in 1860 he had instigated a formidable series of murders, including those of two later British emissaries Charles Stoddart and Arthur Conolly, whom he executed after treating them with the utmost barbarity. Burnes was lucky.

He made full use of the Vizier's cordiality to study the inhabitants and commerce of Bokhara. The city's principal feature was the Registan, the great square surrounded by the citadel and two of the religious colleges which gave Bokhara its designation as a holy city. The Registan was a scene of perpetual, multi-racial activity.

A stranger has only to seat himself on a bench of the Registan to know the Uzbegs and the people of Bokhara. He may here converse with the natives of Persia, Turkey, Russia, Tartary, China, India, and Cabool. He will meet with Toorkmuns, Calmuks, and Kuzzaks, from the surrounding deserts, as well as the natives of more favoured lands.

Burnes was also aware that this great Asiatic crossroads was a remarkably filthy place, flyblown and ridden with dysentery and typhoid – aggravated by the drawing of water from the central canal that also served as a sewer.

Burnes was sarcastic about the noisy, formal disputation in the religious colleges, of which there were no fewer than 366. 'The students are entirely occupied with theology . . . A more perfect set of drones were never assembled together; and they are a body of men regardless of their religion in most respects beyond the performance of its prayers.' As an example of Uzbeg hypocrisy he cited the brutal slave market where transactions took place to the accompaniment of a quotation from the Koran. A further official absurdity was the official ban on tobacco. It could be purchased openly, but anyone seen smoking in public was dragged before the *Cazee* and sentenced to be flogged, or paraded on a donkey, with a blackened face. The traveller had to be cautious if he dared to look at the Uzbeg women, who were kept in strict purdah. But Burnes was able to observe that the ladies of Bokhara dyed their teeth black and braided their hair in long tresses. Even in their houses they dressed in huge hessian boots, highly ornamented. 'What a strange taste for those who are for ever concealed, to choose to be thus booted as if prepared for a journey.'

Much of the acclamation which Burnes received for his *Travels into Bokhara* when it was published arose from its sheer novelty and the intrepid character of the author. But the third section of the book contained a great deal that was of immediate interest to the British government. It was a penetrating account of the commercial prospects in Central Asia. He had already spotted the close connection between trade to Bokhara or Toorkistan and to Kabul. As regards the latter he suggested establishing trade fairs to extend British commerce west of the Indus. He added a pregnant observation. 'It would at the same time counteract the intrigues and designs of the great power I have named.' It was Russia that he had in mind.

Russia, he pointed out, could ferry her goods to the confines of Asia by water carriage, 'and it is the superiority and cheapness of our manufactures that alone enables us to appear in the contest by the Indian route.' He admitted that we could not compete with the Russians in metal and heavy goods, but he claimed that if we exported more 'white cloths, muslins, and woollens', we could drive the Muscovites from the market.

> The transport of merchandise by the route of Cabool costs little, and if Russia navigates the Volga, the greatest of the European rivers, Britain can command like facilities, by two more grand and equally navigable streams, the Ganges and the Indus.

Britain's world-wide export of cotton piece goods was already expanding rapidly, but further outlets had to be found for the mills of Yorkshire and Lancashire. This was just what Burnes had proposed – provided that the Indus and the Ganges were fully exploited. To complete his *tour d'horizon*, he confirmed that the Oxus was navigable throughout the greater part of its course. The advantages of using the Oxus, he thought, must be great – both commercially and politically. His analysis provided very palatable grist for the Government mills. Not only were there strategic reasons for pursuing the Great Game to counteract Russian influence. There was also a complimentary commercial one. It is not too fanciful to imagine that many a twentieth-century trading mission would have been glad to include someone with Burnes's vision and application.

Burnes had hoped to travel next to Khiva, but as local feuds made the route unsafe it seemed wiser to attach his party to a caravan heading for Meshed. As an *envoi* to his stay at Bokhara, the Koosh Begee, giving the *cafila-bashee* strict instructions to look after his charges, hoped that Burnes and Gerard would return as 'trading ambassadors'. He asked them to confirm that they had been well treated in Bokhara; Burnes was happy to give him an assurance, certifying that his party had been treated in every way as honoured guests, and that 'their luggage had not even been opened, nor their property taxed'.

The journey to Meshed took nearly two months, with frequent danger from raiding, and slaving, Toorkomans. First, the caravan was halted a bare three days' march from Bokhara while permission was obtained form the Khan of Khiva. Burnes's identity was not at issue, but he was far from comfortable at the delay. The route to Meshed was through the vast Toorkoman desert, unbearably hot, sand always in the nostrils, and no vegetation to be seen except the tamarisk. Perseverance was needed as they wound their slow way – two miles an hour – from well to well, and the *cafila-bashee* enforced strict discipline. Then they came too near the camp of the Khan of Khiva for comfort. An insolent Toorkoman searched the convoy; Burnes pretended to be a Hindoo from Kabul, and proved his point by conversing in the native language with an Afghan in the party. There were other alarms. Tolls had to be paid, and on approaching Meshed Burnes noticed that every field had its tower, built by the cultivator as a defence to which he might fly on seeing the hated Toorkoman. 'What a state of society, that requires the ploughshare and the sword in the same field.'

Burnes was struck by the contrast between the environs of Meshed and the desert he had just traversed. 'A new scene burst upon our view, with a rapidity which one only sees in theatrical representation.' They were in Persian territory, and for the first time in many months he felt he was not subject to the whims of oriental despots who might, on sudden impulse, imprison or execute him for sport as an infidel. He met the Crown Prince of Persia, the son of Abbas Meerza, and listened gravely to the young man's enquiries about the art of staining glass and the whereabouts of the unicorn. A safe conduct was provided to the Prince's camp, about 100 miles further on, and there he was hospitably entertained by three Europeans in the Shah's service. It was a delight to hear English spoken again. In camp he also met Yar Mahomed, the Chief Minister of Herat, a sinister satrap who was to play a leading part in the events leading up to the Afghan war, but on this occasion Burnes saw nothing untoward in his behaviour.

The party now separated, Gerard and Mohun Lal deciding to return to India by way of Herat and Kandahar. Burnes, given a handsome escort, pushed on through the wilds of Khorassan to

Astrabad, recently scourged by plague, where he recorded his horse's hooves echoing as he trod the lonely streets. He reached the shores of the Caspian at Nokunda. It was a moment to savour. 'After we had been so long looking for it and travelled from Delhi to its shores. It now rolled before us like the ocean.' The rest of the journey to Teheran, where a weary, tanned, calloused Burnes reported to Sir John Campbell, the British Minister, was free of incident.

Campbell arranged for him to be presented to the Shah. Burnes, hastily equipped with a ceremonial uniform and carrying his sword, was dazzled by the Aladdin's cave of the audience chamber, the ubiquitous mirrors and the clutch of chandeliers that hung like stalactites from the ornate ceiling. The aged King of Kings, pleased that his visitor could speak Persian, put him through a lengthy catechism. What had led Burnes to undertake his perilous journey? Curiosity, he replied. It must have been expensive? The Shah was amused to learn how Burnes escaped with paying a minimal tribute to the Toorkomans. There were searching enquiries about the state of affairs at Kabul and Bokhara. When asked what was the greatest wonder he had met, Burnes, now skilled in oriental flattery, kept a straight face to reply, 'What sight has equalled that which I now behold, the light of your Majesty's countenance, O attraction of the world.' The aged Monarch graciously assented and Burnes withdrew.

On 1 November he left for Bushire, where he embarked on the East India Company's *Clive* and sailed for Bombay, arriving on 18 January. He spent the rest of the month in quarantine before travelling to Calcutta. In character, Burnes concluded the account of his travels by saying

In the journey to the East, we had marched on the very line of route by which Alexander had pursued Darius, while the voyage to India took us on the coast of Mekran and the track of his admiral Nearchus.

One comment may be added. Unlike an earlier traveller, Pausanias, Burnes did not exaggerate. He did not strain the reader's credibility; nor did he tell tall stories. Byron, the day after the publication of *Childe Harold*, woke to find himself famous, and on arrival in England Burnes might have said the same. At Calcutta Governor-General Bentinck had given him a warm reception, and with good reason, for Burnes could say without immodesty that he had achieved his objectives. Bentinck saw that, in addition to memorabilia about Asiatic *mores*, Burnes's information was highly relevant to the Great Game and sent him to London with his despatches.

Letters from Calcutta, packed with eulogies, had gone before him, and the new-found Marco Polo was the hero of the hour. The Court of Directors at Leadenhall Street treated him with respect; he had long interviews with Lord Grey, the Prime Minister; and he was given an audience with King William IV. The Monarch, surprised that so important a mission had been entrusted to a young subaltern – promotion to captain took place during his stay in England – summoned him to Brighton and paid him the compliment of listening with evident interest to his account. 'Really, Sir,' the King said, 'you are a wonderful man . . . I had heard that you were an able man, but now I know you are *most* able.' The great salons at Holland House and Bowood were anxious to secure his attendance, and throughout the London season few days passed without the receipt of an invitation to a fashionable soirée. Did it give him ideas above his station? Very probably. An officer employed by John Company, who did not even have the cachet of a commission in one of the King's regiments, and who knew more of the ways of Amirs than of society hostesses, was bound to feel flattered. At this stage Burnes's advancement might have been dismissed as the archetypal progress of a Scotsman on the make, which indeed he was. He had, however, one quality to add, for it is clear, both from the way he conducted himself from Delhi to Teheran, and from the manner he adopted in London, that he had flair and he had style. This was the source of much envy.

The social round did not prevent Burnes from visiting the Bow Butts at Montrose, and in his native town he received all the deference which the Scots pay to success. He was made a freeman of the burgh. He could now afford to emulate his early patron Joseph Hume and endow a prize at his old school. Burnes rejoiced in the affection of his family, and dedicated his later volume, *Cabool; A Personal Narrative*, to his father who, he said, 'besides cherishing me in youth, early associated me with himself, and taught me to think and to act as a man when most of my companions had not even acquired the rudiments of their education.' He was particularly pleased when, thanks no doubt to his standing at Leadenhall Street, his young brother was awarded an Indian cadetship.

Burnes was also busy putting the finishing touches to his journal. The King had told him, 'You are intrusted with fearful information; you must take care what you publish.'* The text had to be cleared with the Board of Control, and the effect of their censorship can be seen in the published version, which is innocent of any strategic material or anything that might offend a foreign power. (In December 1838, in a letter to Hobhouse at the Board of Control, Burnes repeated that his journey to Bokhara had convinced him that Russia had ulterior designs eastwards; that he had so expressed himself with some force; but that it was not the policy of the day to take counter-action.)

Burnes took the precaution of getting the distinguished explorer and former Governor of Bombay, Mountstuart Elphinstone, to vet the manuscript, a wise move, since Elphinstone's *Account of the Kingdom of Caubul* – though he did not get further than Peshawar – published in 1815, had long been a model. It is, however, strange that Elphinstone did not query Burnes's ingenuous assessment of the Afghans (page 30). He may have thought that to start an argument on this topic, about which he held very different views, would go beyond acceptable editing. In any event, *Travels into Bokhara; being the Account of a Journey from India to Cabool, Tartary, and Persia: Also Narrative of a Voyage on the Indus from the Sea to Lahore*, was published by John Murray early in 1834. It sold the remarkable number of 900 copies on the day of publication, and was reprinted in 1835 and 1839. Burnes received an initial payment of £800 for the copyright.

Learned bodies were quick to recognise him. The Royal Asiatic Society made him a member; the Royal Geographical Society awarded him their gold medal; and the Athenaeum admitted him to membership by acclamation. At the end of 1834 he went to Paris to address the French Geographical Society and receive their silver medal. There was, it appeared, no one who did not want to

---

*Kaye, *Lives of the Indian Officers*, 1880

honour Burnes, but if his cup was full, the elixir was about to turn slightly acid.

He had naturally been considering how to exploit his success. There was no possibility of transferring to the more fashionable Diplomatic Service, for which he seemed to have all the qualities required – tact, presence, and a facility for languages. Kaye in his history says that Lord Ellenborough, at the Board of Control, offered to use his influence to get Burnes the post of Secretary of the Legation at Teheran with a promise of succession as Minister in charge, but the offer was really much less favourable. Ellenborough, from his journal, was one of the very few who at the time took a cool view about Burnes's ability. He was, after all, the Minister responsible for Indian affairs, although the public appeared to believe that young Burnes was the font of wisdom on that part of the world. Ellenborough was disposed to regard Burnes as something of a bore. All that he offered him was appointment as Second Secretary at Teheran.* Burnes, wanting more, declined, and Ellenborough put him off with a promise to try to get him an Agency in one of the Indian states. But in writing to the Governor-General designate, Lord Heytesbury (who, as it turned out, was replaced on a change of Government before he could take up office), all he did was to enclose Burnes's curriculum vitae, adding, 'What use should be made of his services in India entirely depends on you. It is a matter in which I have no power.'

Ellenborough was an extremely capricious man, and never more so than in his treatment of Burnes. On 10 January 1843, more than a year after the uprising at Kabul, Ellenborough wrote home to Lord Fitzgerald, his successor at the Board of Control.

I have a very indifferent opinion of him [Burnes]. He was intensely vain and self-sufficient and did that which he ought not to have done. Acting as he was for a government to which I was opposed in Afghanistan [the Whigs] he wrote to me from Cabool upon the affairs of Afghanistan. I had not seen him since I was in office in 1835, and have never corresponded with him, and you may be sure that I took no notice of his letter.

This argues some indiscretion on Burnes's part; but it does not enhance Ellenborough's reputation.

*Norris, *The First Afghan War*, 1967.

Meanwhile, in March 1835 Burnes sailed for India. He was disappointed not to get what he wanted at Teheran, but with plaudits still ringing in his ears the future still looked bright. At Calcutta, however, there were those who thought that the encomia on Sikundar Burnes had been overdone and that it was time to clip his wings. He was sent back to his old post as Assistant to Henry Pottinger at Cutch. Pottinger had earlier been one of Burnes's admirers, and had reported favourably on him, but by the end of 1836 they were scarcely on speaking terms.

6

Burnes's next assignment, which took him again to Kabul, was inevitable, unfair, and disastrous. It was inevitable because, if there was to be another trade mission designed to open up trade with Afghanistan and beyond, Burnes was the obvious man to be put in charge; unfair, because the mission acquired a political purpose but he was not given any realistic powers to negotiate; and disastrous for him personally because his advice was ignored and he did not again have any influence on the higher counsels.

Soon after Lord Auckland arrived in India in the spring of 1836 to take up his appointment as Governor-General he received warm greetings from Dost Mahomed. The Dost, who had been distressed by the tacit support which Auckland's predecessor had given to Shah Soojah in his abortive attempt to regain the throne of Kabul, now hoped for some improvement. He was still enraged at 'the conduct of the reckless and misguided Sikhs' in seizing Peshawar, and he made an overt plea for British friendship, to which Auckland replied in very guarded terms. He regretted the dissension with the Sikhs, but sententiously explained that it was not the practice of the British Government to interfere in the affairs of independent states – a doctrine to which he was soon to give the lie. Nevertheless he might soon 'depute some gentleman' to discuss commercial matters with the government of Kabul. So it was that plans were prepared for Burnes's next expedition.

Burnes, when he was in England, had canvassed the promotion of trade beyond the Indus to the point of wearying his listeners. He had talks with the Court of Directors and leading politicians, and not all were impressed. The Court of Directors feared another political involvement, but Burnes – quite unabashed –

wrote to Bentinck, the retiring Governor-General, that the Prime Minister took too parochial a view of the possibilities. The celebrated young explorer was taking much, probably too much, on himself, but his objectives were consistent with Auckland's own long-term plans for peaceful expansion. In the event Burnes soon received his orders from Calcutta.

The objects of Government were to work out its policy of opening up the river Indus to commerce, and establishing on its banks, and in the countries beyond it, such relations as should contribute to the desired end.*

He was to be assisted by Lieutenant Robert Leech of the Bombay Engineers, Lieutenant John Wood of the Indian Navy, and Dr Percival Lord. They sailed from Bombay on 26 November 1836.

In the meantime Westminster had begun to take serious alarm at the apparent spread of Russian influence. Ellis, the Envoy at Teheran, reported that the Shah of Persia was threatening to attack Herat and that he was in communication with the Kandahar chiefs. It was beyond doubt that the capture of Herat, and an alliance between Persia and Afghanistan, was being encouraged by the Russians. On 25 June the Secret Committee of the East India Company had sent Auckland a minute inviting him to consider what should be done 'to counteract the progress of Russian influence'. He was given discretion to proceed, whether by sending a confidential agent to enter into relations with Dost Mahomed 'either of a political or merely, in the first instance, of a commercial character', or by adopting other measures if he thought the time was ripe 'to interfere decidedly in the affairs of Afghanistan'. Auckland took no immediate action, apart from adding a postscript to his reply to London. He said that by despatching Burnes he had 'in a degree anticipated' the Court's instructions. This was in November, and it was not till the following May that Macnaghten wrote to Burnes adding a vague political element to his instructions.

Burnes, travelling up through Sind, was for the moment enjoying himself. At Tatta he had a shooting match with the local tribe. He was surprised that they could not hit the target, 'and then it was gravely discovered that the shots had been fired in

*Burnes, *Cabool, being a personal narrative*, 1842.

the direction of Mecca, which rendered success impossible'. The Amirs of Sind were no longer suspicious, and at Hyderabad he recorded that 'no one could more heartily appreciate than I did the change of tone at this court.' One chief, Ali Moorad Khan, finding he could not tempt Burnes to turn aside to visit him, 'got politically sick'. Dr Lord cured him with a glass of Maraschino 'which was discovered in Sinde to have effects unknown to us'. On 30 March the party was welcomed with many protestations of friendship by the Vizier of Khairpur at Bukkur. Burnes says that he little thought that on Christmas Day of the following year he would negotiate a treaty placing Khairpur under British protection, or, on 29 January 1839, see the British flag flying over the fortress.

On 2 June he heard news that Dost Mahomed's troops had attacked the Sikhs at Jumrood, at the mouth of the Khyber, in an attempt to regain Peshawar. He thought at first that it had been an Afghan victory, but it had actually been an inconclusive battle, though the Sikhs lost one of their best generals. Burnes did not realise at the time that the Dost's action had not only enraged Runjeet Singh, as well it might, but had also helped to convince Auckland that he could not make any alliance with the Dost without jeopardising his friendship with the Maharajah.

At Peshawar Burnes was welcomed by Avitabile, the Italian-born Sikh Governor. He observed the changes made since the province had been taken from the Afghans, the building of bazaars, the widening of streets, and 'that most conclusive proof of civilisation, the erection of a gallows'. On 20 September he was received 'with great pomp and splendour' at Kabul, when a detachment of Afghan cavalry, under the Dost's favourite son, Akbar Khan, came out to meet him. After Akbar had paid him the signal compliment of seating him on his own elephant, he was given agreeable quarters – as befitted the British emissary – in a garden inside the Bala Hissar, and on the next day he had his first formal audience with the Afghan ruler.

It was as well for Burnes that Dost Mahomed greeted him as an old friend, because the presents he had been authorised to bring were niggardly, and, as was soon to become apparent, he was hamstrung by the instructions that soon reached him. The Dost, for his part, was well aware that conditions on his immediate frontiers were far from propitious. To the east, his hated enemy Runjeet Singh, whose ambition seemed insatiable, was still in possession of Peshawar. In the west, Shah Kamran, the last representative of a rival dynasty, ruled at Herat, along with his unscrupulous vizier Yar Mahomed. The Dost knew that they were plotting with his brother Kohun Dil Khan at Kandahar to overthrow him. Moreover, there were rumours that the Persians were about to move on Herat, and a Russian mission, unsought by the Dost, was said to be on its way to Kabul. Burnes's arrival could not have been more timely.

Unknown to Burnes, Fate was slipping the lead into the boxing glove. He was happy in Kabul; he was well entertained; he was no longer a solitary traveller in Afghan dress; he was the formal head of a British mission, and though he had no military figure he had the personal authority and presence to carry off his uniform. He solemnly outlined the British interest in expanding trade with Kabul. Very well, replied the Dost, but, as a start, what help could he expect from the British to expel the Sikhs from Peshawar? Therein lay the rub, for Burnes could offer nothing. A despatch from Macnaghten, sent on 11 September which reached him while he was still − as he thought − taking the Dost's mood, reiterated the Government's concern for 'the honour and just wishes of our old and firm ally Runjeet Singh'. Burnes was firmly told not to support any 'extravagant pretensions' by the Dost. He was also reminded that he had no direct political power to treat with the Kabul ruler and was to do not more than report via Claude Wade at Ludhiana.

The Dost, though disappointed that Burnes was not forthcoming, addressed him with remarkable frankness. He admitted he had been in touch with the Persians, but only when the British refused to help him over Peshawar. He emphasised time and time again that he wanted no alliance but with the British. Burnes readily approved the letter which the Dost wrote urging his brother at Kandahar not to submit to the Shah. He forwarded a copy to the Governor-General, hoping that he would view it 'in a light that must prove, as I believe, very gratifying to the Government'. He went further, detaching Lieutenant Leech to go to Kandahar with an offer of help, and cash, if it were needed. For this he was strongly reproved by Macnaghten, who was angry that his instructions had been disregarded. (Auckland later admitted that in this instance Burnes had been right.) Rebuffed for his attempt to find a solution at Kandahar, and making no progress over Peshawar, where tentative proposals to restore the Dost's treacherous brother Sultan Mahomed while still paying tribute to the Sikhs failed to win acceptance, Burnes stuck to his guns. He reported monotonously in favour of a concord with the Afghan chief. He was in good spirits. 'I am on stirring ground,' he wrote to a friend, 'and I am glad to say I am up to it in health and all that, and was never more braced in my life.' But the tide was running against him, and to add to his discomfiture the long-expected Russian emissary arrived at the gates.

Captain Vickovich, a Pole who had obtained a Cossack commission, remains a mysterious but attractive figure. He had been detected in the Shah's camp outside Herat; he now appeared in Kabul; and he later persuaded the Kandahar chiefs to sign a treaty with the Persians, underwritten by Russian guarantee. But his credentials were always suspect. Count Simonich, the devious Russian Envoy at the Shah's court, professed to know nothing about him, though this was probably part of the clandestine intrigue. Later, after the Shah had withdrawn from Herat, Vickovich returned to St Petersburg to find that he had been disowned. The legend, not entirely substantiated, is that in the same melodramatic way that he had lived, he retired to his hotel and blew his brains out.

Initially the Dost treated Vickovich with marked coolness. He showed Burnes the letters the Russian had brought ('a blazing letter 3 feet long,' said Burnes), and even offered to evict him from Kabul if the British would give any sign that they were interested in reaching an agreement. The comparison between Burnes and Vickovich, the representatives of the two great powers coming ever nearer to confrontation as they extended their fields of influence, has its own fascination. Vickovich had been to Bokhara – according to Masson he brought with him a French version of Burnes's *Travels* – and they had common interests to talk about. Burnes asked him to Christmas dinner and admitted to a personal feeling of friendship. But he did not see him again, 'as the public service required the strictest watch, lest the relative positions of our nations should be misunderstood in this part of

Asia'. It may be that Burnes also identified something of himself in the volatile character of the Russian adventurer.

On 23 December Burnes wrote a long, reasoned letter to Auckland, again setting out the case for taking Dost Mahomed's side over Peshawar. The argument was a logical one, and the benefit to be gained was, he stressed, immense. In settling the Peshawar affair we would have an 'immediate remedy' against further intrigue; the Afghans would see that they had the sympathy of the British Government; and both political and commercial objectives would be achieved. Auckland would have none of it. Macnaghten sent Burnes a further snub, and the Governor-General wrote personally to the Dost saying he must make his own approach to Runjeet Singh, and 'appease the feelings of the powerful sovereign he had offended'. If he did this, and gave up any alliance with other powers, he could count on British good offices, but no more. The Dost was indignant. The British, he said, asked for everything and offered nothing. Vickovich was now received at the Kabul court with every mark of favour. Burnes, seeing that there was nothing more to be done, asked for permission to withdraw. He left on 27 April.

Masson, a dubious character who is described as 'the British writer in Kabul' and seems in that capacity to have submitted intelligence reports on any subject that took his fancy, recorded with evident satisfaction that 'thus closed a mission, one of the most extraordinary ever sent forth by a government, whether as to the singular manner in which it was conducted or as to its results.' He added spitefully that 'the government had furnished no instructions, apparently confiding in the discretion of a man who had none.'

Despite the failure of his mission, Burnes's *Cabool*, which was published in 1842, is free from recrimination or bitterness. The appendices contain an objective appraisal of the domestic economy of Kabul and the strength and weaknesses of the Dost's régime. He barely touches on the Dost as a possible ally. He merely says, 'The British Government, confident of the success of its measures in Persia, placed no value on an Afghan alliance. Fear, therefore, overtook Dost Mahomed, and it was seconded by appeals to his interest; and thus two of the most powerful motives which influence the human mind inclined the chief to look for support to the west instead of the east.'

There are traces of the old Burnes in the text. From Kabul he paid a brief visit to Istalif and the Kohistan. 'Thessalian Tempe could never have more delighted the eyes of an Ionian, that did Istalif please Boeotian Britons.' (Istalif, one of the most attractive towns in Afghanistan, was later the scene of severe reprisals by Pollock's Army of Retribution.) There was also a plea from Moorad Beg, the Chief of Koondooz, who had once had Burnes dragged before him as a suspected culprit, for help to cure his brother's blindness. Dr Lord, sent by Burnes, failed to effect a cure, though he did manage to recover the books and manuscripts of the late Moorcroft and also sent a vivid description of the prizes awarded to the winners of Koondooz horse-races, usually forty or fifty miles across country.

The first a young maiden, generally a Huzarah or Chitrali, both prized for their personal attractions; the second, fifty sheep; the third, a boy; the fourth, a horse; the fifth, a camel; the sixth, a cow; and the seventh, a *water-melon*, the winner of which becomes an object of ridicule.

7

Burnes had reached Gandamack when a messenger brought him a further despatch (sent before he left Kabul) which finally rejected any compromise with Dost Mahomed. He was still at Peshawar at the end of May when he was told to join Macnaghten at Adinanagar. He set off at once and caught up with the British mission on 17 June. *En route* he had to suppress his annoyance at receiving Macnaghten's request for advice on the best way to counteract the Dost's approach to the Persians and the Russians. Burnes might have said he had already written at some length on this subject, but his reply, written on 2 June, is an important one. But what was Macnaghten doing in conference with Runjeet Singh at Adinanagar? The answer lies in the fertile mind of the Governor-General.

In the autumn of 1837 Auckland set out on a lengthy tour of five and a half months, to Simla. During his ceremonial progress he kept in touch – so far as he could – with mail from London, which took between two and three months in transit, and with Envoy McNeill who had left Teheran to join the Shah in his camp outside Herat. Surveying events at the end of April 1838, Auckland could find only one ground for satisfaction. He had at last got a new treaty with Sind, where the Amirs had been induced by Henry Pottinger to accept a British Resident at Hyderabad. So that part of his frontier was now secure. Elsewhere the prospects were less promising. McNeill reported that he could not persuade the Shah to raise the siege of Herat; it seemed likely that the city would fall; and the Persian/Russian threat to British dominion throughout India would be magnified. At Kabul, Burnes had, as Auckland saw it, failed to get Dost Mahomed to come to his senses and accept the *status quo* at Peshawar. The Dost's brother at Kandahar had reached the stage of a draft treaty with the Persians. Auckland was not by nature aggressive, but the advice from Palmerston in London, McNeill at Herat, and the day-to-day reports from his closest advisers, Macnaghten, Colvin and Torrens, all combined to convince him that the time had come 'to interfere decidedly' in Afghanistan, and create a buffer state against Persian/Russian encroachment. We need not follow Auckland's reasoning, or heart-searching, further than this. In his view the only stable element was the friendship of Runjeet Singh. Dost Mahomed, on the other hand, was known to be a man of war; he would not make peace with the Sikhs; and he and his brother were intriguing with the Persians. A British operation to secure Afghanistan could be mounted only through Runjeet's territory, and with his compliance. This meant that an understanding with the Dost, which would antagonise Runjeet, was out of the question. If the Dost resisted, he must be removed.

Once this was decided it was an apparently logical step to select as his replacement the former Kabul ruler, now a pensioner in exile, Shah Soojah. He had at least been friendly to the British when last in power – though that was a long time ago.

That in brief was Auckland's reasoning when he sent Macnaghten to negotiate a tripartite treaty with Runjeet and Soojah. Macnaghten found the task to his liking, and by 20 July he was back in Simla with an agreed document. It provided for interference with a vengeance. As finally adjusted, the plan was for a British army, along with levies raised to give Soojah a presence of his own, to advance on Kabul through the Bolan pass by way of Quetta and Kandahar. A Sikh contingent (Runjeet never intended to commit more than a token force) would at the same time take the more direct route through the Khyber.

Burnes's part in all this was a melancholy one. A letter which he wrote on 2 June is highly significant, and in time he was severely criticised for it. Earlier, writing from Jalalabad on 30 April, Burnes, who had long been an interventionist, had urged the need for 'prompt, active, and decided counter-action' against Russian activities. On 2 June that was still very much his view, and he was emphatic on two points. First, British policy must aim at a United Afghanistan. 'Divide et Impera is a temporising creed at any time.' Second, British arms must be involved, 'that is, it must not be left to the Sikhs.' Burnes agreed that since Dost Mahomed had gone over the Persians he had lost much of his popularity and the way was open to restore Shah Soojah. In a crucial sentence he advised that

The British Government have only to send Shuja-ool-Moolk to Peshawar with an agent and two of its own regiments, as an honorary escort, and an avowal that we have taken up his cause, to ensure his being fixed for ever on his Throne.

Although he must have known that it would be unacceptable, he could not resist making a last plea for his friend the Dost.

He is a man of undoubted ability, and has at heart high opinions of the British nation; and if half you must do for others were done for him, and offers made which he could see conduced to his interests, he would abandon Persia and Russia tomorrow.

Auckland would not entertain the idea of supporting the Dost. His mind was made up, and he paid special weight to Burnes's opinion that Soojah could easily be restored, since Burnes was inclined to favour the Dost. Before long the Army of the Indus was being mobilised to march on Kabul.

It cannot be said that Burnes's one fatal sentence decided Auckland's course of action. Apart from Macnaghten, Wade at Ludhiana, the adventurer Masson who had also been in Kabul, and Mackeson (then agent for navigation on the Indus) all thought the Soojah plan was feasible. But Burnes knew more of the Afghan scene than anyone, and he had consistently argued the Dost's case. Why then did he change horses at the last moment and tell Auckland what he wanted to hear? Was it cynical opportunism, arising from his anxiety not to be left out of the enterprise of great pith and moment that was now afoot? This is the Burnes enigma. He was strongly criticised as a turncoat, and, since he had been the man on the spot, as the architect of the whole misguided expedition. When his despatches were published in London in the *Official Blue Book* – at first in an unscrupulously edited form – there was a strong tendency to make him a scapegoat.

Burnes had been engrossed with the rival claims to Kabul ever since he met Soojah at Ludhiana in 1831. From the start he had no great regard for Soojah's ability, and in that letter of 2 June he had written, and then crossed out the words, 'Of Shah Soojah-ool-Moolk personally I have, that is as ex-King of the Afghans, no very high opinion.' Later, in the historical sketch included in his *Travels*, he thought that Soojah's fitness for the status of sovereign 'seems ever to have been doubtful'. He concluded that the restoration of Soojah was most improbable. 'The dynasty of the Suddozyes (Soojah's tribe) has passed away, *unless it be propped up by foreign aid*'. His account of Dost Mahomed, in contrast, was always complimentary, but there is an interesting passage in the *Travels* where he declares that the whole of the Dost's family 'entertains a dread of Shah Soojah-ool-Moolk, and the Prince Kamran of Herat. The one, *if aided by the British*, would drive them from their usurped authority: and the other, if assisted by the Persians, might perhaps find himself on the throne of his ancestors.' The phrases underlined by the author provide a pointer. Burnes preferred the Dost, but he had no doubt that what mattered was British intervention – which he believed would be successful.

It is a generality that every public servant must be ready to see rejected the course he recommended and then have to carry out an entirely different policy. There is something of this in Burnes's case, but he was aware of the charge of inconsistency, or worse, and tried to find a reason for reconciling himself with the Soojah plan. Writing to a friend on 10 September 1838, he said that when first asked for his views he had replied, 'Self-defence is the first law of nature. If you cannot bring round Dost Mahomed, whom you have used infamously, you must set up Shah Soojah as a puppet, and establish a supremacy in Afghanistan, or you will lose India.' To his mind the need to counter the Russians was paramount. In a letter to Hobhouse in December 1838 he stuck to the same theme. 'We can have no security for the future without rearing a solid fabric westward of the Indus . . . the basis of the present law is self-defence, the first law of nature.'

To sum up, Burnes can justly be arraigned, like many others, for advocating British intervention in Afghanistan. If it was not to be in support of Dost Mahomed, he was content that it should be to restore Soojah. But he is not to be convicted of time-serving for his final advice to Auckland and it does not reveal a flaw in his character. That comes later.

8

During the summer of 1838 regiments were warned for service in Afghanistan, and in December the various components of the Army that was to elevate Soojah started to move. The Bengal Division under Major-General Willoughby Cotton marched from Ferozepore, where it had been reviewed by Auckland and Runjeet Singh, down the left bank of the Indus, while Sir John Keane was bringing a Division of the Bombay Army up from the coast. The intention was that they should meet at Roree and cross the river by way of Bukkur, before heading north through Shikarpur, where Keane would assume overall command. Soojah and his levies, who had crossed higher up, were also moving downstream.

Burnes, when he arrived at Simla on 20 July, hoped that he would be the principal political officer to accompany the Army. He did not know what role he would be assigned, but, he wrote, 'if full confidence and hourly consultation be any pledge, I am to be chief. I can plainly tell them that it is *aut Caesar aut nullus*, and if I get not what I have a right to, you will soon see me *en route* for England.' He was disappointed, for Auckland had already made his choice. Macnaghten had volunteered to go and had also put forward Henry Pottinger as a candidate, but Pottinger, who had a fairly intractable reputation, was busy coercing the Amirs of Sind to accept the passage of British troops. So Auckland designated Macnaghten as 'Envoy and Minister on the part of the Government of India at the Court of Shah Soojah-ool-Moolk'. Burnes was not even considered. Compared with Macnaghten he was too young, too junior, and he was still suspect for his endorsement of Dost Mahomed. He was bitterly disappointed, the more so since he had been made much of by the Governor-General. He was even more chagrined than he had been three years earlier when he failed to get the job of Minister at Teheran, and he at once applied for home leave.

Auckland persuaded him to withdraw his application, but Burnes still grieved. Writing to his brother on 23 August, he claimed that Sir Henry Fane, the Commander-in-Chief, India, had wanted him for the chief political job, but 'as for Macnaghten, he was not sorry to see Dost Mahomed ousted by another hand than his'. About this time Burnes began to imagine that Macnaghten would not stay long at Kabul and that once Soojah had been restored the Envoy would return to more congenial employment in India. Burnes could not believe that he would be passed over a second time. The injury to his pride was somewhat softened by a letter Auckland wrote to him on 5 November in which he admitted that the balance of opinion supported the action Burnes had earlier taken in trying to win the Kandahar chiefs from the Persians. Auckland was glad that Burnes's 'ability and indefatigable zeal' had been recognised, and with quaint grace invited him to look at the superscription of the letter. Addressed to Lt. Col. Sir Alexander Burnes, it was the first intimation that he had been promoted and awarded the accolade. With equal grace, in a letter to Hobhouse, Auckland said he had never been served by anyone who had so much vigour and elasticity of action, or more willingness for good, than Burnes.

If he had not secured the appointment he wanted he was still to outward appearances highly successful, and in November he was told that he was to have an important, though subsidiary, task in accompanying the Army. He was to go ahead of the Bengal column and carry out all necessary negotiations with the chiefs *en route*. It was an assignment for which he was well suited, and Burnes applied himself to it with characteristic energy. First the Khan of Bahawalpur was induced to allow passage and provide fodder for the advancing troops, which he did with some reluctance because the Bengal Division and its camp followers consumed all the provisions in his area before they swept on like locusts to Khairpur. By then Burnes had persuaded the local Khan to accept British protection and allow the troops to occupy Bukkur, the key fortress in the middle of the Indus. This was not Burnes's first visit to Khairpur, and he made good use of the friendship he had formed on his earlier mission.

Macnaghten joined the Bengal column at Shikarpur on 31 January. He was not pleased to learn that Burnes had been a party to diverting a force to compel the Amirs of Sind to accept conditions more onerous than their lately signed treaty. They were now required to allow troops to use the Indus (cancelling the previous prohibition) and to compound twenty years of tribute to Soojah. After first refusing, they agreed to the harsh terms only when they were threatened by a pincer attack from the Bengal column and the Bombay contingent advancing up the river. Macnaghten was furious at the delay and there were ominous signs of disagreement between him and Burnes.

There was more dissension over Burnes's negotiations with Mehrab Khan of Khelat. While the Bengal column was threading its way through the dreaded Bolan Pass Burnes came to an agreement with Mehrab Khan that in return for a modest subvention he would acknowledge Soojah's supremacy. He also undertook to restrain his Baluchi tribesmen from marauding (an undertaking impossible to fulfil), and to procure supplies (which he could do only to a limited extent as his own people were barely at subsistence level). Burnes tactlessly reported to Macnaghten that Mehrab had forecast eventual disaster for the British force and that though Dost Mahomed might be replaced by Soojah, 'even in our present mode of procedure, we could never win over the Afghan nation by it'. Macnaghten, who was not satisfied that Mehrab had tried to fulfil his bargain, came to regard him as an 'implacable enemy', and later took a savage revenge. As for Burnes, Macnaghten thought he had been too gentle with Mehrab and had been too intent on conciliation.

The Army of the Indus, wracked with disease and thirst, struggled through Quetta, Kandahar and Ghuznee. The Commissariat arrangements were deplorable; tribesmen continuously raided the baggage train, even carrying off elephants; but there was no organised resistance except at Ghuznee where fierce hand-to-hand fighting ensued when the gate had been blown in with a massive charge of gunpowder. Dost Mahomed gathered his forces for a final stand in the defiles at Arghandeh, but when his men would not follow him he quit the field and fled towards Bameean. Shah Soojah made his formal entrance into Kabul on 7 August 1839, to be greeted with indifference, acquiescence, but no wild enthusiasm. Macnaghten the Envoy, Keane the Army Commander, and Burnes alone rode beside him. Burnes's uniform was 'a cocked hat fringed with ostrich feathers, a blue frock coat with raised buttons, richly embroidered on the collar and cuffs, epaulettes not yielding to those of a field marshal, and trousers edged with very broad lace'. But though he might rejoice in his place of honour, though he was to be made a Knight of the Order of the Douranee Empire which Soojah soon instituted, though he was officially Resident, he was to spend the rest of his life doing that which was hardest for him – nothing.

The next two and a half years, until the final withdrawal from Kabul under humiliating and disastrous terms at the end of 1842, were notable for the insensitivity which the British showed to local conditions and the temper of the Afghans. Macnaghten might refer to the 'miraculous tranquillity' throughout the country and claim that all was peace from Dan to Beersheba, but these soporific phrases merely exemplify Toynbee's view that a superb administrator may be a purblind statesman.

In fact, the whole of Afghanistan was simmering with discontent, as was evident from the rash of sporadic uprisings. There were small battles, not much more than skirmishes; the British usually won; but in sum they signified widespread hostility. At Kabul itself the chiefs and tribesmen did not resent the race meetings, the cricket matches, the gymkhanas to which the British garrison gave themselves over with joyful vigour. They were sportsmen too. Nor did they take offence at the arrival of the *memsahibs* to join their husbands in the cantonment; their own ladies might be freer from importuning. But they were appalled at the seeming permanence of the British occupation. Soojah, they well knew, could keep his throne only so long as the pennants of the British regiments fluttered alongside the Bala Hissar. Soojah was increasingly detested and the infidels were hated for organising and maintaining his puppet régime.

Shah Soojah-ool-Moolk might be king in Kabul, but he was a disconsolate figure. Painfully aware that even his own mercenaries were officered and paid by the British, that the real source of power lay in the cantonment, and that such minor policy decisions as he was allowed to take had to be approved by Macnaghten, Soojah developed compensating illusions of grandeur. He insisted on all the minutiae of royal protocol at his court; chiefs were kept waiting for hours before being granted an audience; and there was great bitterness that the most lucrative posts were given to the cronies who had kept him company in exile. But taxation was the real cause of complaint. Those who had suffered under the Dost hoped for better things under the rival dynasty, but Soojah, who had promised much, did little for them. His tax-gatherers were as over-zealous as the Dost's had been. When those oppressed appealed for some relief Macnaghten's men would forward their grievances to Soojah. The complainers were then punished for complaining. As the British became more intimately associated with Soojah's malpractices, the Afghans' hatred for the *feringhees* grew.

The tinder was ready when Macnaghten lit the spark with his economy measures. The Eastern Ghilzyes had traditionally enjoyed a subvention, in return for which they refrained from plundering convoys on their way to Kabul. At Auckland's insistence, in the autumn of 1841 Macnaghten reduced the subsidy. The Ghilzyes at once closed the passes and the rebellion was under way. The initial signal was the murder of Burnes.

The British would have been better equipped to analyse events and to take precautionary measures if there had been even a semblance of harmony in their own camp. Unfortunately the leading military and civilian personages could not have been more ill-assorted. Macnaghten's relations with the soldiers were singularly abrasive. He did not get on with Cotton, who had succeeded Keane. Cotton in time gave way to the pathetic, well-meaning, invalid General Elphinstone, but there was no improvement in relationships. Macnaghten could make nothing of Elphinstone's impotent temporising, and he found Elphinstone's second-in-command, Brigadier Shelton, a curmudgeonly boor and extremely objectionable. So did everyone else. Collectively, the military men were not impressive, and some of them earned

Macnaghten's contemptuous epithet of 'croakers', but the Envoy was also at fault. For example, he took violent offence at criticism from the knowledgeable Brigadier Abraham Roberts, who was in charge of Soojah's troops, and Roberts (father of the future Lord Roberts) was replaced by the more compliant Brigadier Anquetil. The move cost Anquetil his life.

Macnaghten's attitude to his civilian colleagues was no better. When Rawlinson, the political officer at Kandahar, and Eldred Pottinger at Charekar both warned him repeatedly that rebellion was brewing, he would not listen. He reproved Rawlinson for not looking at things 'a little more *couleur de rose*', and dismissed Pottinger as an alarmist. None of his immediate juniors could pierce his self-confidence, or his belief that all was well.

But what of Burnes, the Resident, next in seniority to Macnaghten? Before the Army occupied Kabul there had been suggestions that Burnes should be the Agent at Kandahar, or at Herat, but he refused both offers. He was certain that he would soon succeed the Envoy; he would do nothing to impair his chances; in practice he did not do anything at all. The trouble was that Macnaghten, the deskbound scholar and administrator, and Burnes the wayfarer were entirely antipathetic. Macnaghten in his letters said tartly that Burnes was painting a gloomy picture in order to enhance any success he might gain when he reached the highest post.

Only twice in these two years did Burnes play a role of any importance. When Macnaghten accompanied Soojah to spend the winter at Jalalabad, where the climate was less severe, Burnes was left in charge. Later, when Sale took his Brigade to the Bameean area to seek out the elusive Dost Mahomed who had reappeared in some strength, Burnes went with him as political officer. The Afghans had the better of it in the fighting at Purwundurrah, though they did not press home their advantage. Burnes was sufficiently alarmed to send an urgent despatch from the battlefield recommending that outposts should be withdrawn and that all troops concentrated at Kabul. But before this could be acted upon the Dost decided that, despite his partial success at Purwundurrah, further resistance was useless. He rode into Kabul and surrendered to Macnaghten personally. The Dost had an affectionate interview with Burnes before he left for exile at

Ludhiana (on the same quarters where Soojah had been housed) and made him a present of his sword. Their mutual respect survived hostilities.

Otherwise, Burnes, seeing his advice rejected or ignored by Macnaghten, declined into indifference. He was now, he wrote,

> A highly paid idler, having no less than 3,500 rupees a month, as Resident at Caubul, and being, as the lawyers call it, only counsel, and that, too, a dumb one – by which I mean I give paper opinions, but do not work them out.'

His letters now boasted of his sybaritic breakfasts of 'smoked fish, salmon grills, devils, and jellies', not to mention the select wines to which he entertained his dinner guests. But when he asserts, 'I lead, however, a very pleasant life, and if rotundity and heartiness be proofs of health, I have them,' it had a defiant air. This was a sad falling-off for the man who had said that difficulties were his brandy.

It is even sadder to note Burnes's idling when it is clear from his letters that he saw that Macnaghten was laying up a store of trouble by interfering too directly in affairs at Soojah's court. In June 1841 he wrote to his friend Major Lynch that he was opposed to any further fighting in Afghanistan, since the country would never be settled at the point of the bayonet. He knew very well that he should have added his weight to the disquieting reports from Rawlinson and Pottinger, but he remained silent.

In the autumn of 1841 it was confirmed that Macnaghten was to go to Bombay as Governor, but there was as yet no news of his successor at Kabul. This started a last period of dreadful agonising for Burnes. He had been taking refuge in reading – Tacitus, the letters of Horace Walpole, the life of Sidney Smith – which he claimed supported his view that 'all great men have more or less charlatanerie'. On 16 October, in a moment of self-criticism, he wrote in his journal that he had been wondering whether he was as well suited for supreme control as he thought. But he was convinced that second best would not do. 'In it my irritation would mar all business.' On the 31st, twenty years to the day since he first landed in India, he was convinced that the news simply must come.

> Ay! What will this day bring forth? . . . it will make or mar me, I

suppose. Before the sun sets I shall know whether I go to England or succeed Macnaghten.

But no despatches arrived. The next day, swallowing his disappointment, he went to congratulate the Envoy on leaving at a season of such tranquillity and to wish him Godspeed on his journey to Bombay. Then he returned to his Residency.

He was not to leave it alive. Two Afghan chiefs had of recent weeks been fomenting a conspiracy to raise the country against the hated *feringhees* and they now decided that the signal for rebellion should be the death of Burnes. They had four reasons for selecting him as their victim. First, Burnes had recently discovered one of the chiefs – Abdoolah Khan – intriguing with the insurgent Ghilzyes and threatened to crop his ears. Abdoolah wanted revenge for the insult. Second, the Afghans were aware that Burnes was likely to be Macnaghten's successor. They also knew that he was much better versed in their affairs than the departing Envoy, and they did not relish the prospect of his taking over control. Third, Burnes's Residence in the city, protected by only a small detachment, was an easy target. Fourth, as the other conspirator, an old rogue called Amenoolah Khan, said, 'Everything we do is made known to Burnes; *lose no time*; attack the Kafir at once in his house, before he can know our plans.'

During the day the bazaar was full of rumours and Burnes's Afghan servants warned him that he was at risk. In the evening his loyal *moonshee* Mohun Lal – the one man to whom he might have listened – repeated the warning, but, according to Mohun Lal's account, 'Burnes stood up from his chair, sighed, and said, he knew nothing but the time had arrived that we should leave this country.'* He may have had a premonition, but he would not act on it. He refused to go to the cantonment or ask for the guard to be strengthened. He had done the Afghans no injury, he told his worried servants; why should they harm him? The same evening Taj Mahomed, a friendly chief, told him he was not safe, as did Osman Khan, the chief Afghan Minister, early the next morning. A large crowd was now pressing round the house, but Burnes still believed it was only a local riot, which would soon subside.

*Kaye: *Lives*.

From the stones and imprecations that were being hurled at the Residency, and the brandishing of knives, Burnes at last realised that help was needed. He sent a message to Macnaghten in the cantonment; but it was too late. The mob of fanatics, stirred up by Abdoolah Khan and his associates, was screaming for Burnes's head. He harangued them from the gallery overlooking the courtyard – the parallel with Gordon at Khartoum is inescapable – but the mob fired at him. His companion William Broadfoot was shot at his side. Then the rebels set fire to the stables and shouted to Burnes to come down. He offered them money to spare himself and his brother Charles, unhappily a guest at the Residency. A mysterious Kashmiri told the brothers to put on native dress and follow him. It was a trap. As soon as they reached the garden the Kashmiri shouted, 'Here is Sikundar Burnes!' The mob fell on them and hacked them to pieces.

It was a tragic ending. Burnes might be said to have brought it on himself, since he had certainly been warned. He was too concerned about succeeding Macnaghten to pay attention to the immediate danger. But there was more to it. He was too cocky; too self-assured, and he could not imagine that he would be singled out for attack within reach of the main British garrison. This one aberration, though it cost him his life, does not, however, provide the answer to the Burnes conundrum. Was he inconsistent, unstable, too impulsive and too ambitious, as his critics claimed? As late as the end of September 1841 Colvin was writing to ask whether Burnes, who admittedly possessed 'a peculiar experience and perhaps a peculiar influence' which might be most valuable, was 'really a fit and safe person to be appointed Envoy at Cabool?'

The charge of inconsistency is not proven. As already explained, he did not support the plan to restore Soojah till his eloquent and oft-repeated arguments on behalf of Dost Mahomed had failed; he offered to leave India; and only Auckland's personal plea that 'it would be desertion at a critical moment' persuaded him to remain. Nor was he particularly unstable or impulsive. His recommendations were invariably well documented, and if his life style was more extravagant than that of his rivals he could always carry it off with flair. (There was a strong undercurrent of rumour that Burnes antagonised the chiefs by his *affaires* with their women; but there is no real evidence to justify the allegation.) Ambitious he undoubtedly was, but ambition and energy were prerequisites to success in the service of the East India Company.

Burnes had great resilience and an unusual insight into the oriental character. The early momentum of his career was to seize opportunities which came his way, or which he made for himself. He was happiest, though he may not have realised it, sharing the friendship of his travelling companions and the tribesmen he met in deserts and high places. It seems probable, however, that the success which he enjoyed in London in 1834 went to his head. He began to nourish unjustifiable ideas of his own importance – he became disillusioned and idle and flaccid. The Burnes of the Bokhara travels would never have been trapped and cut down by the Kabul mob. To use Hazlitt's words, Burnes was one of those who felt that

Greatness is great power, producing great effects. It is not enough that a man has great power in himself; he must show it to all the world in a way that cannot be hid or gainsaid.

3
The Other Eden

I

The most influential woman in British India while George Eden, second Baron Auckland, was Governor-General was his sister Emily. No one doubted that she was closer to her brother than any of his nearest official advisers. Emily took the relationship so much for granted that, in the voluminous letters she sent back to England, she mentioned it only in passing. 'It is odd', she wrote in July 1836, 'that whenever G and I are alone we invariably find ourselves talking hard English politics... Indian politics are clearly not half so amusing.'* Two years later she was more explicit. 'G, who has always been a sort of idol to me, is, I think, fonder of me than ever, and more dependent on me, as I am his only confidante. I feel I am of use to him, and that I am in my right place when I am by his side.' Writing to Charles Greville from the heights of Simla in June 1838, she described the Governor-General's lonely responsibility – no Ministers, no Parliament, and his Council down at Calcutta. 'To be sure,' she went on with a touch of irony, 'as you were going to observe, *if* he ever felt himself in any doubt, he *might* feel that he has my superior sense and remarkable abilities to refer to, but as it is, he has a great deal to answer for by himself.' She was assured enough to make light of the bond between them.

There is only one recorded instance when Emily was in real dispute with her brother. When Auckland returned to England in 1842 his reputation was at its nadir. His successor, the Tory Lord Ellenborough, who felt he had been left with a mess to clear up, had made it so brutally clear that he dissociated himself from Auckland's activities that there was a party dispute among the Whigs whether a vote of thanks to Ellenborough in Parliament should be resisted.

*Emily Eden, *Letters from India*, 1872.

They resolved with only two dissentients [wrote Charles Greville] that the vote should not be opposed. Auckland took no part, of course, but entirely concurred. His sister Emily Eden, who has great influence over him, and who is a very clever and wrong-headed woman, was furious, and evinced great indignation against all their Whig friends, especially Auckland himself, for being too prudent and moderate, and for not attacking Ellenborough with all the violence which she felt and expressed.

Greville's judgement is harsh, particularly since he had enjoyed a long and intimate correspondence with Emily. He had previously treated her with good-humoured respect, but now he thought that her intemperate defence of her brother's actions showed the distorting effect that sisterly affection could have. Perhaps too she had some feeling of personal guilt, having herself been a party to many of Auckland's decisions. But Emily was no fool.

Born in Old Palace Yard, Westminster, in 1797, she was the seventh daughter out of fourteen children of William Eden, the first baron. Her father had a successful diplomatic career, holding posts as Minister to Versailles before the Revolution and later as Ambassador to Spain and Holland. Her mother, Eleanor Elliot, was a sister of the first Earl of Minto, an earlier Governor-General of India. Her father died in 1814; his widow four years later; and Emily and her younger sister Fanny set up house with George.

It was a highly political family. George became a fairly undistinguished President of the Board of Trade, and then, in a Cabinet reshuffle, First Lord of the Admiralty. Emily, intelligent and articulate, relished her role as a leading Whig hostess. Her eldest sister, Eleanor, had an affectionate interlude with William Pitt, but eventually married Lord Hobart, later the Earl of Buckinghamshire. Emily remained on close terms with Eleanor and two friends in particular, Theresa Villiers, the sister of Lord Clarendon, and Pamela Fitzgerald, later Lady Campbell. With all of them she corresponded at great length throughout her stay in India.

Auckland and Fanny both died in 1849, but Emily lived for another twenty years, latterly in poor health which restricted her scope as hostess. She remained a zealous Whig. Her *Letters from*

India, edited by her niece, were published in 1872, and another collection, this time edited by her great-niece, Violet Dickinson, appeared in 1919. This was not the sum of Emily's writing. *Up the Country* (1866), an account of her journey from Calcutta to the Upper Provinces, is her most substantial work. In the dedication she hoped that the details of an expedition that was 'picturesque in its motley processions, in its splendid crowds' and in its 'barbaric gold and pearl', might be thought amusing. It is still highly regarded for its wit and vivid descriptions. Though gossipy, it is seldom malicious. On her return to England she wrote two novels, *The Semi-Detached House* (1859), soon followed by *The Semi-Attached Couple*. A faint flavour of Jane Austen pervades them, but they lack the vigour of the Indian writing. (All three volumes have been reprinted in paperback.) Lastly, in the fashion of the time, Emily was a keen amateur artist, and her *Portraits of the People and Princes of India* (1844) is now a collector's piece. Her accomplishments are not in question.

In April 1835 the short Tory interregnum came to an end. Lord Melbourne was once again Prime Minister and offered Auckland the Governor-Generalship of India. Emily received the news without enthusiasm. To her friend Lady Campbell she complained about the 'awful change in our destination' and taking leave of friends she would never see again.

Besides, what is there to say, except, 'God's will be done.' It all comes to that. I certainly look at the climate with dread, and to the voyage with utter aversion . . . One thing is certain, I could not live without George, so I may be thankful that my health has been so good this year that I have no difficulty on that account, as to going with him. And as other people have liked India and have come back to say so, perhaps we shall do the same.

She did not find her hope fulfilled, but she was soon busy with preparations to face 'the deep-seated real Indian calamity'. It was irritating to need so many things.

A cargo of *large fans*; a *silver busk*, because all steel busks become rusty and spoil the stays; nightdresses with short sleeves, and net nightcaps, because muslin is too hot. Then such anomalies – quantities of flannel which I never wear at all in this cool climate, but which we are to wear at night there, because the creatures who are pulling all night at the punkahs sometimes fall asleep. Then you wake from the extreme heat and call to them, then they wake and begin pulling away with such fresh vigour that you catch your death with a sudden chill.

Her distemper was only slightly mollified by a cordial letter from Melbourne, with whom her name had once been linked, and a gracious one from King William. His Majesty was not surprised that Miss Eden and her sister 'should have determined to accompany so affectionate a Brother even to so remote a destination'.

2

On 3 October 1835 the Governor-General designate and his sisters sailed on board the *Jupiter*. With them went their nephew William Godolphin Osborne, who had already seen service in India with the 16th Lancers and was now appointed Military Secretary. High-spirited, excessively keen on shooting tigers, much addicted to practical jokes, he had an underlying shrewdness that later appeared in his account of the mission to the court of Runjeet Singh. In these days the journey to India was a hazardous one and not all ships that sailed from Portsmouth reached the mouth of the Hoogly. Shipwrecks and piracy were common occurrences, but the *Jupiter* survived with a single dismasting. There were formal entertainments at Funchal, Rio, and Cape of Good Hope, and Emily's main grievance was about the constant creaking of the ship's timbers. (She did not like the horseplay in the ceremonies when they crossed the Equator.)

On 2 March, after seventy-two days at sea since the Cape, they sighted the Indian coast. Emily wrote that, according to protocol, 'Sir C. Metcalfe (the provisional Governor-General) gives us a great dinner *at* Government House, and then leaves it *to* us in the evening.' It was not to be. The steamer towing them upstream was caught in an eddy and drove the *Jupiter* aground. Auckland's official yacht, the *Soonamookie*, which was being towed astern, collided with them, and the embarrassed party had to transfer to the steamer. No one would admit that there was anything ominous in the accident, but it was late at night when they reached their destination.

The First Lady and her sister quickly adapted to the formality of their new establishment. Receptions, levées, dinners at which eighty or more sat down to table, bearers in perpetual attendance, sentries presenting arms whenever they emerged from their rooms, all were a source of interest, but no more. On their first Sunday the Governor-General and the Misses Eden drove in state to church. Three velvet chairs, with a railing round them, were placed in the middle of the cathedral aisle. There they sat, as new exhibits. Emily observed that some of the ladies came without bonnets and fanned themselves unceasingly with large feather fans. 'Otherwise it was very much like an English church. Great part of the service very well chanted.'

Regrettably, Emily soon found that she hated India. Of course she had to preserve a façade, and this she did with some success, but in her letters she could not conceal the depth of her detestation. Much of her writing is concerned with the trivialities that might be expected from one newly exiled, and she was always anxious about the uncertain arrival of letters from home. (Lieutenant Waghorn, 'dear Mr Waghorn', had been sent to Cairo to investigate a regular overland mail service by way of Suez. Otherwise, letters, frequently lost in transit, took five or six months.) She was an avid reader. Charles Lamb, Dickens, especially *Pickwick*, Hannah More and the twenty-two volumes of Saint-Simon were among her favourites, and she welcomed pirated editions to speed up delivery. But there is a recurring theme. Quite simply, she abominated her new country, and it is clear from the regular pattern that her comments were not prompted by occasional bouts of depression or homesickness.

As early as April 1836 she was writing home, 'I cannot abide India, and that is the truth, and it is almost come to not abiding *in* India.' A year later, 'As to India; looking at it dispassionately and without exaggerating its grievances for fun, I really think I hate it more now than at first.' The first letter in *Up the Country* refers to a place 'where there is little society and few topics'. Emily did not take kindly to travelling or living in tents, even in the style the Governor-General could command. Her own tent had been christened 'Misery Hall'. Auckland humoured her by calling his own 'Foully Palace'. Cawnpore was one of 'those dreadful large stations', and at Meerut there was nothing to see or draw. From Kurnaul she wrote in March 1838, 'I believe it has taken us forty English years to do those two Indian ones; but it shows what time and longevity will effect.' When she returned a year later she thought 'this place looks quite as ugly as it did last year; all barracks and plain, and not a tree in sight. I cannot think how people bear their cantonment life as well as they do.' She had already written from Amritsar that life was passing away and that she was in the wrong place. In January 1840 she wrote to her sister, Eleanor, 'I want to talk to you and never see these brown, arid plains, and browner, arider people any more, and, as for staying here a whole year that ought to be passed in England, I can't.'

There was more than a touch of desperation when she saw release in the offing. 'George is writing home by this post to say that he positively goes next February, and I mean to look over that letter before it goes, to be sure he makes no mistake.'

Auckland did not find India so uncongenial. He had gone out with high hopes of a peaceful administration. Events in Afghanistan and in China (which also came within his purview) gave him a much rougher ride than he expected, but he remained conscientious, hard-working, mildly amused by the ambience of Government House. His younger sister Fanny too was more tolerant of her new environment. More lighthearted than Emily – who commented tartly that Fanny had to have excitement – she was not so influential in Auckland's counsel. But she was an engaging figure. The (belatedly discovered) journal she wrote on a tiger-shooting trip with her nephew to the Rajmahal hills gives some indication of her temperament. The expedition was an informal one for these days, although they had 260 people in their camp. Fanny was intensely proud of returning as the only white woman in India, apart from the dedicated huntress, Mrs Cockerell, who had seen a tiger killed. Other species of game were also encountered.

March 1st. I have been out from six till ½ nine . . . Our safety consists in being in the thick of the shooters, who have no time to think about us, but would naturally shoot any animal that would attack us, because it is the object they are after. Very soon the elephant we were on and two others near gave a roar, and an immense rhinocerous started up within a yard of us. All those near shot, and all declared it was hit, but if it were bore it very philosophically. While we were chasing that, our elephant still was snorting. Then we found a young rhinocerous was left, not much larger than a great pig. They wanted to take him alive, but he showed much more fight than the mother – charged a line of sixteen elephants and made them roar and turn round, for they hate a small live thing. The *mahouts* threw themselves off, to bind it with cords, but though they caught it three times, at last it fairly got the better of them and escaped to the thick jungles.

Ten minutes after, we found another old rhinocerous, probably the respected father, a very magnificent looking beast. The chase after him was beautiful. All the elephants get so eager and press on as hard as they can. He made his escape, too, which I was not as sorry for as I ought to have been, for the half-hour's chase was just as grand to see. After that I left them to come home across what was called a safe bit of country, and in that same bit, within a quarter of a mile of the camp, they killed their first tiger ten minutes after I left them. Mrs. C. came home smaller and fresher and better dressed than ever, quite delighted, and only wishing it had showed more fight.

March 2nd. Last night, just as I was going to bed, they came and told me a rajah had brought a spotted deer, two peacocks and a pot of honey. As they were jungle productions I was not to refuse them. I sent my salaams, wondering what on earth I should do with the peacocks, but he made such a point of making his salaam to the *lady sahib*, I went out in a pink flannel dressing-gown, which I hope he thinks an approved English mode of dress. There he was, in a gold kincob dress and turban, with his servants holding torches and the peacocks and the deer, which turns out the greatest of pets, follows me about, and lies by me on the sofa like a little dog.

March 9th. Elephants are the best beasts to see much of – I cannot say the respect I have for them.

She has a very pert comment to add about brother George.

March 15th. ... He was growing very despotic when I left home; he may have committed any atrocity during our absence – he has probably cut off the heads of all the aide-de-camps.

3

Before analysing Emily's observations on the most significant event during her brother's tenure – the circumstances that led to the destruction of the British Army in Afghanistan – her general attitude to those she met is of interest. Socially, she was completely confident, and felt no need to assert her primacy over Anglo-Indian society, such as it was, in Calcutta, in the stations she visited, or in the summer capital in Simla. She was also aware

[67]

that she could look forward to an end of her 'term of transportation', unlike others who were there for longer or not infrequently for life. India, she still thought, was a dreadful place, but, she went on,

> I do not mean so much for us, who come for a short time and can have a fleet, or any army to take us anywhere if we have pains in our sides, but for people who earn their bread in India, and must starve if they give it up.

She was very sympathetic to those from remote stations who came to pay their respects to the Governor-General on his travels from Calcutta to Simla. Often they had no European companionship: they seldom heard English spoken; and the chance to hear a regimental band playing for Auckland's entertainment was an unusual delight. Emily was gracious to them all. But she could not refrain from writing, 'How some of these young men must detest their lives!' She was more acid about her own sex. Did she find any pleasing or accomplished women among her European acquaintances?

> Not one – not the sixth part of one: there is not anybody I prefer to any other body .. It is a gossiping society, of the smallest macadamised gossips, I believe, for we are treated with too much respect to know much about it: but they sneer at each other's dress and looks, and pick out small stories against each other by means of the Ayahs, and it is clearly a downright offence to tell one woman that another looks well.

She grieved for the eventual fate of the 'fishing fleet' who came out in search of husbands. After a ball at Meerut she wrote sadly about some of them. They had arrived just in time for the high season; they would have the choice of three regiments; but they would get a false impression of the usual tenor of life in the cantonments. Cruelly, if they failed to find a mate and went home unmarried they would be contemptuously known as 'returned empties'.

Both Emily and her sister were inveterate matchmakers. They rejoiced when they organised an engagement between Cecil Beadon (later Governor of Bengal) and Harriet Sneyd. The marriage took place in a tent during the progress up the country, Emily improvising an altar from the 'state housings of the elephants', with four armchairs for railings. She was, however, disenchanted with the balls she had to attend. Perhaps there were too many of them. Perhaps it was because the Misses Eden were the only two ladies who never danced. At all events, such enthusiasm as she could muster was obligatory. Anything out of the ordinary would attract her attention. At Kurnaul, for example, she noticed European soldiers dressed up as footmen, '*real, red plush trousers*, with blue coats and red collars, and white cotton stockings, and powdered heads, and they carried about trays of tea and ices'. The artificial nature of the society over which she presided sometimes came home to her. At the Queen's Ball at Simla she could not avoid remarking on the contrast between 105 Europeans eating imported salmon and sardines to the accompaniment of the band playing *I Puritani* and *Masaniello*, and the 3,000 natives who surrounded them. 'I sometimes wonder they do not cut all our heads off, and say nothing about it.'

In *Up the Country* Emily is determinedly discreet. Few are identified by name, and she often changed initials. But there were two who could not remain anonymous. First, the Eden sisters' bland superiority was set at nought by the indefatigable Mrs Parkes who pursued them from Benares to Delhi and Simla. 'If she were not so fat, I would say she was something supernatural. My spirit is broken about her. We shall find her settled in our home at Simla, and shall not have the strength to turn her out.' The second lady was celebrated in a wider context. In September 1839 Simla was excited by the arrival of the newly-married Mrs James, whose beauty drove the other ladies to distraction. Emily was much taken with her. 'Undoubtedly very pretty, and such a merry unaffected girl.' She would have needed a crystal ball to foresee that Mrs James was to become the mistress of the King of Bavaria – and to be better known as the notorious courtesan Lola Montez.

In an age when the British in India kept their distance from the native population, Emily and her sister were refreshing exceptions. An earlier *memsahib*, when asked what she had seen of the people of India, replied, 'Oh, nothing at all about them, nor I don't wish to. Really I think the less one knows of them the better.' The Governor-General and his sisters reached Cawnpore at the height of the 1838 famine, when over a quarter of a million

Indians died. Emily's letters were full of compassion. 'The women look as if they had been buried, their *skulls* look so dreadful . . . I am sure there is no violent atrocity I should not commit for food, with a starving baby.' She rescued one child and, despite her doctor's advice, preserved it by feeding it in her tent four times a day. It was not only enormous disasters that affected her. She was distressed by a visit to the 1,200 life prisoners in Alipore Jail. It was melancholy to see old men who had been in fetters for so many years, often for crimes that would have incurred lesser penalties at home, but worse to observe boys of nine and thirteen already chained for life. On the way back from Lahore to Simla she bought two little orphans for three pounds and in time handed them over to the orphanage at Calcutta run by Mrs Wilson, a lady whose work she greatly admired.

Emily was often impatient with protocol. She warmly approved of her brother's action, during the journey upstream from Calcutta to Benares, in going ashore to see the Bullgha horse fair. Macnaghten and Torrens, the two officials present, were aghast, and Torrens danced about the deck with rage. Macnaghten said the Governor-General should never appear in public without a regiment, but when he added that there was no precedent Emily retorted that they had one now and that it would be his duty to take the next Governor-General, however lame and infirm, to the identical fair.

Emily had a keen feeling for the underdog, especially those who suffered from rigid social distinctions. At the prize-giving at the Hindu College in Calcutta she was delighted when Auckland rescinded the order that the pupils were to appear barefooted. They were allowed to wear shoes. At Simla, when Emily learned that the ladies were going to boycott her ball because the Sikh envoys had been invited, she descended upon their unfortunate spokeswoman to say that, since she had asked forty natives to every dance she had given at Calcutta, it was too late to object. When the evening came, there were only three defaulters. (Conversely, at an earlier ball at Dinapore, she noted that the Rajahs who were present thought the ladies who danced were 'utterly good for nothing, but seemed rather pleased to see so much vice'.)

Her genuine sympathy for the underprivileged is best seen in her attitude to the Eurasians. A series of plays had been arranged for the Simla theatre, the proceeds to go to the starving people of Agra, but some actors fell out – one man assigned a woman's role would not shave his moustache, and another went off to shoot bear.

So when the gentlemen gave it up, the 'uncovenanted service' said they wished to try. The 'uncovenanted service' is just one of our choicest Indianisms, accompanied with our very worst Indian feelings. We say the words just as you talk of the 'poor chimney sweepers', or 'those wretched scavengers' – the uncovenanted being, in fact, clerks in the public offices. Very well-educated quiet men, and many of them very highly paid; but as many of them are half-castes, we, with our pure Norman or Saxon blood, cannot really think contemptuously enough of them . . . amongst them are several thorough gentlemen . . . and I never saw better behaved people.

Emily insisted that the Eurasians should be allowed to take part in the dramatics. Unrepenting, she remarked that 'a great many of the *gentry* were even above going to see them act. However we went, and lent them the band, and the house was quite full.'

4

The picture of Emily which emerges so far is of a liberal-minded, sympathetic Victorian, anxious to do her duty, though she loathed the country. She was not going to let her brother down. Auckland was not the most decisive of men, and it was only after months of vacillation that he took the most important decision of his time in office. This was to send Macnaghten to negotiate a treaty with Runjeet Singh which would enable the British, with Sikh support, to invade Afghanistan. As we have seen, it was a disastrous move. There can be little doubt that Emily was privy to her brother's communings. We do not know exactly what passed between them, but the incidental observations in her letters give a good idea of her attitude, which seems to have been more frivolous than anything else. Her comments on the various military and other leaders whom she met before the storm broke give a foretaste of her reaction to the 'signal catastrophe' that followed.

At Meerut she found Major-General the Hon. John Ramsay, the Governor of the District, a good-natured old man who had lost his memory and said the same thing ten times over. When Auckland asked him how many men he had at Meerut, he replied, ' "I cannot just say, my Lord; perhaps sax and twenty thoosand" – such a fine army for a small place.' On the way to the great durbar with Runjeet Singh at Ferozepore, Emily was allowed to go half a mile in advance, to avoid the dust. This shocked Sir Henry Fane, the Commander-in-Chief, who never even let a little dog precede him on the march. When Emily passed him and his suite – 'a very large body of cocked hats' – by the side of the road, she felt that

> It was too awful a military moment for speech. I was not sure whether it was irregular to kiss my hand; however, I ventured on that little movement, which was received with a benign 'clignotement de l'oeil' signifying 'wrong, but I forgive it for once.'

Military pomp is none the worse for mocking, and on this occasion Emily may be forgiven her frivolity.

Like all who met him, she was intrigued by James Skinner, the son of a Scottish father and a Rajput mother, who raised the regiment of horse that bore his name. She visited the bizarre church in Delhi which he had sworn to build if he survived his wounds. Skinner, she said, had done all sorts of gallant things. He had 'his zenana and heaps of black sons like any other native . . . In short, he is one of the people whose lives ought to be written for the particular amusement of succeeding generations.' Skinner sent Emily and her sister a pair of cashmere shawls, saying that if they returned them he would imagine they looked on him as a native, and not as an old British soldier. They kept the shawls.

Sir Willoughby Cotton, who was soon to lead his troops into Afghanistan, was evidently regarded as something of a buffoon. He seemed to think that one of his most luminous achievements in life was to have got himself expelled from Rugby for having led the school mutiny forty years before and never tired of retelling the story. He had been too long in India and Sir Henry Fane wrote of him that 'I don't think Cotton has a mind which carries away much of verbal instruction', a polite way of saying that he was both slow and stupid. Emily describes him arriving at Ferozepore not so fat as he was at Calcutta. When she told him he had grown thin he replied that the courtiers had assured George IV, when he was at his most obese, 'Your Majesty is regaining your figure.' So much for the Commander of the Bengal Division.

Auckland had an uncanny gift for choosing the wrong man, none worse than General Elphinstone, whom he later appointed to succeed Cotton at Kabul. Emily, who already knew 'Elphy Bey', saw him at Futtehpore on his way to take up his new post and realised he was in poor shape.

He is in a shocking state of gout, poor man! – one arm in a sling and very lame, but otherwise a young-looking general for India. He hates being here... He is wretched because nobody understands his London topics, or knows his London people... He went off with a heavy heart to his palanquin, which must be a shaky conveyance for gout. One sees how new arrivals must amuse old Indians. He cannot, of course, speak a word of Hindoostanee.

Elphinstone complained of the difficulty in making his bearers understand him and regretted he could not bring his favourite negro with him. Emily supposed he meant a native, since he could hardly have picked up 'a woolly black negro who speaks Hindoostanee'. She did not comment on the folly of sending this pathetic invalid to take charge of the British force in a hostile country.

She was not cordial towards William Macnaghten, the Political Secretary. Each was probably suspicious, if not overtly resentful, of the other's influence on the Governor-General. She first refers to him – with measured coolness – as clever and pleasant, speaking Persian 'rather more fluently' than English, Arabic better than Persian, but preferring Sanskrit for familiar conversation. She wrote to Charles Greville describing Macnaghten as '*our* Lord Palmerston', and referring again to his linguistic ability. Everyone was aware of Macnaghten's reputation as an oriental scholar, but the identification with Palmerston is of interest. On the surface, it might mean no more than that the Political Secretary was Auckland's principal adviser on relations with foreign powers – though Auckland notoriously made up his own policy – or it might be sarcastic, because there could be no greater contrast than that between the suave bureaucrat and the imperious Foreign Secretary at Westminster. There is no answer to this problem, as Emily passed no later judgement on poor Macnaghten, whose obstinate determination to believe what he wanted to believe led to his murder by Dost Mahomed's son. Emily referred only once to Macnaghten's wife – 'on whom we depend for our *tracasseries* to repeat all that any of the company have ever said of the others'. Lady Macnaghten, who eventually joined her husband at Kabul, was a formidable *memsahib*, preoccupied with her jewellery, her cashmere shawls and her cats. If she was not sufficiently obsequious towards the chatelaine of Government House, she endured months of captivity after her husband's assassination, and spent much of her widowhood in an acrimonious dispute about her pension.

Emily was mistaken in her reaction to Captain Claude Wade, the Political Agent at Ludhiana, merely noting that he had 'lived so much with natives that he has acquired their dwindling soft manners and their way of letting things take care of themselves'. Wade was in fact an ambitious careerist. He added his own dissentient comments to Burnes's despatches from Kabul, and was one of the foremost of those who assured Auckland that Shah Soojah would be acceptable to the chiefs if restored to the Afghan throne.

The more glamorous aspects of the oriental courts attracted Emily, but the barbaric splendour affected by the potentates dazzled her to their real character. This was especially apparent at the Ferozepore durbar – Fanny and Emily were the only two English ladies allowed to attend – when Auckland and Runjeet Singh solemnised the treaty that was the prelude to the invasion of Afghanistan. With a keen eye for detail, she describes Runjeet's arrival for the start of the ceremonies. 'He is exactly like an old mouse, with grey whiskers and one eye.' He later sat for Emily to do his portrait, when she observed that

> He had a curious and constant trick, while sitting and engaged in conversation, of raising one of his legs under him on the chair, which he used in compliance with the customs of his European visitors, and then pulling the stocking from that foot.

He was also presented with a portrait of Queen Victoria which Emily had painted for the occasion, and gravely replied that it would be hung in front of his tent and received with a royal salute from his cannon. Emily soon tired of the repetitive ceremonies, both at Ferozepore and later at Runjeet's court at Lahore. The nautches were not so good as she had seen at Benares and Delhi, and Runjeet's addiction to strong liquor was an embarrassment.

He began drinking that horrible spirit, which he pours down like water. He insisted on my touching it... and one drop actually burnt the outside of my lips. I could not possibly swallow it... All these satraps in a row, and those crowds of long-bearded attendants, and the old tyrant drinking in the middle – but still we all said; 'What a charming party!' just as we should have said formerly to Lady C's or Lady J's.

The surface nature of her assessment of Runjeet appears in her conclusion.

He is a very drunken old profligate, neither more nor less. Still he has made himself a great king; he has conquered a great many powerful enemies; he is remarkably just in his government; he has disciplined a large army; he hardly ever takes away life, which is wonderful in a despot; and he is excessively loved by his people.

This is all right as far as it goes, but her nephew Osborne gives a different version in his *Court and Camp*. Although commending Runjeet's insatiable curiosity and his personal courage, not a common quality in the Sikhs, he thought the Maharajah would sooner face Dost Mahomed and his Afghans than any of the *houris* who formed his Amazonian bodyguard, and he has this to say about Runjeet's rule.

His executions are very prompt and simple, and follow quickly on the sentence: one blow of an axe, and then some boiling oil to immerse the stump in, and stop all effusion of blood, is all the machinery he requires for his courts of justice. He is himself accuser, judge, and jury: and five minutes is about the duration of the longest trial at Lahore.*

(This is nearer the mark than Emily – or Burnes at his earlier visits to the Sikh court.)

Emily did not suspect the sinister reality that lay behind the elaborate ceremonial. She admired Heera Singh, Runjeet's catamite, finding him a very handsome boy, without realising that he had obtained his place of favour in a manner, according to

---

*W.G. Osborne, *The Court and Camp of Runjeet Singh*, 1840.

Osborne, which in any other country would have made him infamous. Nor could she know that within a few years all the glorious Sikh chieftains, including Kharak Singh, with whom she made a pretence of flirting, and the jolly Shere Singh who kept turning up at meal times to watch her, would have died violent deaths. Later she was sad to hear of the *suttee* at Runjeet's funeral. 'These poor dear ranees, whom we visited and thought so beautiful and merry, have actually burnt themselves.' Meanwhile she was more sympathetic to the problems of Auckland's negro chef, who told her:

Il ne faut pas tuer un boeuf, à cause de la religion de ces maudits Sikhs; enfin j'ai de la poussière pour sauce. Mon dieu, quel pays!

When Dost Mahomed surrendered to Macnaghten in Kabul he was taken down to Calcutta as an honoured captive. He was not received by the Governor-General in full durbar. That would have been overdoing it. He was, however, allowed to pay a 'common morning visit' to Government House. 'George sat on his sofa, with the secretaries and the aides-de-camp on the rows of chairs all bolt upright and doing nothing, and I flatter myself that the Dost thinks that is the way in which he passes his day.' Emily watched from a peephole in the door of the billiard room. She thought the Dost a fine-looking man, imperious in his own house, but very easy and frank.

Dost Mahomed spent four months in Calcutta before being returned to Ludhiana. There is some irony in the way in which he became almost a favourite with the Misses Eden. He told Emily he missed not having his own *zenana*, but knew that if he did set up a temporary establishment his wives in Ludhiana would hear of it and make their resentment known when he rejoined them. But he still professed himself enchanted with everything he saw, from the giraffe in Emily's private menagerie at Barrackpore to the paddle-steamer on the river. Emily played chess with him and he sat for his portrait.

He would have made a great sensation in a London room with his sons and suite standing round him, in their immense turbans and with flame-coloured, or scarlet, or blue dresses embroidered in gold. Dreadfully hot, poor dears! but I suppose they would not think muslin quite correct. Perhaps they are not more picturesque than the other natives, but they are quite different and look new; they are very Jewish in countenance and colour.

An interesting comment since the Afghans proudly believed themselves to be descended from the lost Ten Tribes of Israel.

Emily's appreciation conveniently forgot that this was the ruthless chieftain of the Barukzye tribe, who had seized the Kabul throne and kept it with a mixture of adroitness and savagery.

5

The First Afghan War takes on a different colour when seen through the eyes of Emily, first from the refined seclusion of Simla, which she reached after the journey up the country, and latterly from Government House when she returned to Calcutta.

Her first references are to what she no doubt regarded as a tiresome interlude at Herat. In the autumn of 1837 the Persian army, with Russian support, attacked the frontier town, but with Eldred Pottinger's assistance the Heratis survived ten months of siege. James McNeill, the British Envoy at Teheran, had gone to the Persian camp to persuade the Shah to desist, but, finding he could make no progress, he severed relations and withdrew. Auckland had ordered the despatch from Bombay of two steamers carrying a military detachment, to be at McNeill's disposal should he decide to return by way of Bushire. The British force occupied the island of Karrack; reports of the size of the contingent were greatly exaggerated; and this token of British strength eventually influenced the Shah to abandon the siege and go back to Persia.

Emily knew all about Herat. It was widely recognised as the most likely route through which the Russians might descend on Hindustan, the 'gateway of India'. The imminent fall of the town, which was daily expected throughout the summer of 1838, was prayed in aid by Auckland as a main pretext for going to war. Emily's reaction was characteristically frivolous.

One serious grievance is that the steamer which was to have taken our letters home this month was ordered off to Persia to bring away

Mr McNeill, if he wished to come, and our letters are 'left lamenting' like Lord Ullin on the beach at Bombay. That is the sort of thing that George does in the plenitude of his power . . .

The next mention of Herat follows four days later (14 June 1838). The Russians, she said, were egging on the Persians. Two Russian letters had been intercepted and sent to Auckland, 'highly important, only unluckily nobody in India can read them'. The aides-de-camp were busy making facsimiles in the hope of finding an Armenian to translate them. Emily thought it would be amusing if they turned out to be 'some Caterina Iconoslavitch writing to my uncle Alexis about her partners'. On 24 October, when it was learned that Herat was saved, she expected that the 'Cabul business would now be so easy'.

And so indeed it was, at least initially. The Army of the Indus reached Kandahar without a single pitched battle; only at Ghuznee was there any organised resistance; in August 1839 the British flag was flying on the Bala Hissar at Kabul; Shah Soojah was once more on his throne; but Dost Mahomed had escaped.

The Misses Eden shared the general air of optimism. Fanny had written on 9 December 1838 that they thought that the Dost would give in without fighting. On 17 August 1839 she said that with the capture of Ghuznee 'that war is *warred* and done, and we expect you to send us word that you are exceedingly satisfied with our manner of doing things.' Throughout the rest of the year and most of 1840 the euphoria continued. At Simla Emily was mainly concerned about the lack of male company. There were sixty ladies whose husbands were in Kabul and who would not appear in public without them. 'Very devoted wives, but if the war lasts three years, they will be very dull women.' Emily was at pains to organise tableaux (scenes from *Kenilworth*) and other entertainments. Keane, the Army Commander, wrote 'most cheerfully' from Kabul. In November, at Umballa on her way back to Calcutta, she met some officers of the 16th Lancers, back from Afghanistan. They had taken their pack of foxhounds with them to Kabul and said that they had suffered only from a lack of wine and cigars; they all looked uncommonly fat. 'That does not look like having undergone great privation,' she commented tartly.

Emily's account of the fall of Khelat (November 1839) shows

how out of touch she and her brother were with the realities of the Afghan campaign. The reasons that led Macnaghten, with dubious justification, to propose the deposition of Mehrab Khan, the Khelat ruler, have been described in a previous chapter. Auckland gave his authority, and the deposition was duly carried out by General Willshire. Emily, like everyone at Auckland's headquarters, was delighted. 'The Khan and his principal chiefs died sword in hand, which was rather too fine a death for such a double traitor . . . Another man has been put on the Khelat throne, so that business is finished.' It did not prove to be so.

In July 1840, Emily, now in Calcutta, was still writing complacently about Auckland's great venture. 'Our George has done very well in India,' she wrote to Lady Campbell. 'You know we always thought highly of him even in his comical dog days . . . '

One of the first signs that all was not well in Afghanistan was not regarded as serious. At Kahun in the southern provinces Lieutenant Clark was killed by marauding tribesmen and Captain Brown reported that he was besieged. But soon came news that he had survived. 'I am so glad,' Emily wrote. 'It was such a horrid prospect to be starved out by these Belochees and then cut to pieces, and he was so spirited about it.' In November came disturbing news that the British force had not acquitted itself too well when Dost Mahomed made his final despairing reappearance at Purwundurrah. The 2nd Bengal Cavalry refused to charge when ordered, leaving their five British officers to advance alone, a feat which greatly impressed the Dost and is said to have convinced him that the British were unbeatable. Emily found the behaviour of the Indian troopers unaccountable; they did not run away, but just did nothing – 'natural, but wrong'. She was relieved to hear that the Dost had ridden into Kabul to give himself up.

The next year saw continuous, though as yet isolated, uprisings, but Macnaghten's despatches from Kabul were monotonously confident. It was not till 13 November – three days after Emily had been to see *Macbeth*, and had been pleased to see so many natives in the audience – that her letters disclosed that the news from Kabul was unpleasant, uncertain, and alarming. She was quite right. The Eastern Ghilzyes were in open revolt, Sale was shut up in Jalalabad, Burnes had been killed, and from then on the tragedy generated its own impetus. The heroic Lady Sale had managed to smuggle out a letter from the besieged Kabul cantonment. It gave a realistic account of the garrison's plight, but Emily was still inclined to discount the danger. She could not believe that '3,000 of our troops, Europeans or Sepoys, will allow themselves to be massacred, and, though of course there must be many painful casualties, I cannot see it quite in this despairing line.' Was her reaction courageous, insensitive, or simply ignorant? It was probably a mixture of all three.

The situation continued to deteriorate, although there was some slight comfort in Sale's vigorous resistance. Emily conceded that there were 'bad bits in life certainly', and this was not a good month, but she could still write on 10 December that her 'chief amusement' had been 'packing'. She was preparing to accompany Auckland, who was awaiting the arrival of his successor, back to England. The order of release was at hand.

On 6 January 1841 she reported the contents of another letter from Lady Sale. 'Nothing can seem more hopeless . . . Her letter is wonderfully composed, and indeed very spirited.' Spirited it may have been, but by the time Emily heard from Lady Sale the demoralised British force had straggled out to meet its end in the snow. Emily, however, thought she would try a few days on the river, on board the *Soonamookie*. By 30 January she had seen further letters from Jalalabad and learned of the annihilation of Elphinstone's army and the surrender of the women and children to the doubtful care of Akbar Khan, the murderer of Macnaghten. 'It is utterly inexplicable', she wrote, 'these unfortunate women, too, in the hands of such savages.'

The last comment on the Afghan war that finds a place in her letters was on the (incorrect) report that Elphinstone and his second-in-command Shelton were the only officers to survive. 'People are becoming rabid to hear their story; they must have some excuse that has never transpired.' Emily was still taking refuge under the umbrella of incredulity. In her final letter from India she wrote about Lord Ellenborough's reception, as incoming Governor-General, at Calcutta. 'I declare I have been more amused for these twelve days than I have been since I came to India.' A revealing *envoi*.

It may seem that these extracts from her letters show Emily in an unduly unfavourable light. She was not in charge of British policy towards Afghanistan, and there was little that Auckland could do once the British troops were cut off north of the Khyber. But she was intelligent, and sympathetic, and she was her brother's most intimate confidante. Auckland was full of good intentions. He had, admittedly, an extremely difficult decision to take in sending the Army of the Indus into Afghanistan – a decision independently endorsed by the Government at Westminster. Thereafter, however, he was unbelievably bemused by Macnaghten's complacent reports. It is hard not to believe that he discussed these letters and despatches with Emily in his long hours of heart-searching. With all her wit and intellectual capacity, she was no help to him. She wanted to go home. But at least let it be remembered to Auckland's credit that after the catastrophe he insisted upon every effort being made to secure the release of the British prisoners in Afghan hands, to whose fate his successor, Ellenborough, showed a callous indifference. 'After the outbreak,' wrote Colin Mackenzie, 'he [Auckland] did all that was done. The whole of the force with which Pollock made his victorious march was sent up by Auckland; not a man was added to it by Ellenborough.'

4
Châteaux en Espagne

I

Major D'Arcy Todd's political career came to an abrupt end when he earned the wrath of the Governor-General. Some, particularly those who echoed Fortinbras in saying that 'he was likely, had he been put on, t'have proved most royally', felt that he had been unjustly treated. The contrary view was that, regrettably, he exemplified Tacitus's description of a man by everyone's consent worthy of governing – provided he did not govern. Either way there is much of interest in Todd's career.

Elliott D'Arcy Todd was one of the young men who embarked for India last century to seek military service with John Company because the family fortunes had foundered. He was born on 28 January 1808 in Bury Street, London, the third and youngest son of Fryer Todd, a Yorkshireman, and his wife who is best remembered as Coleridge's Mary Evans – her maiden name. Widowed when Elliott was only three, Mary was in some difficulty, but fortunately her brother William, who held the office, more prestigious than its name, of 'Baggage Warehouse Keeper' with the East India Company, took charge of young Elliott's education. In 1822 Mr Evans, through his interest with the Company, secured for his nephew a nomination to the military seminary at Addiscombe. Elliott showed great promise as a cadet, and obtained a commission in the artillery. He passed his final examination in December 1823 and sailed for India on the *Duchess of Athol*.

After a year and a half at the headquarters of the Bengal artillery at Dum-Dum, he was assigned to a foot company, which he accompanied to the siege of Bhurtpore. There is no record of his distinguishing himself in that memorable battle, but he had got his first taste of gunpowder. He was next posted to the Horse Artillery, but on promotion to 1st lieutenant he was again attached to a battalion of foot. This was not a welcome move since it meant laying out substantial funds on new uniforms and equipment, an expense which the young subaltern could not afford. He successfully appealed to the Commander-in-Chief to be sent back to the mounted branch and was posted to the Horse Artillery at Meerut. 'From what I have observed of the different services,' he wrote home in glee, 'I now say that I would rather be in the Horse Artillery than any service in the world.' After a spell at Kurnaul, ill health compelled him to go to the hills for convalescence, and there he developed an enduring friendship with James Abbott, whom he had known at Addiscombe.

Abbott inspired affection, sometimes tempered with criticism, through his career. Honoria, Henry Lawrence's wife, records meeting him much later. Writing home from Haripur in Hazare in February 1852, she says:

Among these people Major Abbott lives as a patriarch. It is delightful to see a British officer loved and respected as he is and the province he administers, larger than Wales, so peaceable and prosperous. I do not mean that he is perfect, for he has some failings that make it difficult to deal with him officially, and he gives Papa [Henry] more trouble than many a man of not a tenth of the merit. The more so because Papa has so high a regard for him. Abbott is morbidly sensitive, and he has lived so long without coming in contact with other educated minds that he cannot apprehend any views but his own. He is aged about forty, small make, with eager black eyes and well marked features. I suppose it is many years since shears or razor approached him, and his hair and beard are silver white.

Abbott lived to reach general rank. His immortality was assured when the Gurkha depot at Abbottabad was called after him.

In April 1833 Todd had a stroke of luck. He was selected to join the military mission to the Shah of Persia, with the special task of instructing the Persian gunners. 'There will probably be a good deal of fighting,' he wrote in the first flush of enthusiasm, 'and abundance of opportunity of displaying the stuff a man is made of.' It did not turn out like that. The British mission was diplomatic, rather than military, in origin and purpose. Its job was to bolster up the confidence of a precarious regime, and, more important, to prevent the Russians from gaining a foothold at the court of the Shah-in-Shah. As many found over the last century, the role of army officers in such a situation is not satisfactory. It is ill-defined and lacks responsibility.

By August 1834 Todd was bored with idleness.

I consider the Persian appointment as sheer humbug; the climate is the only desirable thing in the country. The people, especially the people about Government, are a lying, deceitful, procrastinating faithless race, with whom to hold any communication can only be a source of disgust and disappointment. I would never have left Cawnpore had I known the prospects of an officer in Persia.

Todd's annoyance continued. The Persian Kaim-Makam (Prime Minister) was evasive, and would not give him a proper remit. He might be recognised as an instructor, but that was the limit of his authority. Some of the other officers in the provinces fared better, since the local governors were less strict in insisting on protocol. Major Farrant commanded the whole cavalry corps at Zenjan and Major Rawlinson was in charge of the province of Kermanshah. But at Teheran Todd was less fortunate.

Soon the British were involved in king-making. Shah Futteh Ali died on 23 October 1835. According to Todd, he had

at the time of his death, the most valuable of his jewels with him; the great diamond, called from its splendour the 'durya-i-noor' (sea of light), placed in a casket at the foot of his bed, was the last object he beheld before his eyes closed in the sleep of death. The disorder which ensued when the frail thread which bound together the disorderly spirits about the royal camp was broken, may be imagined.

The British detachment was engaged in an exercise at Khoi, ninety miles north of Tabriz. As soon as Mahomed Meerza, the eldest son of Abbas Meerza, was proclaimed King, taking the name of Mahomed Shah, the British broke camp and joined him at Tabriz. Henry Ellis, the British Envoy, had been authorised to support Mahomed Shah, but there were three competitors who each proclaimed themselves as successor to the throne. Mahomed Shah, with his British contingent, at once marched on Teheran. Meanwhile it was learned that Zil-i-Sultan, Prince Governor of Teheran, 'a man infamous for his vices and notorious for his weakness of mind', had crowned himself, but during Mahomed Shah's advance the rival suppliants retreated to a respectful distance and the gates of the city were thrown open to welcome him. Todd's training of the Persian gunners was not tested.

Thus ended our first bloodless campaign! ... In former days this farce would have been succeeded by a tragedy – heads would have been lopped off by the hundred, and eyes would have been plucked out by the bushel – *vide* Aga Mahomet's conduct fifty years ago; but the young king has behaved on the present occasion admirably; his late opponents have been dealt with in the most lenient manner, and many of them have in consequence become his staunch friends and supporters.

Todd was detained in Teheran for the avowed purpose of being put in charge of the Shah's artillery, but it was not till the Persian Commandant died of cholera that he obtained preferment, and then it was only temporary. On 31 July 1835 he wrote to his brother.

When the King heard of his death, he sent me a *firman*, placing the control of all matters connected with the Artillery in my hands, until a Persian 'fit for the situation' should be appointed. He will have to wait for some time before he finds such a person. If a man like the late Commandant is appointed, I shall give up all hopes of making myself useful in my profession so long as I remain in the country.

Things took a turn for the better when Henry Ellis decided that Todd would be a useful recruit to the diplomatic service, and wrote about him in warm terms to Auckland.

He belongs to the Bengal Horse Artillery, is most intelligent and clear-headed; he has given much attention to the question of possible invasion of India from the north-west, and is fully alive to and well acquainted with the views and designs of Russia; in short, I know no one whom I would employ with more confidence.

Ellis put his name forward for appointment as Political Agent at Kabul. Todd, though heartened, did not deceive himself that he would get the job (in fact no appointment was made) but he felt certain that Ellis's recommendation would help him and that he would not have to return to regimental duty on leaving Persia.

In the autumn of 1836 he was at Tabriz, acting as Military Secretary to Sir Harry Bethune who commanded all the troops trained by British officers. In 1837 he was back in Teheran, and was promoted to local brevet major, though, as he commented ruefully, without any increase in pay, but at the end of the year

James McNeill, who had succeeded Ellis, appointed him Secretary of the Legation. No sinecure, Todd observed, reporting that on a single day he had written forty-eight pages, foolscap, of Persian translation, as well as his normal work in English and French. A more exciting assignment lay ahead.

2

From the moment of his ascent to the throne Mahomed Shah had entertained thoughts of conquest in the direction of Herat and Kandahar. Relations between the Persian court and Shah Kamran at Herat became increasingly strained, and despite a stern warning from Palmerston, delivered through the British Envoy, the Shah set off to lay siege to Herat. To mark British disapproval, McNeill refused to accompany the Shah's entourage to Herat, as protocol would normally have required, and merely sent Colonel Stoddart as a liaison officer. In time, however, as both Calcutta and Westminster took ever more seriously the possible threat to British India through Herat, McNeill, who had been given discretion to act on 'his own excellent judgment', felt it expedient to make his representations in person at the Shah's camp.

Todd was to accompany him. On 8 March 1838 he wrote:

The whole of the orchestra will not accompany the leader of the band, but the acting second fiddle must, of course, be in attendance, and I am preparing to start from this in about four days, with Mr McNeill and Major Ferrant, who is acting as his private secretary. We take four sergeants and fifteen or twenty Persians, armed and mounted, in case we should meet with some of the roving bands of Turcomans who infest the road between Shahrood and Herat. As I have no hankering after a pastoral life, I hope that you will not hear next of me, or from me, tending the flocks and herds of the Turcomans.

They arrived at Herat on 6 April, having done the 700-mile journey in 26 days. Their caravan consisted of 60 laden mules, and for the last few marches they were accompanied by a train of 500 camels carrying provisions to the camp. Todd was impressed by the strength of the Herat fortifications. He observed that the Shah's batteries (which he had trained) had knocked down some of the upper defences, but no attempt had been made to effect a breach.

Todd's view is contrary to that of Eldred Pottinger who was directing operations from behind the Herat ramparts. (Lieutenant Pottinger, on a solitary mission to collect Afghan intelligence, had reached Herat just before the siege began. He threw off his disguise and took a prominent part in the defence of the city.) Even after the siege had been lifted Pottinger could not understand how the Persians, with their Russian advisers, had failed to take Herat. He was firmly convinced that a concerted attack would have overrun the defences, and blamed bad leadership for the Persian failure. No doubt it all seemed very different, depending on whether the situation was seen from outside or inside the walls, but it is likely that Pottinger's opinion was the more realistic. He was present during the whole ten months of siege and often took part in the hand-to-hand fighting. On one point Todd was certainly wrong. He said that Herat had provisions for two years; but we know from Pottinger's detailed account that near-famine conditions prevailed inside the city.

The Shah had no warm welcome for McNeill and the British party. He knew that McNeill would try to dissuade him from pursuing the siege, and at first he refused to see the envoy. But McNeill persisted; he was granted an audience; and eventually the Shah agreed that the British should mediate between him and Herat. As a first step, Todd was sent through both sets of lines. He was received in Herat with wonder. He was the first British officer to appear in the city wearing full regimentals, and his 'tight-fitting coat, the glittering epaulettes, and the cocked hat, all excited unbounded admiration'. His message found a ready response from Shah Kamran, who was willing to listen to anything that the British Minister might propose. Kamran gave Todd his own cloak as a singular mark of esteem. If Pottinger and Todd thought there was anything odd in the negotiations between these oriental potentates being carried out by officers from the Bengal and Bombay Artillery, they kept their thoughts to themselves.

Todd returned to camp with high hopes, but he was soon disappointed. 'The Persians have been playing their usual dirty game, shuffling and shirking, and eating their own words, so that at present there seems to be but little probability of matters being satisfactorily arranged.' Kamran was again cooperative; but the Shah's demands were impossible to meet and nothing came of the negotiations. McNeill decided to send Todd to Simla with despatches for the Governor-General.

Todd was delighted. He looked forward to the chance of making his number with Auckland, and felt he could not do so under better auspices than as the bearer of important despatches, and as the possessor of the latest news from the Persian front. Writing on 8 March, he had hoped that this journey would materialise. 'But all this may be a castle in the air; but I am, and ever have been, fond of constructing châteaux en Espagne.'

Now, on 8 May, he reported that he would start in the next few days. He added tartly that he would travel as an Englishman, since 'all the difficulties that Europeans have encountered in these countries have arisen from their foolishly endeavouring to personate natives'. Thinking primarily of Pottinger and Burnes, he said that their success had generally been as great as Chinamen would meet in attempting to carry themselves off as Englishmen on the strength of a pair of tight breeches. With a light heart he quitted the 'filthy nest of all possible abominations' in the Shah's camp.

Todd left Herat on 22 May 1838, and arrived at Simla on 20 July. An account of his journey was published in the *Journal of the Asiatic Society of Bengal* in 1844. 'Mostly jotted down either on horseback, or after being in the saddle for twelve to fifteen hours out of the twenty four', it is written by a man with an eye for country and a shrewd sense of the tactical implications.

His assessment of Herat, after he had left it, was more measured than his first impressions had been. The ruined walls of houses and gardens, he noted, afforded cover to the besiegers, almost up to the edge of the fortifications. The city's very size was also a weakness. Todd thought that a garrison of at least 10,000 would have been needed against an active and enterprising enemy, whereas the estimated force inside Herat was no more than 2,500 fighting men, little artillery, and cavalry. On the other hand, he was convinced that the walls could be breached by gunfire. He must, however, have learned from Pottinger what the temper of the defenders was, and he concluded that if they had time to carry out the necessary works, 'the place supplied with guns and a sufficiency of ammunition, and the works defended with common bravery, the capture of Herat even with European troops, would be tedious and difficult.' Four month later, the Persians and their Russian advisers took the same view and gave up the siege. It had been a near thing, but the threat to British India was eased.

At Subzawaur, ninety miles from Herat, he came upon Shahzadeh Iskunder, the son of Shah Kamran and governor of the district.

> He seemed to be a half-witted and imbecile person. He made no attempt to succour his father, or even to divert the attention of the Persians. The surrounding country was in a state of utter disorder. Bands of plunderers roving about in every direction, and these men were described as acknowledging neither God nor King.

Three hundred miles took him to Kandahar. He thought it a place of no strength, which could be taken by escalade, though this would be deemed hazardous. Four 12- or 18-pounders would effect a sizeable breach in the course of a day. This was also the Afghans' appreciation, and a year later they did not defend Kandahar when the Army of the Indus advanced against the city.

Todd's estimate of the defences at Ghuznee is more open to question. He found the approach from the south highly picturesque, but the citadel presented a formidable appearance. He jotted down that the garrison had four small guns and one much larger one. (This may have been the brass 48-pounder which the Afghans nicknamed 'Zubur-Zum', the 'hard-hitter'.) Todd was writing before the British invasion had finally been decided upon, but, as a good staff officer should, he commented that an army advancing from Kandahar would have to capture Ghuznee. He was, however, wrong in thinking this would be an easy task. A year later, when Keane reached Kandahar he took the remarkable decision to leave there his siege train of artillery, which had been laboriously dragged through the Bolan Pass. It is widely believed that this foolish action owed something to Todd's advice. He was an experienced artilleryman, and he had been to Ghuznee, but he should have known better. At all events, the fall of Ghuznee was accomplished only after a deserter had revealed that one of the gates had not been properly bricked up and was vulnerable to a massive charge of powder. Keane still regretted the absence of his heavy artillery.

Todd's reaction to the Bala Hissar, the citadel that broods over Kabul, was also different from that of the Army of the Indus. He dismissed it as 'being commanded by the heights in the vicinity'. There are admittedly surrounding hills, but there was a good body of opinion among the British officers when beleaguered in the Kabul cantonment that the best thing that they could do was to get into the Bala Hissar as fast as they could.

Two other comments may be extracted from Todd's report, which in general is a good military appreciation of the terrain. He does not fail to consider whether the roads were passable for guns, whether the rivers were liable to flooding, what was the likely disposition of the tribesmen, and all this before Keane's army had its first skirmish. On the way to Jalalabad, after leaving Tezeen, he recorded 'a steep ascent for about five miles, mountains covered with pine and holly oak, magnificent scenery, road impassable for guns, abrupt descent for about two miles.' He encountered Akbar Khan encamped with his troops in the valley of Agaum, and noted that he was 'certainly the least unpopular of his family', with a high reputation for courage. Ironically, it was Akbar who watched the final destruction of the British force as the soldiers tried to tear down the breastwork which the Afghans had constructed in the pass at Jugdulluk out of the very holly oak that Todd had seen.

3

At Simla Todd was the man of the hour. He brought despatches from McNeill, and he could add his own eye-witness account of affairs at Herat. The way had been prepared by a letter which he sent to Alexander Burnes and which reached Simla on 12 July, a week before he arrived himself. In this letter he gave his opinion that a force of three or four thousand men would have been enough to make the Shah abandon the siege, and he added, 'The slightest demonstration on our part in the Persian Gulph would have had the same effect.' This was just what Auckland wanted to hear. Thinking to safeguard McNeill's withdrawal from Herat, he had already given the orders which led to a British contingent occupying the island of Karrack on 19 June – a move that started the chain of events that frightened the Shah into his retreat from Herat. So Todd found he had unwittingly earned a good reputation with Auckland and his staff.

There was time for some relaxation among the ladies of the Governor-General's entourage. In *Up the Country* Emily Eden gives an account of her 'Fancy Fair' – a long booth for the ladies who sold goods for charity, with the 'Bower of Eden' in the centre, and Henry Torrens acting as auctioneer. He is quoted by Emily:

> I have kept this gem till now – I may call it a gem, the portrait of Gholam, the faithful Persian who accompanied Major L [Todd] from Persia to Herat! I may say this is a faithful likeness of a man who witnessed the siege of Herat. Will the great diplomatist, Major L, who is, I know, anxious to possess this perfect picture, allow me to say eighty rupees, or seventy, or sixty?

The portrait was evidently a sketch done by Emily, but Todd's reaction is not known.

On more serious matters, Simla was alive with preparations. On the very day that Todd arrived Macnaghten had returned from Ludhiana, bearing Shah Soojah's signature to the treaty with the British and Runjeet Singh, and the pace quickened. Auckland took a liking to Todd – heady stuff for an ambitious young officer. Writing to his brother, Todd said:

> Lord Auckland has asked me to enlist, and I do not see any prospect of returning to Persia under existing circumstances, I have accepted the offer, but I know not in what capacity I shall be employed. I am not even aware whether civil or military duties will be allotted to me. I trust the former, as I am heartily sick of drilling recruits.

He could have been given command of the artillery to accompany Soojah's levies, or appointed brigade major with the artillery in the Bengal Division, but military glory had lost its charms for him. He held out for a post in the political department and he got his reward when the Simla Manifesto was promulgated on 1 October. He was gazetted as Political Assistant and Military Secretary to Macnaghten, the Envoy to Soojah's court.

As the various components of the Army of the Indus started their respective marches to the rendezvous across the Indus at Shikarpur, Todd travelled with Soojah's camp. Macnaghten did not catch up with them till 31 December and meanwhile Todd was the senior political officer, having, in effect, political charge of the 22,000 assorted troops and camp-followers in attendance on the Suddozye monarch.

From daylight to midnight I was employed in listening to complaints, settling disputes, answering chits, attending to applications, and suffering annoyances of every conceivable description. All this time I was exceedingly unwell, and living on tea and physic.

Soojah, seeing the throne at Kabul once again within his grasp, became daily more arrogant. Complaints filtered back to the Governor-General, and Auckland told Todd that Soojah was to be left in no doubt that he was to adopt a conciliatory and properly liberal demeanour towards his own people. It was essential for the credibility of British policy that Soojah should be received with enthusiam by the Afghans. Macnaghten, who had reported that Soojah referred to his loyal subjects as a 'pack of dogs', promised to make him mend his ways. For a time he was successful. James Outram, at the start of his distinguished career, had volunteered for service in Afghanistan and been appointed an extra ADC to Keane, the Army Commander. In his *Rough Notes on the Campaign* Outram observes that it was customary to approach and leave the Shah with much ceremony, and that this etiquette was scrupulously followed by the British officers. But Soojah had learned part of his lesson and Outram thought him very affable and of mild manners.

Todd got on well with Keane, whom he described as soldier-like and gentlemanly. Keane was not, however, universally popular – as will become apparent in the chapter on General Nott. He was generally regarded as foul-mouthed, of coarse personal habits, and greatly given to magniloquent despatches. But he was a competent soldier, and a fortunate one. A Peninsular veteran, he had been tempered in a hard school. For example, while commanding a brigade during Wellington's pursuit of Soult, he wrote on 17 March 1814 to his old colleague Charles Colville:

Poor Parker was cut in two by a cannon shot close to the God of War. Taylor was wounded in the neck but is up again. Greenwell severely; Carr ditto – ball entered the chin and lodged in the roots of his tongue. It has been cut out and he is doing well. Elliott severely in the belly, but also doing well. Poor Nugent dangerously in two places, but there are some hopes. Baldwin severely, right arm broken. Capt McDermot, 88th, only joined the day before, with his Victoria wound open, was killed.*

It needed some fortitude to write with such equanimity.

If the Army of the Indus did not meet the enemy in any great strength on the way to Kandahar, there were plenty of incidental hazards. The climate was insufferably hot; the transport and supply arrangements were inadequate. The commissariat departments acting for Soojah and for the Bengal and Bombay Divisions fought with each other to line their own pockets. At Quetta the Bengal Division had rations for only ten days, and the troops' issue was halved. It is generally supposed that the problem was that a barren country, whose inhabitants were barely at subsistence level, could not suddenly provide food and fodder for a vast army, but Honoria Lawrence, writing four years later, had another explanation. The army, she said, was in danger of starving, not for want of grain – of that there was plenty – but for want of women to grind it. 'No man ever dreamed of such an occupation. And when the Commissariat Officer indented at each stage for so much grass, grain, etc., there was likewise an item for so many women to grind.'

Keane did not have to fight anything approaching a pitched battle till he debouched in the plain before Ghuznee, but the tribesmen harried him unceasingly. Outram summed up the Afghan tactics.

Permitting the main army to surmount the [Bolan] pass unmolested, and then letting loose swarms of marauders on our rear, to cut off our supplies while, at the same time, they destroy everything in our front, they take the only possible mode of opposing us with success.

The horses and draught animals were in a terrible condition and vehicles and guns had to be manhandled through the gorges, but Keane's force pressed forward. On 25 April Soojah made his formal entrance into Kandahar. There are conflicting reports about his reception, either then or at the ceremonial review on 8 May. Despite the euphoria of Macnaghten's despatches, it appears that enthusiasm was pretty muted, and resignation was

---

*Sir John Colville, *The Portrait of a General*, 1980.

the prevailing mood. This was the first small sign, ignored at the time, that the Soojah plan was not going to be a success.

For the British troops, after the near-famine and privations of the last few months, arrival at Kandahar was like reaching the promised land. Here was food and fruit in abundance. Colonel Dennis of the 13th thought the mutton was the best he had tasted; a special liquor ration was issued to celebrate the Queen's Birthday; and over-indulgence in fresh fruit soon caused an epidemic of 'Kandahar tummy'. Todd, on good terms with Keane and enjoying Macnaghten's confidence, thought there was much to be said for the diplomatic life. He did not know that he was about to be sent on his fateful mission.

4

A cardinal feature of British policy was the maintenance of friendly relations with the ruler of Herat, Soojah's nephew Shah Kamran. The Persians had already laid siege to the city, and though they had eventually withdrawn, there was no saying that they would not make another attempt. Reports from Eldred Pottinger, who had been rewarded for his efforts during the siege by being appointed Political Agent there, were not encouraging. They spoke of the corrupt, two-faced nature of the Herat government, particularly the activities of Yar Mahomed, whom Pottinger suspected of conspiring with the Persians. Sir John Kaye, the historian of the Afghan War, described the Herat Vizier as the most unscrupulous 'of all the unscrupulous miscreants in Central Asia'.

Macnaghten was annoyed by Pottinger's despatches. They were not what he wanted to hear. Everything was going swimmingly for the Army of the Indus, Macnaghten's plans were maturing, and it was too bad that Pottinger should strike such a consistently discordant note. He wanted someone with a more emollient touch in Herat. Yar Mahomed, with cynical effrontery, had been one of the first to offer his congratulations to Soojah on his return to Kandahar, and this overture seemed to Macnaghten to provide an opening to send a Special Mission to Herat. Ostensibly it was to be in addition to Eldred Pottinger, but there is no doubt that Macnaghten always intended that he should be replaced by Todd.

The mission had first been offered to Burnes who, seeing that it was very likely to end in failure, declined. So, as Outram wrote in his diary,

> It has been determined to depute Major Todd to Herat as Envoy, together with certain Engineer and Artillery officers, who are to strengthen the works of that fortress prior to the advance of troops, in advance of the Shah of Persia returning to besiege it; but of this intention on his part, no authentic accounts have yet been received.

On 21 June Todd rode off from Kandahar to the accompaniment of an eleven-gun salute to mark the importance of his extraordinary mission. He had with him, as Political Officers, his friend James Abbot and Lieutenant Richmond Shakespear of the Bengal Artillery. Captain Sanders, a distinguished Sapper, and Assistant-surgeon John Login were also included in the party, and as a sweetener Todd took with him 200,000 rupees.

His letter of 10 October 1839 to his brother is full of optimism.

> I received my present appointment under very flattering circumstances, such as to make a youth (don't laugh! you can't see my grey hairs) like myself very vain. As yet I have succeeded in the object of my mission, which was to report on the state of affairs here, and to conclude a treaty of friendship and alliance with Shah Kamran; but the maze of politics here is very intricate, and our relations, notwithstanding my treaty, are not on a very solid basis.

Shortly afterwards (20 November) he wrote again saying that he was 'a very fortunate fellow'. He was now appointed permanently to Herat. Another situation was to be found for Pottinger, who had gone on well-earned leave. Pottinger did not at any stage resent Todd personally; he later complained about the way in which he had been superseded; but he knew when he left Herat that it was unlikely that Macnaghten, with whom he had a most unhappy relationship, would let him return.

Todd's main achievement during his time at Herat was not directly connected with the affairs of Shah Kamran. At Christmas 1839 he sent Abbott, and later Shakespear, to Khiva to obtain the release of the Russian prisoners then in the hands of the Khan. Abbott eventually made his way to St Petersburg, where his appearance caused some embarrassment in diplomatic circles, but the prisoners were released and the Russians deprived of a pretext for invading Khiva and threatening a subsequent invasion further south. In the tortuous diplomacy of the time, this was a major success. As the historian Norris has concluded, 'No one could have stopped the Russians advancing towards Khiva. The *whole* of Britain's Asian policy would then have been in ruins...' Todd was entitled to claim credit for the Khiva mission, which he despatched on his own authority. It gave point to Macnaghten's earlier assurance to him that his office formed a connecting link between European and Asiatic politics.

All was quiet at Herat, Todd wrote on 1 April 1840. He thought he was on the best possible terms with the Heratis, and, naively, that Yar Mahomed was beginning to realise that honesty was the best policy. Disillusion soon followed. A few days later Todd received, by a roundabout route, a copy of a letter from Kamran to the Shah of Persia. In it, according to Login, Kamran declared himself to be the faithful servant of the Shah-in-Shah; he merely tolerated the presence of the English Envoy from expediency; and his own hopes were in 'the asylum of Islam'. The Heratis' policy was, quite simply, to milk the British Treasury by promises of fidelity while at the same time getting ready to undertake a doublecross as soon as the occasion arose. To outwit the devious Yar Mahomed would have required the sophisticated skill of Machiavelli, and was asking far too much of poor Todd.

Yar Mahomed knew that Todd was wise to his duplicity and in order to demonstrate his loyalty (*sic*) he proposed an immediate attack on the frontier town of Ghorian, then in Persian hands, but after he had drawn a further subvention from Todd to equip his force he found a frivolous excuse for calling off the sortie. He even warned the governor of Ghorian that while the British had urged him to advance on the fortress, he really had no intention of doing so. In November 1840 Todd reported that Yar Mahomed had threatened to attack Kandahar in an attempt to obtain another large bribe. (The Vizier did not know that in September the Supreme Government of India had told Macnaghten that no more money was to be poured into the Herat quicksands.) Todd was also aware that Yar Mahomed was in correspondence both with the Persians and with the disaffected Douranee tribes in Afghanistan.

The miserable British officer was in a most invidious position. The Governor-General, although he had stopped the regular subsidy, did not want an open breach with Herat. He believed that even a doubtful alliance with Shah Kamran was to be preferred to the expense and trouble of occupying his kingdom, and he turned a deaf ear to Macnaghten's plea for an outright expedition against the Heratis. Yar Mahomed realised that the British did not want the connection severed and became daily more impertinent in his demands. It so happened that there had for long been a plan to station a detachment of troops under British officers at Herat. Yar Mahomed now said he was willing to admit the British contingent in return for a large lump sum and increased monthly payments. To test his sincerity, Todd demanded that the Vizier's son should be sent to Ghirisk to escort the troops to Herat. Yar Mahomed did not intend to do this; Todd said that no money would be forthcoming; the Vizier replied that in that case the British mission must leave.

Shah Kamran had already told Login that, had he not extended his personal protection, not a *feringhee* would have been left alive. Assassination seemed only too probable. Todd, 'baffled and disgusted', thought his best course was to close the mission, and on 9 February he and his colleagues quitted the city. In a letter of explanation to Macnaghten he said:

My departure from Herat may appear to you unnecessarily precipitate, and it is possible that I might have remained for a few days longer, but had I done so I should have exposed the officers of the mission to certain insult and danger, and thus have prevented the possibility of a future amicable adjustment of our differences with the Herat Government. The Wuzeer has latterly been constantly in a state of intoxication, and the project of seizing us and plundering our property was seriously discussed, by himself and his drunken associates, as the readiest mode of replenishing his coffers.

Todd deserves sympathy. He had to deal with the most treacherous and avaricious of the Afghans. He was in Herat on sufferance. He never had adequate funds to satisfy Yar Mahomed's intemperate requests; yet he knew he was meant to foster friendly relations. No one accused Todd of cowardice, and it can be argued that he took the prudent, if not the only, course open to him. Yar Mahomed sent him a long, speciously friendly, letter of self-abasement. 'O brother of my soul! My heart is torn in pieces by separation from you,' and much more in the same vein, but Todd had no qualms about what he had done. In one of his letters he confessed that, should a punitive expedition against Herat be decided upon, he expected to return with it as Political Agent.

It was not to be. Auckland was furious when he heard of Todd's departure. The Governor-General's policy remained unchanged, namely that Herat should be encouraged to stay independent and should not be occupied by the British unless such a course became imperative in order to forestall an enemy. A stern reproof reached Macnaghten.

His Lordship in Council has read the account of Major Todd's proceedings with extreme surprise, concern, and disapprobation. They are directly at variance with all the orders received by him. They are inconsistent with the most obvious dictates of sense and prudence . . .

As if that were not enough, Auckland wrote personally to Macnaghten that he was

writhing in anger and bitterness at Major Todd's conduct at Herat, and having seen no course open to me in regard to it, but that of discarding him and disavowing him and we have directed his dismissal to the provinces.

On any appreciation, Todd was harshly treated. (Emily Eden could do no better than exclaim that 'Major Todd has brought Herat into a mess!' That was how it appeared at Auckland's headquarters.) True, he had no authority for his final confrontation with Yar Mahomed, or for his decision to leave. But it was scarcely dereliction of duty. He did not present his case for explicit approval by his superiors, but he had left Macnaghten in no doubt, over a lengthy period, about the Vizier's machinations. In the final crisis he did not have time to wait for the transmission of letters which might, or might not, have endorsed his action. Todd was not unique in being crushed by the dispositions of the hierarchy, and it was cold comfort to be assured by Macnaghten that 'his conduct had been as admirable as that of Yar Mahomed had been flagitious', and that he had so informed the Governor-General.

Still smarting at what he regarded as his unwarranted disgrace, Todd went down to Calcutta, and submitted a memorial to the Court of Directors, but got no reply. He was granted an audience with Auckland, who received him courteously but did not give him an opportunity of explaining his motives in abandoning the Herat mission. Ellenborough took over from Auckland as Governor-General on 28 February 1842, and Todd hoped for a fresh review of his case. He was to be disappointed once more. The new Governor-General, who had little sympathy for the political service, also received Todd cordially but told him frankly that he could hold out no hope of reemployment in the political department, and advised him to rejoin his regiment. Ellenborough had enough to think about in relation to Afghanistan, where the news could scarcely be worse, without bothering about a single officer whose career had perished there.

Todd reported to the artillery depot at Dum-Dum. A year later he married the daughter of the surgeon attached to the 16th Lancers, and there followed a period of agreeable tranquillity, ending with his wife's much mourned death. Sir John Kaye saw him frequently at this time and was emphatic that Todd's character had not been eroded by that most insidious of emotions, bitterness. Todd wrote to Durand, Ellenborough's private secretary, seeking permission to use official material in compiling a memoir of his experiences in Afghanistan, but nothing came of it. He was given command of the troop of Horse Artillery in which he served as a subaltern, and in the Sikh War was killed at the battle of Ferozshuhur, when a round shot blew off his head.

Any verdict on Todd would give him credit, as a geographer, for his report on the journey to Simla, and for his initiative in securing the release of the Khiva prisoners. It might have been so much more. The victims of the Afghan War did not all die in Afghanistan.

5
He Rode upon a Razor

1

On an evening in April 1842 the watchful calm that lay over General Pollock's camp at Jalalabad was disturbed by an unexpected arrival. Ten days earlier Pollock had ridden in to relieve Brigadier Sale and to be greeted sarcastically with the old Jacobite air 'O but Ye've Been Lang o'Coming'. Just before Pollock arrived at the end of his triumphant march through the Khyber pass, Sale had made his own sortie to disperse the rebels who had kept him penned up in the fortress for the last six months. For the present, all was deceptively quiet, but marauders, 'the brigands of the country, who, even in times of peace, are always to be found where there is a prospect of plunder', were still lurking in the foothills, and no one knew when Akbar Khan might not reappear. Extreme vigilance was called for, and with officers in the camp like Pollock, notorious for his attention to detail, and the martinet Henry Havelock, sentries knew they had to be on the alert.

At dusk on the 25th the picket looked out across the plain to see three horsemen approaching. From their dress they were Afghans, they rode listlessly, as though overcome with fatigue, and one of their mounts was lame and stumbling. The sentry challenged. The leader of the party, his face scorched by the sun and his lips swollen, muttered in English that he was a British captain. The subadar of the guard was summoned, and, overcoming his surprise, saw that the dusty traveller was indeed a European. He called for an escort to take Colin Mackenzie to General Pollock's tent. It was the most dramatic moment of Mackenzie's career. He was thirty-six years old, and he had already experienced more than his share of military vicissitudes.

2

Colin Mackenzie was born in London on 25 March 1806, the youngest son but one of Kenneth Francis Mackenzie. The family, although not of pure Highland descent, boasted an ancient Scottish lineage which they claimed went back to Donald, Earl of Mar, the nephew of Robert the Bruce. Colin's grandfather married the beautiful Mary Cochrane, granddaughter of Sir John Cochrane of Ochiltree, the second son of the first Earl of Dundonald. Traces of the verve and impertinent gallantry that were the mark of the Cochranes through many generations can be found in Colin's exploits.

Kenneth Mackenzie (b. 1748) read for the law, and at the time of the French Revolution was, improbably, Attorney-General in the island of Granada. When French agitators stirred up an insurrection and captured the Governor, Mackenzie refused to negotiate with the rebels, held out for six months till reinforcements arrived under General Sir Thomas Hislop, and then tried and executed the ringleaders. Colin later wrote with approval of his father's action.

> I have remarked that in all cases of misplaced humanity, and I am personally cognisant of many, the effects have been disastrous to all parties. Rose-water surgery never yet cured a deep-seated ulcer.

It may sound callous, but Colin was by then very familiar with the wiles of native insurgents.

His childhood was unhappy. His mother, Anne Townsend, was the first Englishwoman to marry into the line, an impassive, self-effacing figure, and his father's virtues did not extend to understanding his children. The family's frequent moves meant that Colin received a very broken schooling – at a seminary in Cumberland where the cane was the main instrument of instruction, at the stern Scottish academy at Dollar, and at Dr Donne's at Oswestry. By the time he left school his father had lost money by investing imprudently in an estate in Demerara, and there was no prospect of sending young Colin to the university. The best opening for him, as for many younger sons, was service in India, and a cadetship was obtained for him in the Madras Army. On 15 November 1825 he sailed for India in the *Ganges*. Among his companions were two who later made names for themselves in Afghanistan, Christopher Codrington (killed at Charekar in the Kohistan) and George Broadfoot who engineered the defences at Jalalabad.

Fair-haired and strikingly good-looking, Colin was the epitome of a young sprig keen for action, but he saw no fighting on his first tour of duty, when he was attached to the 10th and later the 48th Native Infantry. Instead, his time was occupied with long marches and game shooting in the Nagpur area. As is the way with young officers, he was highly critical of his seniors. He described his commanding officer as a man who never exerted himself, but who was

> not a bit worse than the general run of the old Indians who commonly present an awful picture of the low state of degradation into which a man will fall by yielding habitually to vice, sloth and enervating luxury . . . they dwindle into second childhood ere they reach what is usually considered the prime of life, and sink into the grave, their minds and bodies equally decayed, without even the power of feeling remorse for the past, or hope for the future.

After two severe attacks of Nagpur fever, Colin was ordered home, and embarked from Calcutta on 1 March 1830.

His convalescence, longer than he would have liked, depressed him. 'To have lost at the age of five and twenty, absolutely from disuse, the faculty of enjoyment, might seem hard to some.' The young subaltern resigning himself to a lifetime of melancholy cuts something of a comic figure, but he was evidently attacked by what Thomas Love Peacock called the 'blue devils' of despair. Restored to health, at least physically, he joined an ill-advised attempt to ship arms to the Polish patriots in their struggle with the Russians; acquired a wife (Adeline Pattle); and by October 1832 was back with the 48th at Madras.

He got his first taste of action two years later, in the Coorg campaign. A force of 6,000 men, including the 48th, was despatched under Brigadier Lindesay to free the populace of the hill country to the west of Mysore from the oppression of the local Rajah. Colin distinguished himself leading troops in hand-to-hand fighting at the battle for the river Kavari. After the Rajah surrendered, Colin found a strange example of the potentate's vanity. He came across a grave with the skulls of 200 elephants, each with a hole bored in the middle of the forehead to make it appear that the Rajah had shot the animals through a part of the skull which was actually bullet-proof. (Years later, when the Rajah came to England to sue the East India Company for compensation, he often called on Mackenzie. They dined together and the Indian prince developed a strong taste for 'mutton chop and currant tart'.)

After Coorg, the regiment moved to Palaveram, the Madras cantonment, and then to the Straits of Malacca. Mackenzie was bored, but in January 1836 he found an outlet for his energy by joining Captain Chads of HMS *Andromache* in an expedition to suppress piracy in the Straits, and enjoyed some strenuous months chasing pirates and leading boarding parties. Meanwhile, his wife, who had sailed for home in an attempt to restore her fragile health, died at sea. Sympathetic colleagues arranged for him to be sent on leave to Manila, but a year later he was declared to be suffering from 'general atrophy', and again ordered back to England, which he reached in the autumn of 1838.

Two occurrences in the next eighteen months greatly altered his habit of life. In an age when military men believed that God was the senior officer in the British Army and were wont to invoke scripture in moments of stress or self-exculpation, there is no doubt that for Mackenzie the Christian religion was a matter of strong personal faith. At home in England he was greatly attracted by the evangelical preaching of the Rev. H.H. Beamish at Trinity Chapel, Conduit Street. His doctrinal attitude hardened, and he became strongly Puritanical in outlook. (Ever since his time in Manila he had naively equated Roman Catholicism and Mahomedism as forms of idolatry.) More surprisingly, he fell in love with the daughter of Admiral Douglas. Her parents insisted on a four years' delay before they would consent to the marriage, and the disappointed suitor decided to return to duty.

3

At Calcutta Mackenzie was warned for political service in Afghanistan. The British had occupied Kabul in August 1839, but Dost Mahomed, who had been put off his throne in favour of Shah Soojah, remained at large, and did not surrender till

November 1840, after an inconclusive battle at Purwundurrah, north of the capital. The British garrison settled down for a long stay, and remained impervious to the growing hostility of the Afghans towards the puppet Soojah and Sir William Macnaghten, the British Envoy. There are arguments about the justification for going into Afghanistan; there are none about the disaster that was to follow.

Mackenzie left Calcutta on 15 July, in the company of his friend George Broadfoot. As he made his way up country he noted in his diary the ominous news from Afghan territory: any soldier who strayed outside the cantonment was liable to be attacked, and Soojah's régime had no friends. This did not prevent him from enjoying the countryside on his march. He describes an antelope hunt. When the quarry was sighted, a hunting leopard (cheetah) was unhooded.

Glancing round with an eye of fire, he slipped down from the cart, and singling out his victim, in an instant dashed after it . . . In less than a couple of hundred yards the last fatal bound was made, the death-stroke fell, and at the same time the cheetah's fangs were sunk deep in the jugular of the unhappy deer. Hastening up, we found the conqueror lying on his prey, of which he retained his hold with the tenacity of a thorough-bred bulldog. To loose him it was necessary to obtain a ladle full of blood by cutting the throat lower than his grip, and pushing the cheering cup against his nose. The smell and taste overcame his obstinacy, and after lapping the seductive draught with great gusto, he allowed himself to be reconducted to his cart, on which he jumped of his own accord.

Mackenzie's orders were to proceed to Ludhiana and escort the former ruler, the old, blind Shah Zemaun, with his family and that of his younger brother Soojah, to Kabul, but he was discomfited to learn that this meant taking charge of the 900 inmates of two royal seraglios. Luckily for Mackenzie, the departure of this mobile *zenana*, which with attendants comprised some 6,000 bodies and required 1,500 camels for their carriage, was delayed because of reported disturbances beyond the Indus, and he was allowed to go on his own, leaving the escort to Broadfoot.

At Ferozepore he met Brigadier Shelton, about to march at the head of the regiments assigned for relief duty at Kabul. He later had good reason to resent Shelton's behaviour, and with something of a premonition he recorded, 'He has been very civil; but I shall not join his brigade.' Shelton's force consisted of the 1st Troop of Bengal Horse Artillery, 5th Bengal Native Cavalry, the Queen's 44th, and the 27th and 54th Native Infantry, and from Mackenzie's journal we get our first glimpse of the brigadier's short-comings.

As I expected, Shelton has marched the brigade off its legs, and has brought the troops into the field the next thing to being wholly inefficient. A bad feeling exists between the Queen's 44th and the native troops. Swords and bayonets have been drawn between them . . . Beasts of burden, camels, etc., have died in great numbers and will continue to die from overwork . . . Shelton's gross want of arrangement and the unnecessary hardship he has exposed the men to, especially during their passage through the Khyber, have caused much discontent. Part of the horse artillery on one occasion mutinied and refused to mount their horses.

On 14 November he watched the troops being played over the Sutlej bridge, but he did not think they were going to their doom. In little more than a year their corpses were lying frozen in the ice of the Khoord-Kabul pass.

On 11 December he reached Peshawar to find Dost Mahomed under guard, waiting the arrival of his family before being taken to his place of exile at Ludhiana. Many of the young officers regarded Dost Mahomed with some respect, but Mackenzie was not one of them. In his view, the Dost had led his troops from the rear at Purwundurrah. 'Do not fancy the Dost is anything of a hero,' he wrote. The Dost had addressed himself to flight 'so dexterously as to pass his own people without being recognised'. This comment is not supported by other evidence.

Mackenzie called on General Paolo Avitabile, the Neapolitan-born Governor of Peshawar, who was always sensitive to British opinion and kept open house for officers passing through his province. His appearance, thought Mackenzie, was

rather *outré*; a tall burly man, ordinarily apparelled in a magnificently-laced Horse Artillery jacket, wide crimson Turkish trousers drawn in at the ankle, a golden girdle and a very handsome sabre; his large Jewish features and bronzed countenance adorned with fierce mustachios which look like twisted bayonets, with a thick grey beard; the whole surmounted by a gold-laced forage cap which he never takes off.

This engaging character's daily routine impressed his guest. He 'hangs a dozen unhappy culprits, looks to the payment of his troops, inspects his domestic concerns (especially his poultry yard, in which he takes much pride), sets a-going a number of musical snuff boxes, etc., all by way of recreation before dinner.' One of his customs was to leave a basket suspended by a cord from an upper window of his palace into which any disgruntled citizen could place his petition knowing that it would presently be hauled aloft by the Governor personally, with no danger of its being intercepted by corrupt underlings. To Mackenzie 'he seems withal to be a good soldier and a just man, that is, impartially stern to Sikhs and Mahomedans . . . a famous man in his way, who certainly keeps his province in better order than any other Sikh governor.'

Pushing on to Jalalabad, which Macnaghten and Soojah were now occupying as a winter capital, Mackenzie noted 'five bodies on a gibbet, two of which were hanging by the heels, a favourite way of dealing with Avitabile, whose ingenuity in these horrors will not bear repetition'. The Afghans, however, fully understood the position and spoke of the Neapolitan for years afterwards 'with the admiration of a troop of jackals for a tiger'. Macnaghten, who perversely resented Avitabile's strong and ruthless government as 'calculated to do us infinite mischief', now assigned Mackenzie to act as Major Mackeson's Political Assistant at Peshawar and he retraced his steps through the Khyber.

He had no illusions about the Khyberees and thought them 'the most savage of the savage', with less than one per cent unscarred by sabre cuts or other wounds. Conditions at Peshawar, despite Avitabile's rigorous discipline, were never less than precarious for the British contingent, but in the early months of 1841 there were no signs of open revolt. Mackenzie's duties were light until, weakened by recurring bouts of fever, he found the hot summer climate (110°under canvas) too much for him, and was sent to Kabul for a respite. In September he made a tour of the Kohistan valley, rhapsodising over the abundant variety of fruit and the generous hospitality he received from the British detachment at Charekar, but these were his last carefree days in Afghanistan. Back in Kabul, he heard that there had been an affray at Zurmat, but he was more interested in the news that Macnaghten had been given the plum job of Governor of Bombay. He saw the departure of Macnaghten as a great loss, being convinced of his worth, 'both as a public servant and a private gentleman'. (He is mercifully silent about the impending move at the same time of the ineffective military commander, Elphinstone.) But before Macnaghten could leave as planned, and before Mackenzie could return to his post at Peshawar, the Eastern Ghilzyes had risen in revolt and the rebellion had started in earnest.

4

Mackenzie was soon caught up in the fighting. The rebels – the 'naughty boys', as Macnaghten contemptuously called them – had to be taught a lesson, and Brigadier Sale was ordered to clear the enemy out of the passes on his way back to India. He took with him the 13th Light Infantry, the 35th Native Infantry and Broadfoot's newly-raised corps of Sappers and miners, and since Broadfoot's unit was short of officers Mackenzie volunteered to go with it. Khoord-Kabul is a truly frightening defile, and in some places less than fifty yards wide, with rocks on either side rising up to 500 feet. The Ghilzyes had occupied the heights and had built a breastwork in the narrowest part of the gorge. As it happened, Mackenzie, who had not taken part in any serious action since the Coorg campaign in 1834, was in the thick of the attack on the breastwork. Under heavy fire from the Afghan jezails, he was soon rallying the Sappers to force the pass. Broadfoot wrote, 'Mackenzie commanded as few officers could have done . . . unquestionably great was the credit due to him.' Mackenzie was recalled to Kabul, but Sale's troops suffered heavy casualties as they fought their way to Tezeen. Sale decided there was no hope of returning to the capital and headed for Jalalabad. The Kabul garrison was greatly weakened by his absence.

Mackenzie's next exploit showed his mettle. He had taken temporary charge of the commissariat for Soojah's troops and was stationed in the fort of Nishan Khan, about a mile and a half from the British cantonment. Early on the morning of 2 November he learned that there had been a riot in the town. (This, though he did not know it, was the murder of Burnes and the sacking of his Residency.) In Mackenzie's words, 'suddenly a naked man stood before me, covered with blood from two deep sabre-cuts in the head and five musket-shots in the arm and body.' He was a messenger, sent by Macnaghten, who had tried to reach the house of Captain Trevor nearby. 'This being rather a strong hint as to how matters were going', Mackenzie closed the gates and stood to arms. In the British cantonment Captain George Lawrence, the Military Secretary, offered to go to Mackenzie's rescue if he could have a supporting detachment, but he was refused permission, and the British garrison remained impotent and inactive.

At midday on the 3rd Mackenzie saw the enemy swarming into Trevor's house. (Trevor, his wife and family made an unlikely escape on foot.) He held out for forty-eight hours, encouraged by the loyalty of some irregular Afghan Jezailchees, till his ammunition was exhausted. Then there was no alternative but to run for it. He severed the arm of one of his assailants but a blow on the back of his head knocked him from the saddle. 'The idea passed through my mind – well, this is the end of my career, and a miserable end to it, in a night skirmish with the Afghans.' But the God of Battles looked favourably on him, and he got through with his men and camp-followers to the British lines. He commented bitterly that a friendly Afghan chief assured him that if he had been reinforced by a couple of regiments they could have remained masters of the city, while Broadfoot sarcastically remarked that Mackenzie had cut his way to the large force who did not seem able to cut their way to him.

The garrison, both the detachment under Shelton which had been sent to the Bala Hissar and the main body in the cantonment outside in the plain, was now under continuous siege. On 6 November Mackenzie was engaged in a fruitless action to recover the main commissariat fort, and lost fifteen out of ninety-five men. On the same day came a plea from Eldred Pottinger, the Political Agent at Charekar, for help against the Kohistanee rising. Mackenzie volunteered to ferry ammunition to the hard-pressed outpost, but he was not allowed to muster the cavalry required, and Pottinger was left to make his own way back with his wounded colleague John Haughton, the only two officers from Kohistan to survive. There is a sad symmetry about the way in which both Lawrence and Mackenzie in turn were prevented from going to the assistance of their comrades. No tactical excuse can be offered, and this callous disregard for the safety of these isolated officers argues both insensitivity and incompetence on the part of the military leaders at Kabul.

With the onset of winter, the threat of famine, and the lack of success when they did attempt to engage the enemy, the garrison became thoroughly dispirited. Everything seemed to go wrong, as much with individuals as with the high command. Even the bulldogs that were cherished by the officers caused problems. An incident in which Mackenzie was involved illustrates the perils the British faced in remote places before the days of Pasteur. One day Mackenzie had called to Captain Troup's bulldog, 'Nettle, Nettle!' Next instant Nettle was clinging like a leech to his right arm, having gone mad. He managed to hold it at arm's length and throttle it with his left hand. 'I never saw anything so hideous as that dog's head, his jaws reeking with blood and foam, his mouth wide open, his tongue swollen and hanging out, and his eyes flashing a sort of lurid fire.' Mackenzie escaped rabies by applying caustic, which left a circular scar nearly two inches in diameter.

He soon got a more serious wound. In the debacle on 23 November, when an attempt was made to dislodge the Afghans from the Beymaroo heights that overlooked the cantonment, Mackenzie had the thankless task of acting as Shelton's ADC and received a bullet in the shoulder, but remained on the field till the general withdrawal.

After days of shilly-shallying Macnaghten concluded negotiations with Akbar Khan and the other Afghan chiefs for retreat from Kabul. Now, when terms, shameful though they were, had been agreed, Akbar speciously suggested a more favourable bargain to test the Envoy's good faith. He offered to meet him outside the cantonment. Macnaghten swallowed the bait and at midday on 23 December, accompanied by Mackenzie, Lawrence and Trevor, he rode out to meet the Afghans. There should have been a mounted escort but the military was as incompetent as usual and the troops were not ready in time. What follows could have come from the pen of a Jacobean tragedian – Webster or Tourneur would have made much of it.

When the British party arrived at the rendezvous, a mere 350 yards from the cantonment, they found Akbar and other chiefs waiting for them on horseback and a carpet spread on the snow. After the usual courteous salutations Akbar suggested that they should all dismount and Mackenzie, who had a presentiment that they had been trapped, did so with reluctance. He now found himself engaged in conversation by an old friend, the former chief of the Kabul police, who took him on one side and anxiously enquired about the whereabouts of his pistols. There was a strong smell of treachery and George Lawrence, who had noticed that a crowd of armed Afghans was closing in on the conference in a menacing ring, suggested that they be ordered back. Quite unnecessary, Akbar assured him jovially; 'We are all in the same boat and Lawrence Sahib need not be in the least alarmed.' Lawrence, far from reassured and 'a very spunky active man' (Lady Sale's description), remained crouching on one knee, close behind Macnaghten. Akbar suddenly shouted, 'Begeer! Begeer!' (Seize! Seize!). Lawrence's arms were gripped from behind, his pistol and sword firmly held, while Mackenzie found himself staring at a pistol levelled at his head by his old friend of the Kabul police. Trevor too had been seized and all three officers were roughly mounted behind their captors who rode at full gallop for Mahmood Khan's fort through a mob of Ghazi fanatics who were aiming blows at the British and screaming, 'Drop the infidel! Let us shed the Kaffir's blood!' Their last sight of the Envoy was of him being dragged head first down the slope by Akbar Khan and his cousin Sultan Jan, the former 'with an expression on his face of the most diabolical ferocity'. They heard Macnaghten give one last despairing cry of 'Az barae Khooda!' (For God's sake!) and then they saw him no more.

The unfortunate Trevor fell or was dragged from his horse and was instantly despatched by the Ghazi knives. Lawrence and Mackenzie clung on desperately while their escorts, at great personal risk, parried the blows of their would-be assassins. At one point in this nightmare ride to safety Mackenzie again found himself face to face with Akbar, who drew his sword and 'laid about him right manfully' in the British officer's defence. Having saved him, he could not resist a gloat. '*You*'ll seize my country, will you?' he jeered; '*You*'ll seize my country?'

Mackenzie presently reached Mahmood Khan's fort unscathed and was locked in a cell with Lawrence. Two friendly Ghilzye chiefs protected them throughout the afternoon, trying to cheer them up by the false assurance that Macnaghten and Trevor were not dead. At one point a hand, recognisably European, was held up at their window, bobbing up and down in mockery on a pole. 'Look well,' screamed the Ghazis; 'your own will soon be in a similar plight.' They were still unaware that it was Macnaghten's when, at midnight, they were taken to Akbar's house in the city. There they were joined by another prisoner, Captain James Skinner ('commonly called "Gentleman Jim" from his more than usually pleasing manners and cultivated mind,' says Mackenzie), who told them that Macnaghten had been murdered and his head and limbs carried in triumph through the streets of Kabul. The trunk, alongside the corpse of Trevor, was hanging from a meat hook in the bazaar.

Sir William, Mackenzie later wrote,

always wore an emerald ring said to have belonged to Muhammed himself. The words 'Mustafa, the last of his race' were engraved on it in the square Arabic characters, and this was on his hand at the time of his murder. He had won rank, fortune, and honour for himself, and left none to inherit them.

The next evening Akbar came to ask them to repair the locks of two double-barrelled pistols which Macnaghten had given him as a present.

Two of the barrels had recently been discharged, which he endeavoured in a most confused way to account for, by saying that he had been charged by a havildar of the escort, and had fired both rounds at him . . . He made his defence without any accusation on our part, betraying the anxiety of a liar to be believed.

No British officer actually saw Macnaghten being killed, but this evidence, confirmed by an intercepted Afghan letter, convinced the British that Akbar himself shot the Envoy. Akbar protested with tears in his eyes (once he wept for two hours to prove his point) that he was innocent of Macnaghten's death, which he blamed upon the uncontrollable Ghazis. It may be true that in the first instance he never intended to do more than kidnap the Envoy and hold him hostage but the evidence is strong that when Macnaghten struggled Akbar lost his head and precipitated the murder with his own hand, shooting the Envoy through the body with one of the pistols which Macnaghten himself had presented to him as a ceremonial gift only days before.

Lawrence was sent back to the cantonment at the insistence of Eldred Pottinger, who on Macnaghten's death had reluctantly taken over the role of negotiator. Pottinger said that Lawrence was the only man with authority to sign bills on the Government of India which the rebels demanded. Skinner and Mackenzie wondered what their fate was to be, but Akbar, anxious to gain some credit for being reasonable, released them to join their colleagues.

5

In the cantonment, despite his vehement protests, Pottinger had been compelled by Elphinstone and the other senior officers to come to terms with the Afghans for withdrawal from Kabul. He was not the only officer who thought this was an act of imbecility, for Mackenzie wrote:

Though we were all starving and eating horse and camel, we could have marched into the Bala Hissar, and held out for a year. In a fortnight the tribes would have melted away.

But Elphinstone was too infirm to contemplate further resistance and Shelton's determination to make for Jalalabad at all costs was decisive. So on 6 January 1842 the grotesque, unmanageable column of 4,500 troops and 12,000 camp-followers straggled out into the snow. The individual acts of heroism which were the commonplace of the dreadful march offer a baroque contrast to the ineptitude of those who insisted on the retreat, but cannot offset its appalling consequences.

In times of stress trivia take on a new significance, and Mackenzie has related how he fussed about finding a suitable mount. He had lost his two favourite chargers. Bucephalus, which had belonged to Dost Mahomed, was given to a friendly Afghan who undertook to carry a despatch to Sale at Jalalabad, and Bob had been taken in the mêlée at the Envoy's murder. Pottinger eventually gave him the horse on which he had made his escape from Charekar. Among those with experience in the field Mackenzie was one of the few who made any attempt to adapt to the stark conditions of the march. When the army halted for the first night at Begramee, a bare five miles from Kabul, many died overnight from exposure, but Mackenzie and his Jezailchees cleared a space in the snow, covered it with their poshteens, and lay in a tightly-packed circle with their feet at the centre. Mackenzie said that he 'scarcely felt any inconvenience from the cold'.

The next week till the last remnants of the British force were destroyed at Gandamack was one of mounting horror. Mackenzie was fortunate in being handed over as a hostage on the morning of the 8th, along with Pottinger, Lawrence, the British wives and families, and some wounded officers. (Indian wives and children were considered expendable.) In time the hostages were joined by Elphinstone and Shelton, who had been decoyed by Akbar to a parley and then made prisoner. Their captivity was to last for eight months. Enduring great hardship, vermin, inedible rations, and the insolence of their captors, they were marched in turn to Khoord-Kabul, Tezeen and Jugdulluk – through passes littered with the bodies of their comrades – and then to Budeeabad where they stayed for eleven weeks till 10 April.

Though not naturally of a humorous temper, Mackenzie was one of the liveliest captives, improvising diversions to palliate the monotony of their confinement. On Sundays he and Lawrence took it in turns to hold a Church parade, with the twin objects of affording Christian consolation and convincing the enemy that the British had their own God to protect them. Only Shelton was uncooperative. When an earthquake demolished part of their quarters on 19 February he rebuked Mackenzie for preceding him, his senior officer, in rushing for safety. 'Mackenzie,' he said, speaking 'in a solemn note to make him feel the enormity of his offence', 'Mackenzie, you went downstairs *first* today.' Mackenzie was stung to an impertinent and impenitent reply. 'So I did,' he replied unabashed, 'I'm sorry. It's the fashion in earthquakes, Brigadier. I learnt it among the Spaniards in Manila.'

In the meantime Sale's men at Jalalabad had repaired their defences. They even sallied out to harass the enemy, and on 7 April when Akbar appeared in person at the head of his troops he was decisively beaten. (Mackenzie was critical about the conduct of the 'Illustrious Garrison' of Jalalabad. He felt that Sale might have controlled the tribesmen if he had marched back to Gandamack as soon as he heard that the retreat from Kabul had started.) Beyond the Indus the Government was gathering its forces; Pollock's Army of Retribution was advancing, and on 16 April he joined Sale. Akbar, smarting at his own defeat, learning of Pollock's arrival, and aware that his authority among the chiefs was declining, began to feel for the first time that the tide had turned against him. Gradually he became ready to listen to advice, and Pottinger persuaded him to send an emissary to the British. According to Mackenzie,

> Akbar and the chiefs consulted who should be sent, and they all pitched on me, for they had got into their heads that I was a Moolah (no doubt from officiating at Sunday worship) and they thought I would come back.

This was not the only hazardous mission accomplished by a single British officer in the Afghan campaign, but it was probably the most dangerous. The country was swarming with hostile Ghazis, and if Mackenzie was recognised as a *feringhee* his instructions from Akbar were likely to be disbelieved or disregarded. He set off in the charge of one Batti Dusd, well known as a robber who had captured Sale's camels *en route* for Jalalabad and then sold them back to him. When they met intrusive tribesmen,

> Batti mounted my horse, causing me to ride behind him with my hands and face enveloped in the folds of my turban and the sheepskin cloak, leaving my eyes scarcely as visible as those of the roughest Skye terrier.

This method of travelling was not only perilous; it was also uncomfortable. Mackenzie was

> perched upon the sharp ridge of the brute's backbone, so muffled up as to be unable to use my hands. Every jolt made me sympathise with Aiken Drum who, as the Scotch song informs us, 'rode upon a razor'.

But Batti was fluent at haranguing the Ghazis in Pushtoo and succeeded in the unlikely task of convincing them that his charge was a minor Peshawar chief sent by Akbar to his native place. In this guise they sneaked through the Afghans to reach Jalalabad on 25 April.

Akbar's official proposal was that Pollock should acknowledge him as ruler of Afghanistan and give him a handsome *douceur* of money, whereupon prisoners would be exchanged and the British would leave the country. Privately he told Mackenzie that he would settle for an amnesty and a large *jaghir* (grant of land). Mackenzie gave Pollock a full report on the strength of Akbar's forces and on the tactical possibility of advancing to Kabul. With commendable restraint he urged that the safety of the British prisoners, which would be jeopardised if Pollock moved against the Afghans, should be regarded as of secondary importance. (Pollock later wrote to Mackenzie, 'You deemed the honour of the British nation and the unsullied character of the British army paramount to any other consideration.') Pollock, from a position of growing strength, refused to treat with Akbar on the terms he wanted. He would promise no more than a ransom of £20,000 for the prisoners and safety for Akbar himself.

Mackenzie ('the modern Regulus', Havelock called him) insisted upon returning to his captors at Tezeen, and Akbar was the only Afghan who really expected him to keep his word. Enraged, however, at the tone and content of Pollock's reply, Akbar ordered the weary emissary to go back to Jalalabad, allowing him only a few hours' rest. Mackenzie's second journey was less eventful, the Afghans having heard that he had earlier kept his word to return, but Pollock was intent on completing his plans for a joint advance on Kabul and those of General Nott from Kandahar. This was no time to make concessions to Akbar, and on 10 May a despondent Mackenzie was once more on his way back to the Afghan chief. He brought little for the prisoners' or Akbar's satisfaction. Though he had accomplished nothing except to gain time for the captives – as both Pollock and Eldred Pottinger separately understood – his behaviour was greatly admired by his fellow officers. George Broadfoot wrote from Jalalabad on 18 May 1842:

Poor Colin Mackenzie, most noble Colin . . . has been in again on his fruitless mission. Heroism like his may gild even defeats like ours . . . His coming in here, and then, with death staring him in the face, going back, even when Muhammad Akbar's conduct seemed to release him; *above all* the motives from which he did it, and the spirit in which he went, raise him to something more than the word hero can express, unless it be taken in its ancient and noblest sense, and then never more worthily applied.

On 16 May he rejoined the captives at a remote village south-east of the Tezeen valley. He had drawn 200 rupees at Jalalabad, which he distributed to his colleagues. (The Court of Directors, well knowing how the money had been disbursed, with typical official parsimony later made him repay it.)

Akbar now sent for Mackenzie to join him, Pottinger and Troup at a small fort near Kabul. There were frequent consultations, and Akbar seemed to prefer Mackenzie who had carried out two embassies for him, though without effect, to Pottinger whose aggressive integrity would admit no compromise. The main body of the prisoners was brought to more agreeable quarters at Shewaki, three miles from Kabul, but they were still in great danger as Akbar was beset with squabbles among his fellow chiefs, many of whom wanted to slaughter all the *feringhees* in their custody.

At the beginning of July Mackenzie suffered a violent attack of typhus and was an invalid passenger until the prisoners were released by Richmond Shakespear and his Kuzzilbashees – sent by Pollock – on 17 September. In the interval Akbar, as soon as he heard that Pollock was on his way, had despatched the unhappy pilgrims, by now near the point of exhaustion, to the wilds of Bameean with the threat that he would sell them individually to Turkestan chiefs. Later, however, another captive, Captain Johnston, and Pottinger, whose authority was unchallenged, persuaded their escort to change sides. Pottinger now took complete charge and the party set off for Kabul before Shakespear, soon to be followed by Sale, effected the happy reunion. During all this time Mackenzie, affectionately cared for by Mrs Eyre and the other wives, had a grim struggle with the illness that weakened him.

Freedom promotes resilience, and in Kabul he recovered quickly to go as Political Officer with the punitive column under General McCaskill sent to visit retribution on the towns of Istalif and Charekar. McCaskill commended him for his services at Istalif. The destruction of Charekar, where their colleagues had been killed at the beginning of the rebellion, was a more poignant moment, and Mackenzie made himself responsible for gathering up the bones of Christopher Codrington who had come out to India with him seventeen years ago.

The army, once Pollock had exacted what he thought was appropriate vengeance by destroying the Kabul bazaar and a couple of mosques, hastened back to India. At Peshawar the saturnine Avitabile greeted Mackenzie with particular respect, and, with tears streaming down his cheeks, 'in spite of the savage cruelty of his nature', embraced the Scotsman, 'pressing me in his arms as if I had been his son.' He had no doubt of the worth of the man, or the fortitude he had shown, and gave him a Persian dress, a bible, and a prayerbook as a mark of esteem. Mackenzie hurried on ahead of the main force to Ferozepore, where the new Governor-General, Ellenborough, was preparing his ludicrously pompous reception for the returning warriors. Ellenborough singled out Sale's Brigade for special honours and named them 'The Illustrious Garrison'. Pollock and Nott got a more muted welcome and the prisoners and hostages were given hardly any sign of recognition. Like the other captives, Mackenzie was practically excluded from the festivities, though they had their own celebration when, with the boorish exception of Shelton, they subscribed to a testimonial to Eldred Pottinger for his services in their months of confinement. It is sad to record the churlish attitude of the Governor-General. Ellenborough ignored the Political Officers, cancelled their appointments, and refused to pay them their arrears of political allowance. Mackenzie had to content himself with the reflection that he had grown to expect more kicks than ha'pence. He sailed for England on furlough in March 1842.

6

The rest of Mackenzie's career – less spectacular but still meritorious – can be dealt with briefly. Soon after he reached home he married Helen Douglas, who had waited for him. (John Haughton had sufficiently recovered from his Charekar wounds to be one of the ushers.) For the next three years the Mackenzies led an active social life, and among their acquaintances were Thomas Carlyle, whose homespun austerity appealed to the Afghan veteran, and Landseer. A reminder of the recent past was provided by the arrival in England of Avitabile, who horrified his hostesses with his enthusiastic tales of executions. Mackenzie spent some time in Germany as an observer at manoeuvres before he was recalled to India.

Since there was no political vacancy for him, he was sent to command the 4th Sikh Regiment at Ludhiana, and there he stayed, his house a rallying point for old Afghan hands, until he obtained command of the Elichpore Division, with appointment as brigadier. He was strict with his officers, his wife noting that 'he would have no intercourse, except officially, with those who were known to be leading immoral lives.' The Reverend Beamish's preaching had not been forgotten. On 28 April 1853 he was at last awarded the Kabul Medal, which he had claimed 'as a right', and the next year he was posted to Bolarum, where he suffered a serious reverse. Faced with an incipient mutiny by native troops, he was wounded while confronting them. After order had been restored, and an enquiry held, Mackenzie was – unjustly, many thought – reproved by Governor-General Dalhousie for his 'intemperate act'.

He was again in England on sick leave when he heard the news of the outbreak of the Sepoy Mutiny. He wrote to *The Times*, denouncing Dalhousie's centralisation as a main cause of the uprising, he made representations to the Court of Directors, and he had a long interview with the Prime Minister, but he did not think that No 10 had much idea of what was afoot. He volunteered to go back to India but reached Calcutta only to learn that the crisis of the Mutiny had passed. There was now no apparent prospect of the active service which he sought and he had to be satisfied with appointment as Agent at Murshadabad, about 130 miles up river from Calcutta.

In 1861 he was made a brevet-colonel, after thirty-five years' service, but following intrigues at the local Nizam's court he was removed from his Agency and given the dead-end post of 'Superintendent of Army Clothing for All India'. His command was now reduced to 900 tailors; there were no chests for stores; and indents for 50 additional sewing machines took two years to reach England. Returning from leave in 1864, he was curtly told that his post had been abolished. On any reckoning he was scurvily treated, and after remonstrating at being informed that he was now 'at the disposal of the Madras Government', i.e. unemployed, he left for home.

The Calcutta *Englishman* (28 December 1865) in a valedictory article described him as 'brave to excess, and one in whom the only qualifications for the highest success in official life that are wanting are a less sturdy independence and a somewhat colder heart'. There is much truth in that comment. The writer evidently knew Mackenzie well; but people are as they are made, and it would have been quite foreign to Mackenzie's nature to crook the pregnant hinges of the knee, where thrift may follow fawning. In 1867 he was, 'somewhat tardily' according to the Madras *Athenaeum*, gazetted a CB, and a year later he obstinately returned to India for a final tour of duty. Obstinately, because though his health was broken and his prospects of further advancement were minimal he still cherished the conception of service. He was fobbed off with a routine appointment at Bangalore – the Commander-in-Chief wondered what to do with him – but he had reached major-general's rank before he left India for good in March 1873.

He was finally made up to lieutenant-general and he had eight more years to live. For one of his active temperament it was a matter of serving on committees and charitable bodies, the usual occupation of those who have reached the plenitude of retirement. He wrote angrily, chiefly in the *Daily News*, against the developments that led to the Second Afghan War and the murder of Cavagnari, the British Resident.

By invading Afghanistan we should play the game of Russia, by forcing the Amir to look to her for help . . . On the most favourable assumption, a triumphal march to Kabul, what are we to do when we get there?

For those who remembered the battles in which Mackenzie had taken part a generation earlier, it had a familiar ring.

It is evident that Mackenzie's later career was a long, frustrated anti-climax, starting from the day he crossed the River Sutlej on his return from Afghanistan at the end of 1842. By then he had earned a high reputation for courage and endurance. Moreover, by twice going back to captivity under Akbar Khan when a case could have been made for staying in the British camp, he preserved what he thought more important, his honour. He exemplified Alfred De Vigny's definition of honour as 'a proud virtue animated by a mysterious vitality, and drawing strength even from our vices, amongst which it dwells in harmony'.* He may have met De Vigny, who was warmly received by London society on a visit to London in 1839, although Mackenzie's friend Carlyle was not impressed, dismissing him as 'a French lionlet . . . with a long Roman nose and no chin'.

On the surface there could be no greater contrast than that between the cragged, Puritanical Scot and the refined, romantic Frenchman. But they had something in common. De Vigny had served for fourteen years as a regular soldier. Both endured long periods of garrison duty; both missed some of the major battles of their time; De Vigny was too young for the Napoleonic Wars and Mackenzie returned to India too late for the Mutiny. One reason for Mackenzie's later disappointments may have been that – apart from the bureaucracy and nepotism common in the army in India – he hated ostentation and display. In his dealings with his superiors he thought, again like De Vigny, that soldiers were too fond of braggarts and that this was because they combined a desire for action with acute mental laziness.

Mackenzie had been tempered in the cruel cauldron of the First Afghan War. Thereafter, this now forgotten soldier relied on his doctrine of 'abnegation', accepting all the buffets of fate, and on his deep religious faith.

*Alfred De Vigny, *Servitude et Grandeur Militaires*, 1835, translation by H. Hare as *The Military Necessity*, 1953.

6
Fighting Bob and the Petticoat Grenadier

I

Kabul can be very hot in July and perhaps Major Hamlet Wade simply got a touch of the sun. Perhaps, on the other hand, he really was psychic and had a vision premonitory of the fate that awaited the British garrison. Either way he was sufficiently impressed to record it in his diary on that same evening in the summer of 1841 when everything in Afghanistan, as Macnaghten liked to say, seemed quiet from Dan even unto Beersheba.

Sir Robert Sale inspected the 44th this morning, [wrote Wade] the colours of the regiment are very ragged, and when they passed in review I was suddenly startled by what I took to be a large funeral procession. What put such a thought into my head I know not, as I was thinking of very different subjects. I cannot help recording this, it made such an impression.

General Sir Robert Sale KCB, who was taking the parade, was a bluff and hearty down-to-earth fighting soldier of so little imagination that it is safe to assume that he did not share his brigade major's eerie experience. After the debacle, when the bones of Elphinstone's force lay whitening in the grim mountain passes, the British public, desperate for assurance, gladly followed Lord Ellenborough's lead in acclaiming Sale as *the* hero of the Afghan War. With considerably more justification they voted his wife, Florentia, the heroine, and when Astley's Circus in London, a year or two later, staged the dramatic finale of *The Captives at Cabool* there was loud applause when, according to *Punch*,*

the meeting between Lady Sale and her husband, for the first time after her imprisonment, took place in the prompter's box through the

* *Punch Almanac*, 1843

[121]

exertions of the call-boy ... The heroic manner in which she fought the double sword combat with six Afghans, whom she put to flight, drew down the loudest praise; and her beautiful sentiment that 'the heart of the Briton, even amidst the snows of India's icy clime, still beats warmly for his native home upon the sea-bound isle' threw an enthusiasm into the auxiliaries never before equalled.

If the real Lady Sale was in the audience her comments are likely to have been sardonic.

2

Robert Sale was born in 1781 and was first commissioned into the 12th Foot, later the Suffolk Regiment. At the age of twenty-seven he married a girl six years his junior, Florentia Wynch, who had been born in India, probably in Madras, and was the daughter and granddaughter of civil servants of the Honourable East India Company. For some years the Sales's married life followed a humdrum regimental pattern at stations in Mauritius, England and Ireland (Sale does not seem to have been drafted for active service in the Napoleonic Wars) until, in 1821, he transferred by purchase into the 13th Foot, the future Somerset Light Infantry. He returned to India with the 13th, taking with him his wife and five children, the eldest aged eleven and the youngest only one year old. Florentia was to bear her husband twelve children in all, of whom the eldest boy, George, died at the age of ten and four more in infancy.

When the First Burmese War broke out in 1823* Sale left his family in Calcutta and went off to war with the 13th to win his nickname of 'Fighting Bob'. When the Burmese had been duly taught their lesson he returned to India and was given com-

*This war, which had been provoked by the rash aggression of the Burmese, produced one of Wellington's many memorable remarks. The British Cabinet sought his advice as to which general should be given command of the expedition which was to take Rangoon. 'Send Lord Combermere,' replied the Duke without hesitation. Combermere, as Stapleton Cotton, had commanded Wellington's cavalry in the Peninsula. 'But we always understood that your Grace thought that Lord Combermere was a fool.' 'So he is a fool, and a damned fool! But he can take Rangoon.' In the event, the Cabinet, presumably more influenced by the first part of Wellington's assessment than the second, did not send Lord Combermere. Archibald Campbell (of whom more later in chapter 7) was entrusted with the command. (G.W.E. Russell, *Collections and Recollections*, 1898).

mand of his regiment. It was no sinecure. The 13th had been ravaged by disease in Burma, and brought up to strength by drafts from England which were described as the sweepings of the London gaols. The regiment, said Colin Mackenzie, was 'in a frightful state of insubordination' and several NCOs and at least one officer were murdered by malcontents. The commanding officer received anonymous threats of death and invariably met the challenge by riding on to the parade ground with the menacing letter in his pocket and ordering the troops to fire a volley with blanks. As the roar of the muskets died harmlessly away Fighting Bob could be heard shouting triumphantly, 'Ah, it's not my fault if you don't shoot me!'

This joviality alternated with savage floggings at the triangles – 800 lashes for attempting to stab an officer, 300 for an insolent retort – and the 13th became so cowed that, as one of their officers said, 'the men became mere babies, you could do anything with them'. Moreover, they could not help but feel an affectionate admiration for their colonel, whose physical courage was beyond question and who always led them from the front. As Mackenzie said of him later, 'nothing could induce him to behave as a general should do. Despite his staff's protests he used to ride about two miles ahead of his troops and in action would fight like a private.' Nor did it lessen his popularity that he almost always contrived to get wounded.

In 1826 Sale was given command of the Agra station, which carried with it the perquisite of a large house 'standing in ample grounds and possessing the luxury of a swimming pool 60 ft by 30 ft'* where he was able to occupy his leisure in chess and gardening, for which, according to his wife, he had a *shoke* or passion. Sometimes, too, he 'amused himself by studying military situations and problems and working them out with blocks of wood to represent the contending forces'. As for Florentia, 'she was a clever woman, had been brought up a great deal with her uncles, from whom she had early acquired literary tastes, which enabled her to instruct while amusing her children.' And so 'with these advantages, household occupations, daily rides and drives, and swimming lessons in the bath, together with the

---

*R. Sale-Hill, 'Major-General Sir Robert Sale, GCB', *Illustrated Naval and Military Magazine*, January 1890.

society of the station, where the Sales were popular, their sojourn at Agra passed pleasantly by.'*

3

When the Army of the Indus mobilised for the invasion of Afghanistan, Sale was overjoyed to be given command of the 1st Brigade of the Infantry Division of the Bengal Column, a brigade which included his own regiment. If Florentia, as she bade him farewell, expected him to get wounded as usual, she was not to be disappointed, but Sale himself enthusiastically subscribed to the belief that the whole affair would be a grand military promenade. When the easy task had been accomplished, he said, Florentia must join him in Kabul, and, yes, their eighteen-year-old daughter could come too. If it was at the back of his mind that Emily might find a husband among the British officers in Afghanistan he turned out to be right.

He was given his first chance of distinction at Ghuznee, which Keane, having left his siege guns behind, saw with dismay was 'a place of great strength, both by nature and art'. The lack of artillery was overcome by the gallant Captain Thomson of the Bengal Engineers, who blew in the Kabul gate with bags of gunpowder under cover of darkness. Sale led the main storming column, which was to follow through the breach immediately behind a 'Forlorn Hope' composed of the light infantry companies of the four European regiments under command of the admirable Colonel Dennie of the 13th Light. The gunpowder exploded, the masonry and beams came crashing down in ruins, Dennie and his men charged into the gateway and drove back the defenders by steady volley firing and hand-to-hand fighting, British bayonet against Afghan tulwar.

Hard on Dennie's heels came the main column, but in the gateway Sale overhead a Sapper officer, dazed by the explosion, saying that the entrance was choked by rubble and that he could not see daylight, though dawn was now breaking. Fighting Bob immediately ordered the bugler to sound the retreat; the call was taken up by the whole column; and everyone halted in confusion. Fortunately Thomson was there to reassure them with the news

---
*R. Sale-Hill, *op. cit.*

that the Forlorn Hope was already inside the fortress; the bugles sounded the advance; Sale's men surged forward; and soon the colours of the British regiments were flapping from the ramparts of Ghuznee in the morning breeze, with only mopping up to be done.

Inevitably, Sale was wounded. Havelock found him rolling on the ground in conflict with a burly Afghan who had felled him with a blow in the face from his scimitar, the brigadier keeping a tight grip on the other's weapon as they grappled together. From his recumbent position Sale politely asked Captain Kershaw of the 13th to 'do him the favour to pass his sword through the body of the infidel'. Kershaw courteously obliged, but his thrust was not fatal and the struggle continued until Sale managed to deal his adversary a sabre blow which cleft his skull from crown to eyebrows. The Afghan gave one loud cry of lament – 'Ne Ullah! (Oh God!)', after which, not surprisingly, 'he never spoke or moved again'.*

The capture of Ghuznee was described to Parliament by Sir Robert Peel as 'the most brilliant achievement of our arms in Asia' ('quite ridiculous,' says Sir John Fortescue curtly), and presently the fountain of honours and awards began to spray its favours. Sale, having nearly muffed the whole operation by precipitately sounding the retreat, was rewarded by being made a Knight Commander of the Bath and Florentia became Lady Sale. Dennie, on the other hand, who had played his part to perfection and who had thirty-eight years' service to his credit, did not even get mentioned in despatches. Keane, who had himself received a peerage and became Lord Keane of Cappoquin and Ghuznee, was said to be a man of 'malignant personal animosities' and was believed to have a grudge against Dennie.

We next hear of Sale in November 1840, when he mismanaged the battle against Dost Mahomed at Purwundurrah. The Dost had refused to surrender when the British occupied his capital and had been continuing the fight in wild country north and west of Kabul. He had already been soundly beaten by Dennie, with only a regiment of Native Infantry, four hundred of Soojah's cavalry and two guns, and had escaped capture through the fleetness of his horse. 'I am like a wooden spoon,' he commented

*J.C. Marshman, *Memoirs of Major-General Sir Henry Havelock*, 1867.

grimly; 'you may throw me hither and thither but I shall not be hurt', and, sure enough, he now bobbed up in the Kohistan with a considerable body of supporters, and it was to the Kohistan that Sale was sent with a small force which was to bring the Amir once and for all to book.

They bumped unexpectedly into each other in the Purwundurrah valley on the clear bright morning of 2 November 1840. The Dost, unprepared for battle, had started to withdraw when he noticed that Sale, perhaps mindful of those tactical problems worked out with wooden blocks in the garden at Agra, was moving his two squadrons of native cavalry to a flank. The Dost at once began to advance slowly and steadily towards the British at the head of a small body of Afghan horse. Captain Fraser, commanding Sale's squadrons, instantly ordered the charge and with his four British officers rode furiously at the enemy but his troopers, with no stomach for the fight, followed only at a slow trot which soon dropped to a walk. Emily Eden, when she heard about it, in her ignorance thought that the troops' inactivity was natural, but wrong. 'Cavalry waiting to receive a charge are lost,' wrote George Lawrence,* 'and our men, after feebly crossing swords with the enemy, turned and fled, leaving their officers to their fate.' Fate was relentless. Lieutenant Crispin, Dr Lord (the Political Officer) and James Broadfoot, George Broadfoot's brother, were all killed and Macnaghten's young cousin Edward Conolly had been shot through the heart in preliminary skirmishing. Fraser, however, managed to charge right through the enemy and now rode slowly back to his infantry, bleeding profusely from several wounds and with his right hand almost severed at the wrist.

Meanwhile small groups of Douranee horsemen had chased Sale's cavalry for a mile or more from the field, while the main body of Dost Mahomed's horse had pushed home their charge almost within range of the British guns, which had been drawn up with the infantry to receive them. 'The gallant old Ameer' (Lawrence's description of a man then exactly fifty years old) knew better than to order his cavalry to charge massed infantry and artillery. He stood there for a time, master of the field and with his blue standard waving in triumph, and then quietly withdrew.

Purwundurrah was at best a draw in favour of Dost Mahomed.

*Sir George Lawrence, *Forty-three Years in India*, 1874.

Alexander Burnes, who had been an eyewitness to the ignominious affair, was so shocked that for once he turned 'croaker' and wrote in panic to Macnaghten to urge that Sale's force should retire on Kabul and that all the British forces should be concentrated in the capital. Macnaghten felt 'rather indignant at this very desponding letter from Sir A. Burnes', and no doubt the finger of criticism would soon have been pointing at Sale had not his luck, as usual, held good. Two days after Purwundurrah Dost Mahomed, his honour now satisfied, rode into Kabul to surrender personally to Macnaghten and to be banished to exile in India. In the euphoria which greeted the seeming end of the Afghan War Sale's inept generalship was happily and at once forgotten. No one noticed that the Dost's favourite son, Akbar, had disobeyed his father's order to surrender to the British and was now somewhere beyond the Hindu Kush, implacably waiting for an opportunity to strike back.

4

By the middle of 1841 the British grip on the country seemed so secure that it was thought safe for the *memsahibs* to come up from India to join their husbands, and among them came Florentia, now gloriously Lady Sale, and her daughter Emily. They travelled up through the Khyber sometimes on horseback, sometimes carried in palanquins, and always at the mercy of marauding tribesmen, but they reached Kabul in safety and life became rosy indeed. Sale was second-in-command of the garrison and Florentia was undoubtedly second-in-command of the *mems*, for only Lady Macnaghten outranked her. Furthermore, the Sales's married quarter was 'the best and most commodious' in the cantonments and incorporated many home comforts which the Sales themselves had suggested when the plans were being drawn up. Attached to it was an excellent kitchen garden in which Sale could indulge his *shoke*, while their Afghan visitors admired Florentia's sweet peas and geraniums. Potatoes, cauliflowers, radishes and cabbage all grew well; and as for fruit, the grapes, peaches, Orleans blue plums and melons of every kind were simply superb.

Emily found her husband and in the summer of 1841 married Lieutenant Sturt, the Garrison Engineer. Florentia approved of her son-in-law and got on well with him. One of the first to become aware of the impending rebellion, he had been alerted by his friends among the Afghan gentry and 'by others of lower degree, who having had dealings with him in the engineer department and public works, and having received kindness from him, gave him such intelligence and warning as was in their power'. The young Sapper duly passed this information upwards, but the warnings went unheeded, so that 'he became disgusted and contented himself with zealously performing his duties and making himself generally useful, acting the part of an artillery officer as well as that of an engineer'.

In the autumn of 1841 Macnaghten, in the interests of the economy which was being pressed on him by Calcutta, took his fatal decisions—first, to halve the subsidies paid to the Ghilzyes to secure the eastern passes; and secondly to halve the strength of the Kabul force by returning Sale's brigade to India. Only two months earlier he had been asking Auckland for five *additional* regiments, two of them to be European, but had hastily recoiled in the face of Calcutta's increasingly strident calls for economy. 'The general impression', wrote Florentia, 'is that the Envoy is trying to deceive himself into an assurance that the country is in a quiescent state. He had a difficult part to play, without sufficient moral courage to stem the current singly.'

Macnaghten, of course, had a particular reason for wanting to keep his copybook unblotted at this moment for he was about to take up the coveted post of Governor of Bombay and any unwelcome show of independence on his part could have dashed the cup from his lips at the eleventh hour. He was planning to leave Kabul before the end of October and with him would go the infirm and incompetent Elphinstone, whose urgent plea to be relieved on health grounds had at last been heeded. 'If anything were to turn up I am unfit for it, done up body and mind,' moaned Elphy Bey, 'and I have told Lord Auckland so.'* For once the Governor-General had listened and Nott had been ordered up from Kandahar to assume command at Kabul. As soon as the takeover had been completed the Macnaghtens and Elphinstone would be on their way to the peace and security of British India. It was not to be.

The Ghilzyes, as we have heard, had responded to the reduction of their subsidies by blocking the passes and were now beating up

*W. Broadfoot, *The Career of Major George Broadfoot*, 1888.

caravans and supply columns with all their old enthusiasm. Understandably, they regarded Macnaghten as guilty of a flagrant breach of faith, for they had scrupulously kept their side of the bargain, as Havelock testifies, and British convoys had been coming through the passes in complete safety under their protection. Macnaghten, who found their action 'very provoking to me at this junction', made light of it. They were simply 'kicking up a row about some deductions which have been made from their pay', and 'the rascals will be well trounced for their pains'. The trouncing would be done by Sale's brigade on its way back to India, and when Sale had cleared the passes the Macnaghtens and Elphinstone would follow him down. With them would come Florentia who meanwhile could stay with her daughter and son-in-law.

Sale accomplished his task after some brisk fighting. His troops fought well, and to George Lawrence it was 'very interesting and exciting to see the gallant bearing of the European and native soldiers emulating each other in ascending and driving the enemy from heights hitherto deemed inaccessible'. Casualties, however, were heavy, and any who fell wounded during a tactical retreat were doomed. 'They were of course abandoned,' wrote George Broadfoot, 'the enemy as they came up falling upon them like hounds on a fox.' Broadfoot applauded Colin Mackenzie's *élan* during the battle (chapter 5). Sale himself restored the record he had temporarily lost by emerging unscathed from Purwundurrah and duly got wounded. 'I could not help admiring old Sale's coolness,' said his brigade major when the General's leg was fractured by a bullet. 'He turned to me and said, "Wade, I have got it," and then remained on horseback directing the skirmishers until compelled from loss of blood to make over command to Dennie.' But his success had been enough to enable his Political Officer, George Macgregor, to 'half frighten, half cajole' the Ghilzye chiefs into accepting a truce. Macnaghten was delighted, opining that 'we are well out of the scrape, as we are positively unable to compete with these mountaineers and their jezails'. But Macgregor's success was a very mixed blessing for it enabled Sale's brigade to continue on its march to India with the result that when Kabul rose in rebellion the eastern passes were again blocked, Sale was on the wrong side of them, and the Kabul garrison was cut off from hope of rescue or reinforcement.

5

In the capital the situation was deteriorating fast. The story of the Kabul risings, which began with the murder of Burnes, continued with the assassination of Macnaghten and culminated in the sorry capitulation reluctantly signed by Eldred Pottinger, has been told elsewhere. Colin Mackenzie casts much incidental light on the tragic sequence – so far as he was involved (chapter 5) – but Florentia Sale's own diary gives the most vivid, eyewitness, account of the rising, the siege, the retreat, her captivity and eventual rescue. It adds a new dimension, and from her very personal narrative we learn what it felt like to be a Victorian *memsahib* exposed to every kind of adversity. She saw the crisis of the campaign, and it was the publication of this journal by John Murray in 1843 (it was reprinted four times, a total of 7,500 copies) that helped to secure her recognition as the heroine she undoubtedly was.* The diary, at least in its published form, starts in September 1841 and ends a year later. 'I believe several people kept an account of these proceedings,' she says, 'but all except myself lost all they had written . . .† I lost everything except the clothes I wore and therefore it may appear strange that I should have saved these papers.' She explains that she kept them in a small bag tied round her waist and added a few lines each day. It may here be mentioned that she also had access to the unpublished journals of Captain Johnson and, according to Kaye, 'used them freely and without acknowledgement'. No one can say to what extent, when revising the diary for publication, she took the opportunity to insert statements which, if they were really made at the time, show remarkable prescience but which may in fact have been the wisdom of hindsight.

The style of writing is simple and straightforward, with no attempt at literary flourishes, but every now and then a lively flash helps to bring to life the whole terrible story. There is an occasional touch of salty humour and there is never a trace of

---

*Lady Sale, *A Journal of the Disasters in Afghanistan, 1841–2*, 1843
†This did not prevent her fellow captive, Vincent Eyre, from publishing *The Military Operations at Cabul* in the same year, 1843.

self-pity as she describes experiences which were sometimes no more than extremely uncomfortable, sometimes terrifying, sometimes downright horrific. She is remarkably generous to the enemy and one thinks all the better of her for it. Thus, in the first week of the rebellion, she is writing:

> I often hear the Affghans designated as cowards; they are a fine manly-looking set, and I can only suppose it arises from the British idea among civilised people that assassination is a cowardly act. The Affghans never scruple to use their long knives for that purpose, *ergo* they are cowards; but they show no cowardice in standing as they do against guns without using any themselves, and in escalading and taking forts which we cannot re-take.

So, too, in the last days of her captivity, after writing that a woman's vengeance is said to be fearful but that nothing can satisfy hers against Akbar Khan, she adds that:

> Still I say that Akbar, having for his own political purposes done as he said he would do – that is, destroyed our army, – letting only one man escape to tell the tale, as Dr Brydon did, – and having got the families into possession; – I say, having done this, he has ever since we have been in his hands treated us well; – that is, honour has been respected. It is true that we have not common comforts; but what we denominate such are unknown to Affghan females; they always sleep on the floor, sits on the floor, etc. – hardships to us.

She does not hide her sympathy for the Afghans' wish to regain their independence. If only Akbar had not stained his hands with the murder of Macnaghten, he might have 'shone as another William Tell; he had been the deliverer of his country from a hateful yoke imposed on them by kaffirs; but here he stands, by his own avowal freely made, the assassin of the Envoy:– not by proxy but by his own hand.' But she adds, fairly, that 'I do believe he only meant to take him prisoner, for the purpose of obtaining better terms and more money; but he is a man of ungovernable passions and his temper when thwarted is ferocious.' What made him even more dangerous was that he was also 'a jovial smooth-tongued man, full of compliments and good fellowship, and has the knack of talking over both kaffirs and true believers.' Indeed he had, and when he died only five years later, reputedly poisoned by his Indian physician, another of his captives, George Lawrence, heard the news 'not without a feeling of regret'.

So far as Lady Sale was concerned, 'Let the Affghans have the Ameer Dost Mahomed back if they like. He and his family are only an expense to us in India; we can restore them and make friends with him.' But first it was imperative that the honour and prestige of the Raj must be restored. So the Army of Retribution must not hesitate out of fears for the safety of the handful of British prisoners in Akbar's power, of whom she herself was one.

What are *our* lives when compared with the honour of our country? Not that I am at all inclined to have my throat cut: on the contrary I hope that I shall live to see the British flag once more triumphant in Affghanistan; and then I have no objection to the Ameer Dost Mahomed being reinstated; only let us first show them that we can conquer them and humble their treacherous chiefs in the dust.

No doubt she meant every word of it. No doubt that she was right and that she exemplifies the spirit that made and kept the greatest Empire that the world has yet seen. No doubt, too, her sentiments would be derided today by the sophisticated. And finally, no doubt that the course which she here recommends is exactly what happened.

She never pulls her punches and writes scathingly of 'the defeatism which so soon became apparent among the British officers in the cantonments'. On 21 November 'it is more than shocking, it is shameful, to hear the way that our officers go on croaking before the men; it is sufficient to dispirit them and prevent their fighting for us.' A day later she notes that

there is much reprehensible croaking going on; talk of retreat, and consequent desertion of our Mussulman troops, and the confusion likely to take place consequent thereon. All this makes a bad impression on the men. Our soldiery like to see the officers bear their part in privation; it makes them more cheerful; but in going the rounds at night, officers are seldom found with their men.

As for Colonel Oliver,

he is one of the great croakers. On being told by some men of his corps with great *jee* [spirit or cheerfulness] that a certain quantity of grain had been brought in, he replied 'It was needless, for they would never live to eat it'. Whatever we think ourselves, it is best to put a good face on the business.

For Oliver himself, the prophecy was quickly fulfilled. On the very next day he was fighting under Shelton's command in a battle on the Beymaroo heights above the cantonments, which he correctly foresaw was going to end in a rout. Being a very fat man, he remarked that he was too stout to run and that therefore the sooner he got killed the better. Thereupon he advanced slowly and alone towards the enemy, who promptly shot him dead. 'Poor Oliver's head and one hand were cut off when his body was found,' recorded Florentia laconically; 'the latter was probably done to obtain a diamond ring which he always wore.'

Towards Shelton her feelings were ambivalent. She was fair enough to admit that 'I believe he possesses much personal bravery' and that in an attack by the garrison upon the Rickabashee fort 'Shelton proved a trump. Cool and brave, he with much difficulty succeeded in rallying the men . . . and they fought like lions.' But in general she was one of the Brigadier's sharpest critics. Determined to get back to India at all costs – and Sir John Fortescue says he was right* – he fiercely opposed the bolder course that was being urged by Sturt and others, to seize the Bala Hissar and hold out there until the spring. 'He averred', wrote Florentia in her introduction, 'that a retreat to the Bala Hissar was impossible, as we should have to fight our way (for one mile and a half!). If we could not accomplish that, how were we to get through a week's march to Jallalabad?' The other argument that was urged against this course in the early days was economy. 'Sturt urges the absolute necessity of our now withdrawing our forces from the cantonments into the Bala Hissar, but is still met by the cry of "How can we abandon the good buildings and property?"'

Florentia saw clearly how unwilling Shelton was to shoulder any responsibility or to give any support to Elphinstone.

He often refused to give any opinion when asked for it by the general, a cautious measure whereby he probably hoped to escape the obloquy that he expected would attach to the council of war. He was in the habit of taking his rezai with him and lying on the floor during these

---

*Sir John Fortescue, *History of the British Army*, vol xii, 1927.

discussions, when sleep, whether real or feigned, was a resource against replying to disagreeable questions.

On 2 November, the day of Burnes's murder, Shelton had marched with a small detachment into the Bala Hissar and he and his officers were entertained to dinner by Soojah, who was pathetically eager for their advice; but Shelton's conduct, says Florentia, 'was represented on the emergency as pitiful and childish in the extreme, not having a word to say nor an opinion to offer'. Six days later, recalled from the Bala Hissar, he marched into the cantonments with six companies of the Shah's 6th, one horse artillery and one mountain gun. 'The people in cantonments expect wonders from his prowess and military judgment,' but Florentia thought otherwise. 'I am of a different opinion, knowing that he is not a favourite with either his officers or men and is most anxious to get back to Hindostan . . . I consider his arrival as a dark cloud overshadowing us.'

Shelton for his part had a certain knack of treading on Lady Sale's toes. With Sale's departure he had become second-in-command of the Kabul force, at a moment when he was encamped out on the Siah Sung hills. He at once put in an official request for either Elphinstone's quarters or the Sales', saying that 'it is very hard that he is kept at Siah Sung when there is a good house in cantonments to which he has a right'. This importunate haste drew from Florentia the tart comment that 'now, as long as Brig. Shelton's duty keeps him at Siah Sung, he has no business in cantonments'. Not long afterwards, when Sale failed to respond to the request to return to Kabul, it was Shelton who maliciously, or perhaps just tactlessly, told Lady Sale that he believed that her husband was acting on the principle of 'being out of a scrape, keep so'.

6

The message of recall had been sent to Sale on 6 November, the move initiated by Macnaghten. Perhaps it was in his mind to get himself a general who would fight, for already Elphinstone's inadequacy in a crisis had become manifest. He had somehow got it into his muddled head that there was a danger, 'a very serious and indeed awful one', as he described it in one of his letters to the

Envoy a hundred yards away, of a shortage of ammunition of which, says Florentia, there was 'at that time a sufficiency for a twelve months' siege!' And so, within four days of Burnes's unavenged murder, Elphinstone was telling Macnaghten not to delay in making terms with the enemy – 'Not indeed humiliating terms or such as would reflect disgrace upon us; but this fact of ammunition must not be lost sight of... Our case is not yet desperate; I do not mean to impress that; but it must be borne in mind that it goes very fast.' And so it did, not because of any lack of ammunition but because of a total lack of leadership.

Macnaghten accordingly wrote to Sale asking him to leave his sick and wounded under guard at Gandamack and bring the brigade back to Kabul. Elphinstone at first agreed to countersign the letter but quickly changed his mind and refused, saying that it would mean abandoning the sick and baggage. Then, all in the course of the same day, he changed his mind back again and endorsed the message. Florentia, however, saw clearly enough that it had been so cautiously worded that it was very doubtful whether her husband would or could take the responsibility of complying. 'He is... to return to Cabul, if he can do so without endangering the force under his command. Now, in obeying an order of this kind, if Sale succeeds and all is right, he will doubtless be a very fine fellow; but if he meets with a reverse, he will be told, "You were not to come up unless you could do so safely!"'

Sale was waiting at Gandamack for further orders, which he had assumed meant that he was to wait there until joined by the Macnaghtens, Elphinstone and Florentia so that they could all travel on together to India. Apparently Macnaghten's first message never got through, but on 10 November, when rumours of some disaster at Kabul were already filtering through to Gandamack, a cossid arrived with a further letter from the Envoy, informing Sale that Burnes and his companions had been murdered and that Kabul was in revolt. 'It alluded in the most desponding language to the progress of the revolt, described the embarrassment of their position and reiterated in pressing terms the request he had previously made for the immediate return of Sale's brigade.' There was a curt postscript from George Lawrence, simply stating that 'they were in a fix', and a message from Elphinstone ordering Sale back to Kabul, 'provided the sick and wounded could be placed in security with the irregulars at Gandamack'.

With his wife and daughter caught in Kabul, all Sale's instincts must have been to go back. But although a lion of personal courage he was something of a donkey when it came to generalship, and now he took refuge in that favourite device for spreading the responsibility that was misleadingly known as a Council of War. At this 'Jackdaw Parliament', as Havelock scathingly called it, many argued for a return to Kabul, and according to Durand they included some of the ablest officers in the brigade, 'foremost among whom was Broadfoot'. Havelock vehemently urged the contrary view. What had really shaken the British hold on Kabul, he argued, was a loss of moral courage by those in command. How could one help a garrison that apparently could not and would not help itself? But then again, how could it be in serious danger? It consisted of between five and six thousand men, with good artillery and an immense stock of ammunition. Nor would return to Kabul be easy, for winter had set in and snow was falling on the passes. Sale's brigade was badly clothed and had lost much of its equipment and nearly all its transport. There was only enough ammunition for three battles, yet the brigade might have to fight its way for every one of the eight marches that a return would entail. There were more than three hundred sick and wounded and to leave these unfortunates at Gandamack, with or without the protection of the Afghan irregulars, would be to abandon them to certain destruction.

Havelock's very cogent arguments prevailed and the Jackdaw Parliament decided to disregard Macnaghten's appeal and to march on to Jalalabad, 'thus', as Sale later explained, 'establishing a point on which the force at Caubul might retire if hardly pressed, and restoring a link in the chain of communications with our provinces.'

It is idle, but interesting to speculate on the outcome if Sale's brigade had returned to Kabul. They had just shown that under proper leadership it was possible to fight one's way through the passes, but they had done so unencumbered by that mass of non-combatant *bouches inutiles* which were to prove a fatal clog on Elphinstone's force. It could well be that good money would have been thrown after bad, and Sale's brigade too engulfed in the holocaust. On the other hand, the effect of his return on the garrison's morale is incalculable.

It will always remain a moot point whether Sale could have returned or not [wrote Sir Herbert Edwardes], and if he had returned, whether it would have saved the Caubul force . . . But there were at least two men with Sale's brigade who would have made all the difference; one – Henry Havelock – who would have recalled the discipline and spirit of poor Elphinstone's subordinates, if mortal man could do it; the other – George Broadfoot – who in the last resort would have dared to supply the army with a leader.

But enough of these ifs and ans; Sale did not march back to Kabul but on to Jalalabad.

7

Back in the cantonments Florentia was noting the deterioration with a clear-sighted pessimism. From time to time Shelton, when sufficiently goaded by Macnaghten, would lead out a detachment to engage the insurgents, and Florentia, determined to miss nothing, would 'take up my post of observation as usual, on the top of the house, whence I had a fine view of the field of action and where, by keeping behind the chimneys, I escaped the bullets that continually whizzed past me'. There is something comic but rather splendid in this fifty-four-year-old lady dodging about among the chimney-pots while the bullets droned past her. It was from this vantage point that she watched the 44th make their first attempt to clear the Beymaroo heights of the insurgents, whose presence there was preventing the villagers of Beymaroo from selling food to the garrison. A cloud of Afghan horsemen charged the advancing column and were greeted by a volley at ten yards' range which failed to hit a single man or horse. 'My very heart felt as if it leapt to my teeth when I saw the Afghans ride clean through them,' wrote Florentia, 'the onset was fearful. They looked like a great cluster of bees.'

A few days later she watched Shelton making another attempt to clear the heights. In this sortie, which saw the death of Colonel Oliver, Shelton reached the summit and there, with monumental stupidity, proceeded to draw up his men in not just one but two of the famous British squares. As Vincent Eyre commented, the square was a formation admirably suited to repel a cavalry charge. But Shelton was securely perched on the summit of a steep and narrow ridge up which a horsed charge was impossible. So 'we formed squares to resist the *distant fire of infantry* against the aim of perhaps the best marksmen in the world'.

The gleeful Afghans exploited the situation by shooting down the British infantry from a safe distance with jezails which far outranged Brown Bess and presently, openly sneering at the useless fire of the British muskets, came so close to the leading square that its officers were reduced to pelting them with stones. The Afghans laughed and threw stones back. Shelton, immensely brave, immensely stupid, stood fast, endeavouring to rally his men, and was struck by five spent bullets; 'one spent ball hit me on the head and nearly knocked me down, another made my arm a little stiff.' The single gun which he had taken with him, in breach of a standing order which had laid down long ago that there must never be less than two, became too hot to fire and fell silent as Shelton's squares broke and fled for the cantonments, chased to the very gates by the Afghans. Elphinstone hobbled down from the ramparts to meet his defeated warriors and a poker-faced Florentia records that she heard him saying plaintively to Macnaghten, 'Why, Lord, sir, when I said to them "Eyes right" they all looked the other way.' Later, during a short-lived truce, the Afghans 'say they cannot understand Shelton's conduct on the hill that day; and that if our Generals can do no more, the Affghans have nothing to fear from them.' It was an opinion from which Lady Sale did not dissent.

The garrison's morale, depressed by these unsuccessful forays, was not helped by the bitter weather. As early as 6 November Florentia noted that 'the men are greatly harassed; their duty is very heavy and they have no cover night and day, all being on the ramparts. The weather is cold, particularly at night.' Again, on the same day, 'the Sipahees complain bitterly of the severity of the weather ... and above sixty men are in hospital at the Bala Hissar already, beside the wounded; they are attacked with pneumonia, which carries them off in the course of a couple of days.' Sturt urged Elphinstone and Shelton 'that the men might have fires at night to enable them to warm themselves and dry their frosted clothes when coming off duty; but no order was given in consequence of this suggestion.' Before the month was out sleet and snow were falling daily, with temperatures at freezing point, and by mid-December almost every day's entry in the diary ends dismally, 'Snow all day.' In their misery the garrison became jumpy and 'last night', says Florentia, 'they popped away 350 rounds at shadows, probably of themselves . . . Nothing is too ridiculous to be believed and, really, any horrible story could be sure to be credited by our panic-stricken garrison.'

Food was running short and the animals were the first to suffer. The trees had been stripped of bark and twigs to supply fodder of a sort, but this source of supply was now exhausted and the horses were reduced to eating their own dung, which was served up to them over and over again. By 29 November, according to Florentia, 'the horses are hard up for grain: those for the artillery have not been much looked after since Lieut. Waller was wounded; and one of them is averred to have eaten his comrade's tail! That he bit if off there is no doubt.' Two weeks later,

our horses and cattle have neither grain, bhoosa nor grass; they have pretty well eaten up the bark of the trees and the tender branches; the horses gnaw at the tent pegs. I was gravely told that the artillery horses had eaten the trunnion of a gun! This is difficult of belief, but I have seen my own riding-horse gnaw voraciously at a cart wheel.

The humans were in little better case, and the wretched camp-followers were living on the carcases of camels that had died of starvation. Early in December a committee was assembled

to value all useless horses in the Bazaar, which are to be destroyed; so there will be plenty of cheap meat, as tattoos [ponies] and camels have for some time past been eaten; even some of the gentlemen eating camel's flesh, particularly the heart, which was esteemed equal to that of a bullock. I never was tempted by these choice viands, so cannot offer an opinion regarding them.

The troops had been on half rations since the start of the siege of the cantonments, 'half a seer of wheat per diem, with melted ghee or dhal, for fighting men; and for camp followers, for some time, a quarter of a seer of wheat or barley.' (A seer was roughly 2lb.)

So they came to 23 December and Macnaghten set out for his fatal parley in the snow with Akbar. A sudden burst of firing was heard and Florentia, like everyone else in the cantonments, was uncertain what had happened, but was told by Waller that 'the Envoy had been taken away by the chiefs'. It was at first the general belief that Macnaghten and his companions had been kidnapped and taken into the city but, on the other hand, they could see 'a great crowd about a body, which the Afghans were seen to strip; it was evidently that of a European.' It was, in fact, Macnaghten's. 'The one thing certain', added Florentia, 'was that our chiefs are at a non-plus.'

At last, on 5 January, orders were issued that the force would march the next morning. 'We were to depart without a guard, without money, without provisions, without wood.' For by now all the firewood had been burnt and 'when ours was gone, we broke up boxes, chests of drawers etc.; and our last dinner and breakfast at Cabul were cooked with the wood of a mahogany dining table.'

On that last evening there was what might have been taken for an omen. Sturt had been sorting his books and Florentia picked up a discard from the floor. It was Campbell's *Poems* and it opened at the one on Hohenlinden.

One verse actually haunted me day and night:

> Few, few shall part where many meet,
> The snow shall be their winding sheet;
> And every turf beneath their feet
> Shall be a soldier's sepulchre.

I am far from being a believer in presentiment but this verse is never absent from my thoughts. Heaven forbid forbid that our fears should be realised!

Next morning the retreat began.

8

Florentia and her daughter rode with the advance guard (the troopers of the 4th Irregular Horse), having been warned by the friendly Taj Mahomed to keep well clear of the other British wives – who were likely to be attacked – and to wear *neemchees* (sheepskin jerkins) and turbans. The laconic entries in the journal make it clear that from the start the march was a nightmare. 'All was confusion from before daylight. The day was clear and frosty, the snow nearly a foot deep on the ground, the thermometer considerably below freezing point.'

The Afghans, who were looting the cantonments even before the rearguard had cleared their lines, now opened fire on the unwieldy column. The camp-followers were as sheep to the slaughter, and 'the whole road was covered with men, women and children, lying down in the snow to die'. Well-disposed Afghans – 'alas, how little heeded!' – had urged the need to get through the Khoord-Kabul pass on the first day at all costs, but that would have meant a march of fifteen miles, something quite beyond Elphinstone's rabble, particularly over ground which was 'a swamp covered with ice'. They had gone a mere five miles when, at 4 p.m., a halt was called for the night at Begramee. 'There were no tents, save two or three small palls that arrived. All scraped away the snow as best they might, to make a place to lie down on. The evening and the night were intensely cold: no food for man or beast procurable.' Florentia was lucky to be given the shelter of a small tent, but 'the wind blew in under the sides and I felt myself gradually stiffening. I left the bedding, which was occupied by Mrs Sturt and her husband, and doubled up my legs in a straw chair of Johnson's, covering myself with my poshteen.'

When dawn broke next morning

we found several men frozen to death, amongst whom was Mr Conductor Macgregor... The men were half-frozen, having bivouacked all night in the snow without a particle of food or bedding, or wood to light a fire. At half-past seven the advance-guard moved off – no order was given, no bugle sounded. It had much difficulty in forcing its way ahead of the baggage and camp-followers, all of whom had proceeded in advance as soon as it was light. Amongst them were many Sipahees and discipline was clearly at an end. If asked why they were not with their corps, one had a lame foot, another had lost his musket: any excuse to run off.

It had at first been intended to get through the Khoord-Kabul pass on this, the second day, but even this proved too much and it was only 1 p.m. when to everyone's dismay a halt was called at Boothak, a bare five miles on from Begramee. 'Here again', wrote Florentia, 'did evil counsel beset the General; his principal officers and staff objecting to a further advance; and Capt. Grant, in whom he had much confidence, assured him that if he proceeded he risked the safety of the army!'

Jalalabad was still eighty miles away and it was plain to Florentia that at this rate supplies would be exhausted long before they got there.

We left Cabul with five and a half days' rations to take us to Jellalabad and no forage for cattle, nor hope of procuring any on the road. By these unnecessary halts we diminished our provisions; and having no cover for officers or men, they are perfectly paralysed with cold. The snow was more than a foot deep.

That night she shared a small tent with eight others, 'all touching each other', after dining on a few Kabul cakes and some tea generously provided by Johnson, the Paymaster, and Captain Troup, the brigade major of Soojah's army.

Again no ground was marked out for the troops. Three fourths of the Sipahees are mixed up with the camp followers and know not where to find the headquarters of their corps . . . Numbers of unfortunates have dropped, benumbed with cold, to be massacred by the enemy: yet so bigoted are our rulers that we are still told that the Sirdars are faithful, that Akbar Khan is our friend!!! etc., etc.; and the reason they wish us to delay is that they may send their troops to clear the passes for us! That they will send them there can be no doubt, for everything is occurring just as was foretold to us before we set out.

On 8 January, the fourth day of the retreat,

at sunrise no order had been issued for the march and the confusion was fearful. The force was perfectly disorganised, nearly every man paralysed with cold, so as to be scarcely able to hold his musket or move. Many frozen corpses lay on the ground. The Sipahees burnt their caps, accoutrements and clothes to keep themselves warm.

Some of the British horse artillerymen gleefully broached a cask of brandy abandoned from the mess stores of the 54th N.I. 'Had the whole been distributed fairly to the men, it would have done them good; as it was they became too much excited.' Sure enough, while everyone waited and wondered why no order to march had been given, a sudden hubbub broke out.

The artillerymen were now fully *primed* . . . They mounted their horses and, with the best feeling in the world, declared that they were ashamed at our inactivity, and vowed they would charge the enemy. Capt.

Nicholl, their immediate commandant, came up, abused them as drunkards, and talked of punishment: not the way, under such circumstances, to quiet tipsy men. They turned to Sturt shortly after their own officer had left them, having showered curses and abuse on them, which had irritated them dreadfully. Sturt told them they were fine fellows and had ever proved themselves such during the siege; but that their lives were too valuable to be risked at such a moment but if need were and their services were required, he would himself go with them. This, to a certain degree, restrained their ardour, yet still they kept on talking valiantly.

A comic little episode if one did not know that all of them were doomed to die within the next few days. As for Florentia,

for myself, whilst I sat for hours on my horse in the cold I felt very grateful for a tumbler of sherry, which at any other time would have made me very unladylike but now merely warmed me and appeared to have no more strength in it than water. Cups full of sherry were given to young children three and four years old without it in the least affecting their heads.

At last the column began the march to Khoord-Kabul, the most dreaded of all the passes, five miles long and shut in on both sides by steep cliffs so high that the rays of the winter sun never reached the valley floor. At noon the first of the force entered the jaws of the defile, Florentia and Emily again riding with the vanguard, but before they had gone half a mile heavy fighting broke out from the hillsides where the Ghilzyes, said Mackenzie, 'had erected small stone breastworks behind which they lay, dealing out death with perfect immunity to themselves'. Afghan chieftains riding herd to the column shouted to them in vain to stop firing, and there was nothing for it but to ride hell-for-leather over ground so rough that 'at any other time we should have walked our horses very carefully'. Emily Sturt was the first to reach the further end of the gorge, her pony wounded in the ear and neck, and her mother was not far behind. Florentia, in her usual laconic way, adds stoically that 'I had, fortunately, only *one* ball *in* my arm; three others passed through my poshteen near the shoulder without doing me any injury.'

Sturt was less fortunate. At the beginning of November he had been badly wounded in the face and neck by a young Afghan who tried to murder him as he entered the Bala Hissar on an errand to

Soojah, but he had made a remarkable recovery and thereafter played a valiant part, insisting while still convalescent on going out to the ramparts in his shirt and what his mother-in-law calls his 'pyjamia'. At Khoord-Kabul his luck ran out. He had reached the end of the pass when he saw a wounded horse which he recognised as belonging to his friend Thain, Elphinstone's ADC, and against the wishes of Florentia and Emily insisted on riding back to look for him. (Thain was unhurt, but was killed at Jugdulluk four days later.) Somewhere in the pass Sturt was hit in the stomach by a Ghilzye bullet and lay helpless until Lieutenant Mein of the 13th and Sergeant Deane, a Sapper, eased him on to a pony and brought him down. He was laid on a blanket in the snow, which was now falling heavily, and Florentia watched while Dr Bryce of the Horse Artillery dressed the wound, but she saw 'by the expression of his countenance that there was no hope'. As an afterthought, she adds that 'he afterwards kindly cut the ball out of my wrist and dressed both my wounds'.

The night was hell. Nearly thirty wives and their husbands crowded into 'half of a Sipahee's pall . . . packed together without room to turn', among them Florentia, Emily and Sturt. The dying man was parched with thirst and Mein went out again and again to get him water from a nearby stream, with 'only a small vessel to fetch it in which contained only a few mouthfuls'. Not surprisingly, 'to sleep in such anxiety of mind and intense cold was impossible', and to make matters worse

> the Sipahees and camp followers, half frozen, tried to force their way not only into the tent but actually into our beds, if such resting places can be so called – a poshteen [or pelisse of sheepskin] half spread on the snow and the other half wrapped over one. Many poor wretches died round the tent in the night.

Next morning, 'before sunrise, the same confusion as yesterday. Without any orders given or bugle sounded, three fourths of our fighting men had pushed on in advance with the camp followers . . . the only order appearing to be "Come along; we are all going and half the men are off, with the camp followers in advance!"' But before they had gone half a mile came the usual counter-order, and they were told to return to their starting point and halt for the day, ostensibly to allow Akbar to complete arrangements for their protection and supplies. The short journey had finished off Sturt, agonisingly jolted along in a camel pannier, 'but he was still conscious that his wife and I were with him, and we had the sorrowful satisfaction of giving him Christian burial' (the only man in the whole force to receive it, says Eyre). By now, according to Florentia, 'more than half of the force is frost-bitten or wounded, and most of the men can scarcely put a foot to the ground. This is the fourth day that our cattle have had no food and the men are starved with cold and hunger.'

Throughout the retreat Akbar had been hovering in the wings with his horsemen, and earlier that day he had insisted upon having Eldred Pottinger, Colin Mackenzie and George Lawrence as hostages to ensure Sale's evacuation of Jalalabad. He kept protesting that he was doing his best to stop the murderous attacks by those dogs of Ghilzyes, but his good faith was always suspect. Pottinger for one had no doubts, for as he rode into the Khoord-Kabul with Akbar he turned to Mackenzie and said with great emphasis, 'Mackenzie, *remember*! If I am killed, I heard the Sirdar shout "Slay them!" in Pushtoo, though he ordered them to stop firing in Persian, imagining that we should understand the last and not the first.'

Akbar now approached Pottinger and his companions with a proposal for saving the lives of the British wives and children. As recorded by Florentia, 'it was that all the married men, with their families, should come over and put themselves under his protection, he guaranteeing them honourable treatment and safe escort to Peshawar.' (The offer, let it here be said, was limited to the British; many of the sepoys and camp-followers were married men too, with wives and children, but *they* were expendable and were not included.) Pottinger was sceptical about that safe conduct to Peshawar and thought it more likely that Akbar was intent on getting his clutches on a valuable collection of hostages, but he could see no other hope of saving their lives. So he recommended the offer to Elphinstone, who accepted it, and the families were handed over. Florentia hardly knew what was happening.

Overwhelmed with domestic affliction, neither Mrs Sturt nor I were in a fit state to decide for ourselves whether we would accept the Sirdar's protection or not. There was but a faint hope of our ever getting safe to Jellalabad and we followed the stream. But although there was much talk regarding our going over, all I personally knew of the affair is that I was told that we were all to go and that our horses were ready and we must mount immediately and be off.

They were taken to a little fort, where the rooms were small, dark and dirty, and where 'at midnight some mutton bones and greasy rice were brought to us'.

Soon afterwards the captives were joined by Elphinstone and Shelton, who had gone to a parley with Akbar and had then been detained by him despite the General's urgent plea that his honour as a soldier would be for ever tarnished if he was not allowed to return to die with his men. It was, therefore, Brigadier Anquetil who now led the remnant of the doomed force, now down to 120 men of the 44th and 25 artillerymen, but still clogged by a rabble of camp-followers, on their hopeless march to Jalalabad, where Sale was waiting.

9

The bush telegraph had been at work and already the Jalalabad garrison knew with a deep instinctive foreboding that some dreadful tragedy had occurred. Every day Sale and his staff went up on the flat roof of the highest house in the town and levelled their glasses across the plain to the point where the Kabul road debouched from the hills, hoping for a first glimpse of the retreating army. They were thus engaged on 12 January when William Dennie was moved to prophesy. 'You will see,' he said sombrely, 'not a soul will reach here from Kabul except one man, who will come to tell us the rest are destroyed.' To Sale, whose wife and daughter were among those at risk, the words must have sounded like a funeral knell, and next day the prophecy was fulfilled. The watchers on the rooftop saw a small dot approaching, and presently 'it was distinctly seen that he wore European clothes and was mounted on a travel-hacked yaboo which he was urging on with all the speed of which it yet remained master.' At that moment Dennie spoke again, his voice, it was later remembered, sounding like an oracle of doom. 'Did I not say so? Here comes the messenger.' He was right, for what they had seen was 'the first, and it is to

be feared the last, fugitive of the ill-fated force at Caubul'.*
Brydon had arrived.†

Although Brydon was presumably able to reassure Sale that his family was safe and had been handed over to the dubious protection of Akbar Khan, Fighting Bob's reaction to the news of the disaster was calamitous. He could see nothing for it but to abandon Jalalabad immediately and try to secure from the Afghans a safe retreat to India. Moreover, with one shining exception, his Council of War agreed with him after a session described by Sir John Fortescue as 'the most astonishing and perhaps the most disgraceful recorded in the annals of the Army'. The exception was the fiery, red-bearded, bespectacled Broadfoot, who attacked this pusillanimous proposal with such incoherent vehemence that the Jackdaw Parliament cackled derisively. Havelock, who could not speak because he was not a member of the Council, but who firmly believed that 'it is our duty to die behind the walls of Jellalabad rather than abandon the country', now coached Broadfoot in marshalling his arguments more logically and one by one the other members were won round till Sale, with deep misgivings, bowed to the wishes of his subordinates and decided to stand fast.

When he first reached the town in mid-November, 'the walls of Jellalabad', said Havelock, 'were in a state which might have justified despair as to the possibility of defending them', the tracing of the perimeter being 'vicious in the extreme'. This was quickly remedied by the skill and energy of Broadfoot, with the result that 'an indefensible heap of ruins was, as if by a magic wand, transformed into a fortification proof against any but siege ordnance'. But in the middle of February, when Akbar was on his way with his army to attack the garrison, all Broadfoot's devoted labours were brought to naught in the twinkling of an eye by a severe earthquake. There was a deep rumble like underground thunder, the earth shook, houses quivered and fell, the ramparts swayed and came down with a crash. If the town had been

---

*Marshman.
†Surgeon Brydon survived the Jalalabad siege and, fifteen years later, the siege of Lucknow. Here he was badly wounded and received the CB for his gallantry. He retired in 1859, forty-eight years old, and died in his bed in his native Scotland in 1873. His wife kept a Lucknow diary (still unpublished) which is evocative, but lacks the pithy comment that came so readily to Florentia.

bombarded for a month, said Sale, it could hardly have suffered more damage than the earthquake wreaked in a few seconds. 'Now is the time for Akbar Khan,' commented Broadfoot ruefully and Akbar thought so too, but on arrival a few days later he was astonished to find that in that short time Broadfoot and his men had laboured to such effect that the ditches and been cleared, the breaches filled and the ramparts doubled in strength. Akbar put it all down to English witchcraft.

At the beginning of April the garrison replenished their stocks by a sudden sortie in which they captured five hundred sheep and goats which the Afghans had unwisely allowed to graze too near the walls. The 35th N.I., saying that meat was more important to Europeans than to Indians, gave their share to the 13th Light Infantry, 'between whom and themselves there existed a romantic friendship which ought not to be forgotten'.*

A week later the garrison again sallied out and inflicted a sharp defeat on Akbar and his army of 6,000 men, burnt his tents, and recaptured four of the guns lost by Elphinstone. Sadly, the veteran Dennie was killed, but, as the official despatch said, 'the defeat of Akbar Khan in open field by the troops whom he had boasted of blockading has been complete and signal'. Akbar, generous in defeat, a week later spoke to his hostage George Lawrence 'in a free and soldierly manner of Sale's victory and his own defeat, praising the gallant bearing of our men, which nothing could exceed, with Sale conspicuous on his white charger at their head'. Back in India, Ellenborough greeted the news with a resounding Order of the Day which was 'to be carefully made known to all troops', in which he bestowed upon the defenders of Jalalabad the name by which they would henceforth be known – 'the Illustrious Garrison'.

Although Sale got enormous credit for this victory, he had been most reluctant to sanction the attack. Havelock had been at him for days, but it was only when the senior officers came to him in a body and urged him to take the initiative that he unwillingly agreed. 'I love the old soldier', wrote Havelock, 'and rejoice that, although he did not listen to my single voice, he was swayed by the united opinion of some older and some younger men, since it redounded to his own reputation and to the good of his country.'

*Mackenzie.

And then, before the end of April, Pollock and the Army of Retribution arrived.

10

Florentia and the other hostages had now spent four months in captivity and had another four months to endure before they were released. There were 55 of them, 21 men, 12 wives and 22 children, of whom no less than 8 belonged to the widowed Mrs Trevor, the youngest being born in captivity. In mid-April old Elphinstone died, worn out by dysentery and tormented by remorse. Akbar chivalrously sent his body under escort to Jalalabad, where it was buried with full military honours and where it still lies.

The captives' experiences had been harrowing enough. At the start, as they were led back to Tezeen, Florentia found

> the road covered with awfully mangled bodies, all naked . . . Numbers of camp followers still alive, frost bitten and starving, some perfectly out of their sense and idiotic . . . The sight was dreadful, the smell of blood sickening, and the corpses lay so thick it was impossible to look from them, as it required care to guide my horse so as not to tread upon the bodies; but it is unnecessary to dwell on such a distressing and revolting subject.

Afghan harridans in the villages through which they passed screamed abuse, describing the British ladies (in Vincent Eyre's account) as 'not only immoral in character but downright scarecrows in appearance and the gentlemen "dogs", "baseborn", "infidels", "devils" . . . the whole being wound up with an assurance of certain death to our whole party ere many hours should elapse.'

They reached the fortress of Budeeabad, where most of their time was to be spent, and settled down to a harsh life of discomfort. They quickly became reconciled to the lack of washing facilities and clean linen despite the unwelcome visitors it brought in its train. 'The first discovery of a real living l-o-u-s-e was a severe shock to our fine sense of delicacy,' wrote Eyre, 'but custom reconciles folk to anything and even the ladies eventually mustered up resolution to look one of these intruders in the face without a scream.' The lice, says Florentia, 'we denominated infantry: the fleas, for which Affghanistan is famed (and particularly Cabul) we call light cavalry . . . Bugs have lately made their appearance, but not in great numbers; the flies torment us and the mosquitoes drive us half mad.'

The food was foul. Two sheep and rations of rice and ottah (a kind of flour) were supplied daily, but

the Affghans cook, and well may we exclaim with Goldsmith 'God sends meat but the devil sends cooks', for we only get some greasy skin and bones served out as they are cooked, boiled in the same pot as the rice, all in a lump . . . The rice is rendered nauseous by having quantities of rancid ghee poured over it such as in India we should have disdained to use for our lamps.

To add to their tribulations, there were the earthquakes, some of them very severe, which became so frequent that on 19 March Florentia thought it worth recording 'No earthquake today.'

Numbers were growing, for on 20 April, 'Mrs Waller increased the community, giving birth to a daughter', and on the 24th July Florentia recorded with remarkable brevity and lack of emotion, 'At two p.m. Mrs Sturt presented me with a grand-daughter – another female captive.' Akbar greeted the news with boisterous good humour, and jovially commented to Lawrence that 'the more of us, the better for him'. He had treated the captives not unkindly, often visiting them, supplying them with money to buy sugar and other small delicacies, and sending them lengths of cloth to make new clothes, which provoked Florentia's cynical remark – 'I fancy he is generous at little cost and that it is all part of the plunder of our camp'. He also allowed parcels to be sent to them from Jalalabad, and Florentia received 'boxes from Sale with many useful things'. So too did Mrs Mainwaring, 'a young merry girl', who 'most liberally distributed the contents among the other ladies, who were much in need'. Not so Florentia. She had plenty of needles, among other things, and Mrs Eyre, who had none, tried through Mackenzie to wheedle one or two out of her. He said later that he had never exercised greater diplomacy, but he failed completely, with the result that for the rest of his days, to the amusement of his friends, he could not resist picking up any pin or needle that he saw lying about.

As the ladies became inured to their life and recovered their morale, snobbery and cattiness reappeared. Some of them, said

Mackenzie, 'gave themselves great airs towards Mrs Riley', which was 'not only unfeeling and absurd; Conductor Riley and his wife were very superior people, he being a gentleman's son who had enlisted.' Then there was Sergeant Wade's Eurasian wife, who let the side down by going off with an Afghan paramour and who is crushingly dismissed by Florentia in a single sentence. 'Of so incorrect a personage I shall only say that she is at Mahomed Shah Khan's fort with her Affghan lover.' The sergeant felt especially bitter because his wife had told the Afghans where his money was hidden, even pointing out to them the shoes in which he had concealed a few gold pieces. The infuriated sergeant was loudly proclaiming that when the Army of Retribution arrived he would ask for his wife to be hanged.

Then at last, in mid-September, came the rescue and the captivity, which had begun in January, was over. Pollock had intended to send Nott, but that officer had refused, saying churlishly that 'Government had thrown the prisoners overboard, why then should *he* rescue them?' So Sale was sent instead, with the 3rd Dragoons, the 1st Light Cavalry and the 13th Foot. First on the scene, however, was Richmond Shakespear with his 600 Kuzzilbashee horsemen, to get a typical greeting from Shelton who 'could not forget the honour due to his rank as the senior military man: and was much offended at Sir R. not having called on him first and reported his arrival in due form.' Sale followed soon afterwards. It was a moving moment. 'All hearts were full,' said Mackenzie, 'hardly anyone could speak.' Florentia, for all her toughness, was overcome. 'It is impossible to express our feelings on Sale's approach. To my daughter and myself happiness so long delayed as to be almost unexpected was actually painful, and accompanied by a choking sensation which could not obtain the relief of tears.' The captives were greeted with a cheer by the infantry

and the men of the 13th pressed forward to welcome us individually. Most of the men had a little word of hearty congratulation to offer each in his own style, on the restoration of his colonel's wife and daughter; and then my highly-wrought feelings found the desired relief and I could scarcely speak to thank the soldiers for their sympathy, whilst the long withheld tears now found their course.

Sale too was overcome by emotion. Mackenzie rode alongside him for a quarter of an hour before he could bring himself to blurt out his congratulations. 'The gallant old man turned towards me and tried to answer, but his feelings were too strong. He made a hideous series of grimaces, dug his spurs into his horse and galloped off as hard as he could.'

11

After that it was all triumph and glory – in the light of Pollock's splendid march. First, India with the bands greeting Sale wherever he went with 'See, the Conquering Hero Comes!' and the great parade at Ferozepore, where Ellenborough had personally superintended the painting of the elephants' trunks and had erected a triumphal arch which looked so like a huge gallows that the Illustrious Garrison marched under it roaring with laughter. Then the Sales, with Emily, returned to an enthusiastic welcome in England. In July 1844 *The Times* reported that 'Major-General Sir Robert Sale, the equally heroic Lady Sale and their widowed daughter, Mrs Sturt, and child' had landed by pilot boat at Lyme Regis from an East Indiaman, and that the inhabitants of the little town 'vied with each other in offering their congratulations, while the church bells poured forth their merriest strains of harmony to welcome the gallant veteran and his truly courageous lady to their native land'. Triumphal receptions followed at Liverpool, Southampton and, rather surprisingly Londonderry; the Queen herself welcomed them to Windsor Castle, and one hopes they found time to see themselves at Astley's circus. At the end of 1844 they returned to India and next year the First Sikh War broke out. On 18 December 1845, on the field of Moodki, Fighting Bob got wounded once too often and died three days later, still fighting at the age of sixty-four. The *Pictorial Times* recorded England's 'sacred and affectionate sorrow for the death of Sale'.

In truth, however, Sale's reputation was hardly deserved. 'Stupid unteachable old Sale', as Fortescue calls him, wins no great marks as a general. He bungled things at Ghuznee and he bungled them again at Purwundurrah. He refused to return to Elphinstone's aid at Kabul, a decision that will always be debatable. He would have surrendered Jalalabad without firing a

[152]

shot if Havelock and Broadfoot had not intervened. His victory over Akbar outside Jalalabad was only achieved because his officers forced him to attack against his own judgement. It just shows how far personal courage and the ability to win the affection and loyalty of subordinates can take a man. Perhaps he only answered to one test of generalship, but that, as it happens, was Napoleon's – he was lucky. He is, too, a perfect example of what is today called the Peter Principle, that is, promoting a man to one job higher than he can manage. Sale was a first-class battalion commander and that is what he should have remained. Above that level he floundered.

But to Florentia, surely, we can readily concede true heroic status, as it is hoped that the extracts from her journal in the foregoing pages demonstrate. Laconically, uncomplainingly, without exaggeration she records dangers and hardships beside which those inconveniences of Indian life about which Emily Eden was always whining pale into insignificance. Many years later a French admirer paid her a generous tribute. 'C'est une vraie voyageuse; elle a bon moral, bon estomac, bonne humeur ... Elle a la sourire des heroines.' And she must, too, have been a good colonel's wife, devoted to the regiment. The toughs of the 13th Light, who not so long before had been threatening to murder their commanding officer, would not otherwise have welcomed her as they did when she was rescued.

She lived out her widowhood in India, on a small estate near Simla, sustained by a special pension from Queen Victoria of £500 a year. Presently Emily Sturt got married again, to an Indian Army officer, Major Holmes, and as they drove out in their carriage at Meerut on 24 July 1857 four mutineers of the 12th Irregular Native Infantry rode up and cut off their heads. Florentia had been spared the knowledge of her daughter's gruesome death. In 1853 she went to South Africa for her health and there, on 6 July in that year, she died. The simple granite obelisk that marks her grave in the Church of England Cemetery at Cape Town bears the splendid and appropriate words 'Underneath this stone reposes all that could die of Lady Sale.'

Years before, in the captivity at Budeeabad, Florentia had taken a liking to young merry Mrs Mainwaring's four-month-old baby son. 'This little fellow was born just before the insurrection broke out in Cabul (in October): his father had gone with Sale's brigade; and we always called him Jung-i-Bahadur.'

Long after her death the Jung-i-Bahadur, now grown to man's estate and an officer in the Indian Army, married Florentia's granddaughter. He returned to Kabul in the Second Afghan War and had a chance meeting with an aged Afghan who wept with joy when he discovered that it was he who, forty years before, had taken the news of baby Mainwaring's birth – in the old Commissariat Fort – to his father, with Sale's brigade. Colonel Mainwaring died in 1922 and fifteen years ago one of us talked to his daughter, Miss Ethel Mainwaring, herself then over ninety (and can thus claim to have spoken to someone whose father was in the retreat from Kabul, 1842, a remarkable link with a past in some ways so far and in others so near). It is Ethel Mainwaring who tells us that Florentia was always known in the family as the Grenadier in Petticoats. One feels that it is a nickname of which the old lady would have been proud.

7
Through the Khyber

I

Few military reputations were enhanced by the First Afghan War. Some of those who underwent the rigours of captivity – George Lawrence and Vincent Eyre, for example – survived to earn fame later, as did others like James Outram and Henry Havelock who had left Kabul before the disastrous retreat. Most were less fortunate. There was, however, one officer whose achievement in the final exploits of the Afghan campaign dwarfed a distinguished earlier career and overshadowed a respectable later one. George Pollock, at the head of the Army of Retribution, forced the Khyber Pass to relieve Jalalabad and went on to inflict a salutary defeat on the main rebel army at Tezeen, doing much, in the course of these victories, to restore tattered British prestige.

George Pollock was born in Westminster on 4 June 1786, the youngest of four sons of a prosperous tradesman who held a royal warrant as saddler to His Majesty. Two of his elder brothers gained distinction in the legal profession, David becoming a High Court judge at Bombay and Frederick holding the high office of Lord Chief Baron of the Exchequer. The Pollocks were to become one of the great legal families of England and in a later generation produced a Master of the Rolls in the person of Viscount Hanworth. Little is known of George's early life, except that he went to school at Vauxhall. From 1801 to 1803 he attended the Military Academy at Woolwich and passed out high enough to enjoy the coveted privilege of turning down a commission in the Engineers for one in the Gunners. Soon afterwards he sailed for India on board the East India Company's *Tigris*, and in April 1804 he joined the Bengal Artillery at their headquarters at Dum-Dum.

One comment on the regiments that made up the Company's military establishments may be apposite. There was little blue blood in the veins of the officers. For the most part they came from yeoman stock; they were often younger sons; and they had to make their own way. The system was not free from nepotism and promotion was largely dependent on seniority. Long periods of boredom were inevitable. Individual messes acquired their own tribal rituals, and their members had a keen appetite for luxuries and delicacies which might have then seemed necessary to palliate the discomfort of living in uncongenial conditions but now appear comically extravagant. Officers kept a copious supply of cosmetics, pomades and unguents. Even a subaltern would have his own silver and wine-cooler, and no regiment expected to take the field without its store of cigars and claret. These affectations were harmless enough and they supported the illusion that those who held the Company's commission had imported the aristocratic way of life to which they were accustomed at home.

It was no more than illusion. Style was important to Indian officers, style propped up by strict adherence to protocol and buttressed by mock-feudal customs, but in effect it was no more than a suburban society, especially when the *memsahibs* joined their consorts. The wide gap which often existed between the peers sent out from England to assume the majestic office of Governor-General and their senior military advisers was not wholly explained by a lack of communication or by conflicts in personalities, but had a wider social origin. Fortunately for the well-being of John Company, however, there were some professional soldiers who were content to practise the military art to the exclusion of everything else. One of these was Pollock.

Pollock's early military service is significant because it had an identifiable effect on his behaviour when called to command in 1842. It is also important because so far as responsibility can be assessed, his was greater than that carried by the other officers studied in this book.

As a subaltern, he was soon blooded. In 1804 the Mahratta War was still dragging on, and in August of that year Pollock, fresh from the gunnery course at Dum-Dum, was posted to join the army in the field and narrowly escaped capture by Mahratta cavalry near Cawnpore. At Agra he saw the reality of war as the mutilated survivors of Colonel Monson's brigade limped into camp. It was a highly mobile campaign, but there were two prolonged sieges, at Deirg and Bhurtpore, and Pollock was present at both. Deirg, a fortress of masonry, protected by a wet ditch and surrounded by marshes, had been thought to be impregnable. The British were encamped outside for five weeks before they gained the outworks, and Pollock, working his cannon for the first time, soon learned the disastrous effects of being outgunned by the enemy. On 24 December he was put in charge of the guns detailed to go with the storming party that was to assault the inner citadel. Here he was lucky. It was not common practice to spend much time on reconnaissance, but Pollock decided to spy out the route in advance. Creeping up by night, he went further than he intended and found himself within the citadel wall, but Fortune favoured him. The enemy had withdrawn and the siege of Deirg was over.

The Mahrattas now concentrated their infantry at Bhurtpore, about thirty miles from Agra. Throughout January and February 1805 General Lake made repeated, but unsuccessful, attempts to take the fort. The assaulting troops could make little progress, and Pollock was horrified to see the men of HM's 75th and 76th Regiments refusing to follow their officers. Finally, the infantry tried to make steps in the wall-face by driving their bayonets into the masonry, but they were repulsed by the enemy firing grape shot and throwing down flaming torches dipped in oil. Bhurtpore was not taken, although the native chiefs, unable to face another blockade, signed a treaty in April. Lake had lost 3,100 men and 103 officers killed or wounded – nearly a third of his strength.

Pollock did not forget the lessons to be learned from Bhurtpore. First, there were the tactical blunders – the launching of storming parties without adequate preparation, and the failure of the Engineers to destroy the outer defences. Then there was the effect on morale. The besieged took heart as they repelled each attack, while Lake's men became downcast, dispirited, and eventually near-mutinous. But there was more to it than this. British prestige had been greatly diminished, and for years afterwards scornful drawings could be seen, even in distant areas, showing British soldiers being thrown from the ramparts of Bhurtpore. In short, the British could not afford a defeat. When they committed a large army to a campaign they simply had to succeed. Pollock had this in mind when, thirty-seven years later, he took his time to ensure the most meticulous planning before he marched on the Khyber.

Throughout 1805 the Mahrattas carried on a form of guerrilla warfare, and Pollock was given command of the artillery in one of the field forces sent to subdue them. On the march the sepoys mutinied and refused to go further till they got their arrears of pay. Pollock was ordered to open fire on them if they continued to disobey their officers, but fortunately money was found and the mutineers returned to arms. There had been an awkward moment when the guns were drawn up and the self-destruction of the column seemed imminent, and Pollock saw how fragile discipline could be, how precarious the hold on disaffected native troops.

From 1806 to 1812, a period of comparative peace in India, Pollock held routine regimental posts and obtained routine promotion. In 1814, eager to see active service again, he volunteered for the Nepalese campaign.

As wars go, this was something of an oddity. A frontier dispute had drifted into open hostilities; the four British Divisions deployed were three times the size of the Ghurka army; but the British commanders, ignorant of the terrain and unaccustomed to fighting in snow at elevations above 5,000 feet, gave a poor account of themselves. It was a recurring feature of Indian wars that British generals, grown fat in the cantonments in the plains, had to learn their business anew. Only after severe initial reverses would someone emerge to demonstrate the art of leadership, and this time it was David Ochterlony. In five months, dragging his guns over the formidable passes, he reduced the Ghurka strongholds one by one till peace was made in March 1816. Pollock as he played his part came to the notice of Colonel Jasper Nicolls who, years later, was Commander-in-Chief, India, when Pollock was selected to lead the Army of Retribution into Afghanistan. For the present, the rising artillery officer had learned at first hand the problems of manoeuvring troops and siting guns against a determined adversary in mountain warfare.

2

After Nepal Pollock returned to Dum-Dum and held various regimental and staff appointments before being promoted to lieutenant-colonel on 1 May 1824. He was well-liked, modest, unassuming, a 'safe man' rather than a flier, but he was steadily extending his knowledge of all the aspects of his profession. His next campaign took him to a scene which could not have afforded a more marked contrast to the heights of Nepal – the swamps of the Irrawaddy. From the start of his involvement in the First Burmese War Pollock manifested one of his constant preoccupations, a healthy, but unusual, concern for logistics. Reports had reached Dum-Dum that the Bengal Artillery units in Rangoon were dreadfully short of bullocks and horses and that there were no ammunition wagons. Before embarking, Colonel Pollock obtained authority to procure all he needed, not so easy as it sounds, and at the Burmese port he spent the next five months re-equipping his batteries, while the main army under Sir Archibald Campbell lay enervated by disease and the rigours of the climate.

In February 1825 Campbell decided that his troops were ready to move and gave the order to march up country. We need not follow the tortuous advance in detail, but Pollock's journal gives some idea of the hazards of the country. Here is a good day.

2nd December . . . we endeavoured to penetrate a jungle, with grass five feet high, and certainly so far succeeded that we kept the wheels of the guns in ruts of an old road, and could see about twenty paces on either side; but as to acting with effect had an enemy appeared, the attempt would have been hopeless.

When he went back to get reinforcement drivers the Military Secretary sent him fifty Burmese, each man with an oar, supposing they were to row boats. Pollock put them to work with the bullocks. Cholera added to the troops' difficulties and the terrain became worse.

16th December . . . Our march during the whole way was through a thick jungle, here and there some superb tamarind trees, and occasionally the small female bamboo growing in clusters, but so contiguous that it appeared impervious; on either side of the road the tops met over our heads, forming an arch, and sometimes completely shaded us from the sun for some hundred yards.

These might be reports by the Chindits during the Second World War.

Campbell's despatch after the fall of Mellown was verging on the euphoric.

Where zeal displays itself in every rank, as amongst the officers whom I have the happiness to command, and all vie with each other in the honourable discharge of duty, the task of selecting individual names for the notice of his lordship becomes difficult and embarrassing.

But Pollock was one of those singled out for special mention. If Campbell's version is to be credited, the gunners must have had a field day. His despatch claims that, of the 304 rockets fired, only five failed to reach the target.

On his advance to Ava, Campbell faced one more substantial engagement, on 9 February 1826. In his general order after the battle Campbell's turn of phrase had not deserted him. Recalling that the enemy, instead of relying on field-works and entrenchments, as was their custom, had boldly tried to outflank the British columns, he noted with pride that 'this false confidence has been rebuked by a reverse, severe, signal, and disastrous', and paid his tribute to all ranks 'with the affection of a commander and the cordiality of a comrade'. Even the austere Havelock was moved to describe the 'deafening peals' of Pollock's guns as succeeding each other 'with a rapidity which suggested the image of unchecked vengeance falling in thunder upon the heads of the deceitful barbarians'.

It had been a long and arduous campaign, not so much in terms of casualties as from the nature of the country in which it was fought. For most of the time the army was far from its bases, or from ports through which supplies could be ferried. Great improvisation was required, and Pollock learned again that attention to detail brings it own reward. There were also lessons to be learned from the treacherous behaviour of the Burmese who signed a treaty which, initially, they had no intention of honouring. When the army returned to India the troops were given a double award of six months' *batta* (field allowance), and, among the honours bestowed, Pollock was made a Companion of the Bath.

Pollock's career seemed to be following a predestined rhythm, as each period of service in the field was followed by a long time of inactivity. He went home on sick leave early in 1827 and remained in England for the next three years. In his absence he was gazetted full colonel on 1 December 1829. He returned to regimental duty at Cawnpore, but subsequent promotion was slow throughout Hindustan. He had temporary command of a division at Sinapore before being given command of the Agra district, with promotion to major-general in June 1838. His hour was approaching.

3

By way of background, the schedule of disasters in Afghanistan during the autumn of 1841 can be briefly summarised. In October the Eastern Ghilzyes rebelled and Brigadier Sale, ordered to discipline them on his march back to India, fell back on Jalalabad instead of returning to Kabul when recalled by Macnaghten and Elphinstone. On 2 November Burnes was murdered and from then on the British cantonments at Kabul were under siege. On 23 December Macnaghten was assassinated, and on 6 January 1842 the British army began its retreat, under promise of protection from Akbar Khan. Within a week the entire force had been destroyed, save for a handful of hostages and wounded officers. One European, Surgeon William Brydon, reached Jalalabad.

Apart from the hostages and prisoners – a useful bargaining counter for the Afghans – the British beyond the Indus were now reduced to three sorely pressed garrisons. Sale was shut up in Jalalabad; General Nott held Kandahar in the west; Colonel Palmer had a small detachment, which soon proved inadequate, at Ghuznee. There was also an outpost at Khelat-i-Ghilzye.

In India, George Clerk, the Agent for the North West Frontier, got the first news of trouble on 14 November, and at once ordered troops forward to Peshawar. On 18 November the 64th Bengal Native Infantry crossed the Sutlej and another Native Regiment followed two days later. Auckland did not hear of the outbreak, or of Clerk's action, till 25 November. He approved the despatch of up to six regiments to Peshawar, but he did not see any point in sending a brigade to Kabul, since it could not reach the Afghan capital in time to be of assistance. On 2 December he wrote to Nicolls, the Commander-in-Chief, that 'at present safety to the force at Cabul can only come from the force itself'. At the end of December Brigadier Wild reached Peshawar with four regiments and a detachment of gunners, but no guns. It had been idly assumed that he could borrow guns from the Sikhs, but since the death of Runjeet Singh the Sikhs were less enthusiastic about the British cause, and, with some show of reluctance, all they would provide were a few broken-down pieces of ordnance.

Wild wanted to await the arrival of the second brigade under McCaskill, but after receiving urgent pleas from Sale he decided to march, and unwisely divided his force in half, sending part to relieve the fort of Ali Musjid, five miles inside the Khyber Pass. He was no match for the Khyberees; his Sikh auxiliaries would not fight; the sepoys broke ranks under fire; and by the end of January a thoroughly discomfited brigadier and his men were back at Jumrood, outside the pass. On 30 January Auckland finally learned of the destruction of the British army on the retreat from Kabul. The shock, it was said, caused him to pace for hours up and down the Government House verandah and at night to throw himself down on the lawn and press his face in agony against the cool turf. Then he rallied and issued a proclamation promising the most active measures for reinforcing the Afghan frontier, 'and for assisting such operations as may be required in that quarter for the maintenance of the honour and interests of the British government . . .' But British fortunes were at their lowest when Pollock arrived at Peshawar on 5 February.

The choice of Pollock to command what was known as the Army of Retribution was at best haphazard. When it became apparent that a senior officer must be sent to take charge of the relief force, Auckland had done his best to choose another Elphinstone, for he wanted to select the invalid Adjutant-General Sir Harry Lumley, but medical advice ruled him out. Nicolls suggested Sir Edmund Williams, a light infantryman, but he had been only two years in India and Auckland would not approve. So *faute de mieux* Pollock was preferred, and on 1 January 1842, while smoking his breakfast cheroot at Agra, he received the order from Nicolls telling him to proceed to Peshawar without delay.

There were arguments against the posting, for he was somewhat venerable at fifty-five, and he had first come out to India as long ago as 1803. Although he had seen much active service earlier in his career, he had not smelt powder since the Burmese

War in 1826. But old soldiers, as they reminisce (too often for some tastes), remember the cardinal features of past campaigns. Tactics had changed little in the last two decades; and weapons, both guns and the Brown Bess musket, the standard infantry issue, were still the same. Many shrewd judges recognised that Pollock was the right man for the job. Henry Lawrence wrote that 'General Pollock is about as good a Commander as could be sent', and George Broadfoot thought that, if not a Napoleon, he was 'superior to any officer I have yet chanced to meet in these regions'.*

4

On his way to Peshawar Pollock overtook McCaskill's brigade, then marching through the Punjab. Seated on a terrace beside the Sikh Governor, Avitabile, he watched the troops march into the city. McCaskill's men made as good a display as they could, but Pollock could not help contrasting Avitabile's hospitable welcome with the attitude of the Sikh soldiery, openly sneering at the British and shouting that they were 'food for the Khyber'. Avitabile himself, assuming that they would simply march blindly into the jaws of the pass, was gloomily convinced that they were doomed to destruction. Pollock had many other problems. It was true that he had wide-ranging powers, both political and military, 'at and beyond Peshawar', and while Sale still held a local command at Jalalabad, it was subject to Pollock's direction. But the questions facing him required diplomacy, not to say statesmanship, in addition to professional expertise. What, for example, was to be done about Shah Soojah, the puppet monarch the British had restored to the throne of Kabul, and then left there? Soojah surprisingly still ruled – mainly because the chiefs were jealous of Akbar Khan – and kept up a stream of letters protesting his loyalty to the British. This quandary eventually solved itself when Soojah, whom the British always suspected, probably unjustly, of complicity in the rebellion, was assassinated on 5 April.

There were other matters to give Pollock unease. What measures could he take to secure the release of the prisoners and hostages? Honour required a determined effort. What links could be estab-

*Sir George Pollock, Life and Correspondence, edited by C.R. Low, 1873.

lished with the isolated garrisons at Jalalabad, Kandahar and Ghuznee? The immediate need was to relieve Sale at Jalalabad. At this stage Pollock's instructions were curiously vague. On 31 January Auckland had told Nicolls that the primary objective was a demonstration of force on the Peshawar frontier. If Pollock could hold Jalalabad 'with due regard to the security of communications through the Khyber Pass', he should do so, 'and it will be highly desirable that he should find an opportunity of asserting our military superiority in the open country in the Jalalabad neighbourhood.' But, Auckland went on, Jalalabad was not a place which he desired to be kept at all hazards. By 10 February Auckland had hardened in favour of a withdrawal as soon as Pollock could bring Sale's brigade away safely. First, however, he had to get to Jalalabad.

The omens were not favourable. Wild's brigade had been severely battered, and there were 1,000 men on the sick list. Pollock diagnosed their illness as partly psychological and partly due to the severe weather to which they had been exposed. He ordered the sepoys to be given worsted gloves and stockings, and in his report he added, 'I shall visit their hospitals frequently, and by adding in any way to their comforts, show that I feel an interest in them.'

At first he had no success; the hospital roll rose to 1,800; but on 21 February he noted 'sick are daily decreasing; today the number is 1,289, and this is a very important point.' It was not only physical sickness he had to deal with. The Sikhs were fomenting mutiny and Pollock gave orders to exclude them from camp. The sepoys declared they would not again enter the Khyber. Native survivors from Kabul came in, showing mutilated hands and frostbitten feet. High-caste Brahmins were making the sepoys swear on the *gunga-paunee*, the sacred water of the Ganges, that they would not advance towards the pass. Many of the officers were disaffected. Eldred Pottinger, in captivity, was horrified when he heard of the regiments which made up Pollock's force, saying he had got some of the worst officers in the army. Morale was at its lowest in the 53rd and 60th Native Infantry Regiments, and reports from their messes revealed that they would prefer to sacrifice Sale's brigade rather than risk their own lives. A captain in the 53rd was on record as saying that 'he would use his utmost endeavours to prevent a Sepoy of his company from again entering the Pass'.

In this unhappy climate Pollock remained patient, tactful, refraining from the punitive action he would otherwise have enforced. He remembered from his Mahratta War days that discipline in native regiments was always on a knife-edge. Nicolls summed up Pollock's behaviour in his letter to the Adjutant-General in the Horse Guards at London. Referring to the mutinous troops, he said

It was as well that a cool, cautious officer of the Company's army should have to deal with them in such a temper, 363 miles from the frontier. General Pollock managed them exceedingly well, but he did not venture to enter the Pass till April (two and a half months after Brigadier Wild's failure), when reinforced by the 3rd Dragoons, a regiment of cavalry, a troop of horse artillery and other details . . . morale must have been low when horse artillery and cavalry were required to induce the General to advance, with confidence, through this formidable pass. Any precipitancy on the part of a general officer panting for fame, might have had the worse effect.

The last sentence is significant. Pollock was not going to move till he was ready. He had logistic problems. He required 271,542 rounds to complete the force to 200 rounds per man, he wrote on 16 February. The ammunition did not arrive till mid-March. When the camel-drivers deserted, having been paid to bring their hired animals only as far as Peshawar, Pollock represented that no army should be at the mercy of the camel owners and that camels must be purchased. Throughout February and March he continued to make the most detailed plans for his advance. He was also, respectfully but firmly, beginning to take an independent line in his communications with the Government. Writing to Nicolls's Secretary on 27 February, he pointed out that if he was to go forward merely in order to withdraw the Jalalabad garrison – as Auckland contemplated – he would have to conceal his intentions; otherwise 'every man will rise to molest our return'. He added that to retire again from Peshawar, unless he first had 'an opportunity of inflicting some signal punishment on the enemy', would have a bad effect far and near.

Meanwhile he could not be unaffected by the pleas for help from both Sale and MacGregor, Sale's Political Officer at

Jalalabad. *Cossids* (native bearers) brought them messages, written in rice water, so that they were legible only with the application of iodine, and baked in cakes. For additional security, they were written partly in French and partly in English, but their import was clear. Sale faced starvation. On 19 February he described how an earthquake (also felt at Peshawar) had destroyed the fortifications he had so laboriously built over the last two months, and how he was now much more vulnerable if Akbar were to attack. (The ramparts were rapidly restored by the exertions of George Broadfoot.) In reply to another urgent plea, Pollock wrote very frankly to MacGregor on 12 March. He referred to the sick roll, and his mortification on learning that 'the Hindoos of four out of five native corps refused to advance'. He had taken measures to 'sift the evil', and there had been a gradual improvement. 'Your situation is never out of my thoughts; but having told you what I have, you and Sale will at once see that necessity alone has kept me here . . . Pray therefore tell me, without the least reserve, the latest day you can hold out.' He ended with a summary:

The case therefore now stands thus:– Whether I am to attempt with my present materials to advance, and to risk the appearance of disaffection or cowardice, which in such a case could not again be got over, or wait the arrival of a reinforcement which will make all sure. This is the real state of the case. If I attempted now, it might risk you altogether; but if you can hold out, the reinforcements would make your relief as certain as any earthly thing can be.

Sale replied on 23 March that the reduced rations of salt meat for his troops would run out on 4 April. He had already destroyed all his camels to preserve the fodder for the cavalry and artillery horses.

Pollock had been heartened when on 5 March he received his first letter from Ellenborough, who had now replaced Auckland as Governor-General. Ellenborough emphasised that he should not run the risk of failure. 'When you strike a blow, let it be a heavy and decisive one. These are my views, and they seem to be yours. Depend on my constant and zealous support . . .' For the moment it was just what Pollock needed. As he waited for reinforcements he addressed his mind once more to the attitude of the Sikhs – still allies under Auckland's Tripartite Treaty. The chiefs were courteous and well-disposed, but the soldiery were insolent. Relations did, however, improve when Gholaub Singh arrived with a further contingent and orders from the Lahore Durbar 'to act in support of the British troops agreeably to the terms of the Treaty'. Pollock was doubtful of their good faith, but eventually accepted Gholaub Singh's assertion that his men were ready to face the Khyber. He had little choice, since the Sikhs in the area numbered over 20,000 men. Pollock felt that at least they would be loyal if he was successful. If he was not, they might quickly become formidable enemies.

This indeed was the crux. As Ellenborough had said, and as Pollock had seen from the dispositions at Peshawar, there must be no possibility of defeat. It is highly likely that Pollock also remembered Bhurtpore, where the memory of an unsuccessful assault had impaired the British reputation for decades. Generals who in the course of their careers are given command at a crucial time can count themselves lucky, but Pollock did not doubt the weight of responsibility he carried. At last, on 29 March, the cavalry and extra artillery came in. He gave orders to break camp and move up towards the mouth of the Khyber.

5

Avitabile, as we have seen, was more than sceptical about Pollock's prospects. The Sikh Governor did not base his opinion on historical precedent, but history would have supported him, for the Khyber had never been forced by passage of arms. Even such fearsome warriors as Tamerlane and Nadir Shah had thought it prudent to buy a safe conduct from the Khyberees. In 1587 Akbar the Great lost 40,000 men trying to fight his way through the gorge, and in the seventeenth century Aurangzeb also failed.

More concerned with survival than his place in the annals, at 3.30 a.m. on 5 April Pollock began his advance on the Shadi Bhagiaree mouth of the pass. Though still short of ammunition and transport, his preparations had been exceptionally thorough. The routes for the storming columns had been reconnoitred. Baggage was kept to a minimum. As Major Smith, on McCaskill's staff, wrote, 'The luxurious magnificence which has sometimes been urged as a reproach to Indian soldiery, has no existence in General Pollock's camp.' The camel train was still enormous, and nowhere was confusion more likely than in the narrow confines of a mountain pass, but an explicit system of signals was devised to maintain march discipline. It was going to be thirsty work before the day was over, and attention to detail extended to providing camel-loads of *lotas* (brass pots) filled with water drawn by the sacred hands of the Brahmins to overcome Hindu prejudices. Finally, on the evening of 4 April Pollock made the rounds of his commanding officers to ensure that each knew what was expected of him.

The Afridis had been busy building a huge breastwork of stones, mud, and heavy branches of trees across the entrance to the pass. Remembering how they had wiped out the remnants of Elphinstone's army before a similar obstacle at Jugdulluk, they were ready to give Pollock's men a hot reception. Pollock, however, was no Elphinstone, and he had a different plan. He was going to crown the heights overlooking the gorge and turn the enemy's flanks. He advanced with three columns. The centre column, which included the artillery and the sappers, marched with Wild in charge of the advance and McCaskill in command of the rear guard. The right column consisted of three and a half companies of HM's 9th Foot, 18 companies of Native Infantry, and 400 Jezailchees, armed like the enemy with the long matchlocks. Under Lieutenant-Colonel Taylor of the 9th and Major Anderson of the 64th Native Infantry, it was to storm the right hill, advancing in successive detachments of two companies, at intervals of 500 yards. A similar column under Lieutenant-Colonel Mosely of the 64th and Major Huish was to crown the left hill.

The troops moved forward in the semi-darkness, silently, without beat of drum or sound of bugle. The Afridis, wrote Matthew Smith, watching from the reargruard, 'appeared to be very soon aware of our approach, and the faces of the lofty hills on either side were studded with signal-fires, as if hung with lamps all over. The effect was very beautiful.'

On the right, Taylor's party stormed up the hillside with great élan, dislodging the Afridi marksmen from their hideouts to gain a foothold on the ridge, only to be held up by a strong body of tribesmen on the summit. Pollock, from his position in the central column, at once ordered Wild to climb the precipitous face with the Grenadiers of the 9th and five companies of the 30th Native Infantry. For a time the issue swung in the balance as Wild was checked by overhanging crags, but the sepoys were not to be thwarted and scrambled to the top. The left column met with less resistance and soon reached its objective. The heights had now been crowned according to plan and the storming troops descended to take the enemy in the rear and clear the road.

While flanking companies were at their work, Pollock kept his cavalry posted on the right in case the Afghans attempted a sortie from the low hills on that side. The guns of the horse and foot artillery and the mountain train were drawn up in battery in the centre and kept up a bombardment into the pass. The Afridis, under fire from front and rear, were driven back, though they fought hard to defend a bridge that offered some cover for defence. The sappers now set about the agreeable business of dismantling the breastwork, and the whole of the central column moved into the pass. By two o'clock they were near the fortress of Ali Musjid, perched on its oblong rock, and had covered five miles since the start of the attack.

'The Sepoys behaved nobly,' wrote Pollock on the following day. 'They merely required a trial in which they should find they were not sacrificed.' He admitted there had been many desertions before the battle began, but now, he recorded gleefully,

They are in the highest spirits, and have a thorough contempt for the enemy. This is a great point gained. You are aware that Mahomed Akbar sent a party, about 800 with one or two guns to oppose us; but they thought better of it, and abandoned the fort of Ali Musjid this morning. I have accordingly taken possession. The Sikhs are encamped near us, and are more respectful and civil since our operation of yesterday.

Pollock, still doubtful of the Sikhs' good faith, had ordered them to attack another entrance to the pass, the Jubogee. This they did successfully, inflicting casualties and causing the Afridis to withdraw part of their main force to oppose them. On reaching Ali Musjid, Pollock agreed with Gholaub Singh that the Sikhs would remain behind to keep open the line of communication with Peshawar.

In all, it had been a classic engagement. Who devised the plan for crowning the heights? Some said Pollock was advised by Mackeson, the Political Officer, who in turn learned it from the Afridis themselves. Perhaps some recollection from the Nepalese War stuck in his mind. No matter, it was his triumph. During the next few days there was some desultory fighting as the long convoy wound its way through the defile to emerge at Lundi Khana. Jezail fire caused occasional alarms at night, but the men suffered less from bullets than from the cold wind which swept down, filling their nostrils, and their beasts', with dust and sand. Bivouacking conditions were bleak, and Matthew Smith envied the *lit de repos* of an artillery officer 'who ensconced himself snugly beneath one of his guns, probably on the principle of the prisoner for debt in "Pickwick" who slept under the table because, he said, he had always been accustomed to a "four poster".'

On 10 April Pollock penetrated to the bank of the Kabul river, opposite Lalpoora. Guns were brought to bear on the fort, which was soon evacuated, but the river crossing was troublesome. No boats were available, some of the 3rd Dragoons and their horses were drowned, and the infantry were ferried across on elephants. The enemy were now making themselves scarce. On the 15th Ali Boghan, about seven miles from Jalalabad, was occupied without resistance and the next morning Pollock rode in to greet Sale, his old comrade from Burmese days. The garrison staged an appropriate welcome, the band of the 13th Light Infantry having buffed up their instruments for the occasion. It was a memorable moment. Pollock had achieved his objective at a cost, in the Khyber action, of 135 killed or wounded out of a force of 8,000 men. The Sikhs lost about 100 from 10,000 in their diversionary action. Enemy losses, more difficult to estimate, were put at about 1,000 from a total strength of 20,000.

But, as arms were piled and rolls called, where was the starving garrison? Where, for that matter, were the besieging Afghans? Pollock expected to find the troops he had come to rescue emaciated and showing the effect of their ordeal. In Smith's words, 'a comical surprise came when we found the European officers and men, all fat and rosy, in the highest health, scrupulously clean shaven, and dressed as neatly as if quartered in the best regulated cantonment in India.' Sale's messages to Peshawar had constantly reported that his rations were all but spent. On 1 April, however, a determined sortie from the fortress had captured a flock of 500 sheep and goats, providing supplies for a further ten days.

In fact, ever since they repaired the damage done by the earthquake, the garrison had been in remarkably good heart. The rigorous teetotaller Havelock said morale was high and discipline good because there was no rum or other spirits to issue to the troops. Certainly Sale was fortunate in having under him some of the best officers in the army – Havelock, George Broadfoot who displayed a genius for improvising the defences, Augustus Abbott, Thomas Monteith, and William Dennie. Late on 5 April they had been alarmed to receive a report that Pollock had been beaten in the Khyber, and this seemed to be confirmed when Akbar's army, encamped two miles away, fired a salute which was actually to celebrate the assassination of Shah Soojah just outside Kabul. Abbott and others thought their only course was to seize the initiative and take on Akbar in the plain, but Sale was still hesitating when he learned that, far from being repulsed, Pollock was on the move to Jalalabad. On the morning of the 7th, 1,800 men, almost the whole garrison, marched out to give battle. Abbott's cannonade was too much for Akbar's cavalry and the Afghans fled the field.

Ellenborough was overjoyed that the fortress was now secure in British hands, and there was an inclination to say that Sale had organised his own rescue. He had undoubtedly gained an important victory over Akbar, but he could not have fought his way, unaided, through the Khyber, and, as he testified in his despatch, the credit for the relief of Jalalabad is unequivocally Pollock's.

6

In the next few months, while he remained at Jalalabad, Pollock showed another side to his character. It could be defined as cussedness, obstinacy, or insubordination. Or it could be regarded as determination to do what he believed was right, whatever the effect on his own fortunes. He had no instructions to go beyond Jalalabad, but he was quite clear in his mind that he was not going to move until he was authorised to advance on Kabul and avenge the humiliation inflicted on Elphinstone's army. From a letter left by James Cumming of the 9th Foot it appears that on 4 April, even before he traversed the Khyber, it was known that Pollock's ultimate objective was the Afghan capital. This view, however, was not shared by the Supreme Government of India.

In the last instruction which Auckland, the retiring Governor-General, sent to Pollock on 24 February, he enjoined him to regard the release of the British prisoners as 'one of the first objects of your solicitude', and to concentrate on measures for procuring the safe return of 'our troops and people detained beyond the Khyber Pass'. This was fair enough while Pollock was still gathering strength at Peshawar. On 28 February Ellenborough took over from Auckland and at once sent his good wishes to Pollock in the letter, received on 15 March, which urged a 'heavy and decisive blow'. While Pollock was putting the finishing touches to his preparations Ellenborough set out his initial policy in a letter to the Commander-in-Chief. He told Nicolls that the overriding factors were the safety of the detached units, the security of the troops in the field, and finally the need to inflict some signal and decisive blow (this phrase occurs twice) on the Afghans. No one would query Ellenborough's appreciation so far, or the operations envisaged, which should be to relieve the garrisons and to release the prisoners, 'an object deeply interesting in point of feeling and honour'. He also recognised the advantages of reoccupying Kabul, so that the British could retire 'as a conquering, not a defeated power', provided Pollock was satisfied with his lines of communication.

Ellenborough soon had second thoughts. He was conscious that Auckland's push forward into Afghanistan had been disastrous; he was not going to make the same mistake; and the letters he wrote in quick succession showed a man at odds with himself. On 19 April he sent his congratulations to Pollock on forcing the Khyber. But he also learned of more disturbing events – Palmer compelled to abandon Ghuznee, Nott outmanoeuvred at Kandahar, and Brigadier England, on his way to reinforce him, driven back at the Haikulzai Pass. Alarmed at these reverses, he ordered Nott to draw off the small force from Khelat-i-Ghilzye, evacuate Kandahar, and withdraw to Quetta for eventual retirement to Sukkur. On the same day he wrote no less than three letters to Nicolls. The first enclosed the order to Nott; the second discussed where Pollock should stay for the hot season, his 'ultimate retirement within the Indus being a point determined upon', and told Nicolls to issue his own orders to Pollock; the third, however, imparted an element of confusion by seeming to contemplate a further advance. On 22 April he forwarded copies of these letters to the Secret Committee in London, emphasising his 'deliberate opinion' that Pollock and Nott would be withdrawn as soon as practicable.

On 27 April Nicolls, who had little or no influence on events, and merely served as a confidante for Ellenborough's vacillations, replied that he had not issued any instructions to Pollock. He may have thought Ellenborough would take a more cheerful view when he heard of the success at Jalalabad, and, he added, 'The General (Pollock) is a clear-headed, good officer, and you have loaded him with heavy cautions; but he will stand alone, and treat those around him (as far as I know) as advisers rather than as his agents.' It was an accurate assessment.

Pollock, busily gathering carriage cattle, camels and provender, was somewhat bemused by the Governor-General's next letter, written on 28 April. In it Ellenborough admitted that Pollock 'might have been led' from the absence of serious opposition, dissension among the Afghan chiefs, and the natural desire to display the British flag in triumph, to advance on Kabul. But 'if that event should have occurred' Pollock was to remember that the Governor-General still wanted the army back within the Khyber as soon as possible. Ellenborough's mood is difficult to interpret. Had he begun to have doubts? At any rate, Pollock regarded the letter, if not as a left-handed authority to go to Kabul, as a sign that Ellenborough's mind was slowly working in the right direction.

As the chess game went on, within a week Pollock was depressed by a contradictory letter, dated 4 May, from Ellenborough's Secretary, Maddock. It argued that with the demise of Soojah there was now no political commitment to stay in Afghanistan, and that His Lordship expected that Pollock would already have made up his mind to withdraw, the first anxiety being to retire 'with honour, into positions of security'. It will be observed that this time Ellenborough conveniently ignored the plight of the prisoners. Pollock now received his orders from Nicolls who, recalling that Nott had already been told to come back, required Pollock to 'withdraw every British soldier from Jalalabad to Peshawar'. Delay would be justified only if negotiations for the release of the prisoners were on the point of settlement, or, improbably, if the enemy should be threatening to attack him.

Pollock saw at once that these qualifications were, at the time, inoperative. He had been given an explicit order to retire. Ellenborough must have suspected that Pollock would be reluctant to comply, but he could not have imagined what Pollock's reaction turned out to be. He decided he must defy what he believed to be a foolish order, and immediately wrote to Nott at Kandahar telling him not to move till he heard from him again. This letter has not survived, but one which Pollock wrote, years later, to his biographer may be quoted.

I felt at the time that to retire would be our ruin – the whole country would have risen to endeavour to destroy us. I therefore determined on remaining at Jalalabad until an opportunity offered for our advance, if practicable . . . Stopping Nott for a few days, after his receipt of orders to retire, was perhaps a very bold step . . . If it had not succeeded, I knew I might lose my commission, but I felt it pretty certain that if we worked together in earnest, the game would be ours.

Nott was almost ready to retreat. He was reinforced by England who reached him at the second attempt on 10 May, and on the 21st he completed his residual task when Colonel Wymer withdrew the weary detachment from Khelat-i-Ghilzye and demolished the fortress. But as soon as he received Pollock's letter he replied that he would stand fast.

Pollock's letter of 13 May in reply to the Governor-General is a masterpiece of non-compliance. He made the point that Ellenborough's letter of 28 April could be taken as giving him discretionary powers, and ingenuously added, 'I much regret that a want of carriage has detained me here.' As regards immediate withdrawal, he went on, 'I fear it would have the very worst effect – it would be construed into a defeat, and our character as a powerful nation would be entirely lost in this part of the world.' He politely remarked that the release of the prisoners could not be overlooked. If we retired while negotiations were in progress, 'it would be supposed that a panic had seized us'. He offered Ellenborough the bait that he could deal with any enemy force sent from Kabul – provided Nott acted in concert. In any event, he could not move in less than eighteen or twenty days and could accordingly wait for Ellenborough's reply. Finally, an oblique promise:'Under any circumstances, I should not advocate the delay of the troops either at Kandahar or on this side beyond the month of November.'

For the next two months this extraordinary correspondence went on, and at times it seemed that each participant was determined not to understand, or admit that he understood, the other's intention. Meanwhile there was no lack of diversion at Jalalabad. Pollock's negotiations with Akbar Khan for the release of the prisoners are described in the chapter on Colin Mackenzie, who was the first go-between. For our present purpose, suffice it to say that in this, as in other matters, Pollock was playing for time. He had the prisoners' welfare at heart, but he was careful not to do anything that would compromise an advance on Kabul – which in turn would achieve all his objectives.

On 5 May Pollock welcomed back Monteith who brought two further infantry regiments and a troop of horse artillery through the Khyber. He was having more success in collecting supplies; 'grain coming in abundance,' he wrote to Clerk at Lahore, but he added that this was possibly only so long as the natives thought he intended to stay in the country. He now felt strong enough to make a demonstration in force, and in mid-June sent Monteith on a punitive expedition into the Shinwaree district where the tribes held booty they had plundered from Elphinstone's troops. Villages and fruit trees were destroyed. 'At one time the interiors of forty-five forts were in a blaze along the valley,' reported Monteith with evident satisfaction.

There was still no order for an advance. To return to the despatch boxes, on 4 May Ellenborough wrote to Nicolls regretfully recognising that it was unlikely that Pollock or Nott would begin the homeward march before October. He claimed he had kept secret his intention to withdraw from Afghanistan, and now suggested, as a decoy, the deployment of the 'Army of the Reserve', ostensibly to be ready to support the troops beyond the Indus. It was a fairly open secret. On 24 May Pollock wrote angrily to Nicolls, 'I heard yesterday that an officer of your staff had written to an officer here that we were ordered back . . . bets were made at the messes as to the probable date of our moving.' Pollock, still hoping for a favourable response to his letter of 13 May, took this much amiss, and on 28 May Nicolls sent him a rocket. He said Pollock had no discretionary powers and the Governor-General had endorsed the order to withdraw.

A lesser man would have given up. Pollock had written on 20 May again asking for agreement to remain till October. Ellenborough for his part was still wavering. He was beginning to realise that both Home and Indian opinion wanted the prisoners released and Kabul reoccupied. On 1 June his Secretary wrote to Pollock in more forthcoming terms. Withdrawal immediately after the relief of Jalalabad would have looked like a successful, even triumphant operation. 'Its retirement, after six months of inaction, before a following army of Afghans, will have an appearance of a different and less advantageous nature.' Since Pollock had not the carriage to return before October, or to move his whole army against the Afghans, he might 'possibly be able to move a part of it rapidly against some portion of the enemy incautiously exposed.'

It might have been more graciously done, but the important thing was that Pollock was now authorised to stay till October. Ellenborough was still peeved that his orders for return had been evaded, and writing home to Peel on 7 June, he complained that

Major Generals Nott and Pollock have not a grain of military talent. The latter has fallen into the hands of two or three young political assistants and has not acted lately upon his own view of what is right. He would otherwise have been before now on the left bank of the Indus, and safe . . .

The significance of this letter lies not in the unfair reference to the political assistants (presumably Mackeson and MacGregor, two very able officers) nor in the inference that everyone is to blame but Ellenborough. It lies in his misjudgement of Pollock. The ineffectual Nicolls had been much nearer the mark when he reported to Ellenborough that Pollock would stand alone. Very much so.

Ellenborough, a confirmed egoist, had been obdurate in the face of mounting criticism about his continued inaction but, as he kept his own counsel, he learned that Nott was in a much stronger position. He had relieved Khelat-i-Ghilzye; defeated the rebels near Kandahar; and had got hold of a convoy of 3,000 camels. Pollock had spent the last months accumulating supplies. The tactical argument against an advance was weakened. Ellenborough had also received a lengthy strategic appreciation from Wellington, revered by his peers as the foremost military authority. Wellington was in no doubt that the Kabul disaster would injure British influence throughout Asia, and concluded that he could not impress too strongly, 'the Notion of the Importance of the Restoration of Reputation in the East'. The phrasing was inelegant, but the message was clear. Wellington's advice and the improvement in the Kandahar sector convinced Ellenborough that, however much it went against his own inclination, the risk could now be taken. On 4 July he sent new orders to Pollock and Nott.

They were, in effect, a complete reversal of his previous instructions. The two generals were to retire across the Indus, but they could so so by advancing on Kabul. The march on Kabul, however, was to be undertaken only if Nott was certain that his resources were adequate. Nott was given the option of a straightforward withdrawal by way of Quetta.

By any reckoning, this was peculiar. On the face of it, the result would be a backward move forward, and Ellenborough was later accused of Jesuitical cunning for leaving the decision to the two officers in the field, while disguising his own change of mind. Ellenborough's supporters have argued that it was right to leave the choice to the men on the spot, and that the Kabul route was to be preferred for Nott's troops, mainly sepoys who would be returning to their base in Bengal. These factors have only a little weight, and though Wellington later described the orders as the handsomest ever issued, it seems more likely that Ellenborough perceived that he did not have the moral authority to compel a withdrawal without first inflicting the 'signal and decisive' blow and securing the release of the prisoners. He therefore adopted a devious solution. The steadfast obstinacy of Pollock had prevailed.

Pollock, naturally, was elated. He had got what he wanted, but only just. He wrote to a friend, 'If I have not lived long enough to judge the propriety of an act for which I am alone responsible, the sooner I resign the command the better. I assure you that I feel the full benefit of being unshackled and allowed to judge for myself.' He had written at once to Nott, and, as he said, 'he will find some difficulty in resisting the glorious temptation; but if he does resist, he is not the man I take him for.' Pollock was anxious lest Nott had already started for Quetta, and, a sign of his impatience, he sent five messages in haste to Kandahar. (One, written in undetectable rice water, was impertinently conveyed part of the way by Captain Troup whom Akbar Khan had sent to Pollock's camp as his latest envoy.) Nott, as will become apparent in the next chapter, was a very different man from Pollock, but he brought the tension to an end with his reply of 27 July. He was going to take the Kabul route.

7

Life at Jalalabad had been far from pleasant. Tempers were frayed by dust storms, and the troops ate, drank, and slept in filth; the temperature was 108°; and ominous tremors recalled the great February earthquake. Now a fresh breeze swept through the camp. It was a time for sharpening axes, checking kit, and reconciling march tables. The morale of Pollock's army, which he had painstakingly sustained through the months of delay, rose steadily. The old war horse 'Fighting Bob' Sale, who had already moved forward to Futtehabad, wrote on 16 August: 'Hurrah! This is good news. All here are prepared to meet your wishes to march as light as possible . . . I am so excited that I can scarce write.' Back in India, however, Nicolls was not so enthusiastic, for the Governor-General had not told him of the orders he had issued on 4 July. In his journal Nicolls noted, as late as 24 August, that he did not know what Pollock and Nott were doing. Three days later he found out, and recorded – with some justification – 'Lord Ellenborough's want of decent attention to my position is inexcusable.' One of Ellenborough's defects was that he thought he was his own Commander-in-Chief.

But matters were out of the Governor-General's hands as the three principal actors began to converge for the next act in the drama. On 7 August Nott emerged from Kandahar with upwards of 6,000 men; Pollock left Jalalabad on the 20th with 8,000; and at Kabul, Akbar Khan, who had fulfilled his threat to send the prisoners off to Bameean, roused his tribesmen for the confrontation he knew must come. Pollock's activity was distinguished by features which by now had become familiar. First, there was his unremitting attention to detail. Though still bedevilled by shortage of transport, he checked and rechecked the commissariat arrangements. Food for eight days had to be carried. He even ordered mounted troops to tie the legs of their spare pantaloons, fill them with grain, and sling them in front of their saddles. Next, he kept the sepoys' spirits high by reassuring them that they would not be committed without certainty of success. Lastly, he showed consummate skill in deploying his regiments in differing conditions of terrain.

It was not a triumphant march. Pollock knew that his, and the army's, reputation was once again at stake. From the depths of captivity, Lady Sale summarised the prevailing mood in her journal of 21 August:

Let us first show the Afghans that we can both conquer them and revenge the foul murder of our troops; but do not let us dishonour the British name by sneaking out of the country, like whipped pariah dogs . . . I have been a soldier's wife too long to sit down tamely whilst our honour is tarnished in the sight and opinion of savages.

If these, or similar, thoughts were not enough to strengthen the purpose of the advancing force, there were other, more visible mementoes of the fate of Elphinstone's army. At Gandamack, where the last remnants of the 44th had been butchered, Augustus Abbott found a hill 'literally covered with skeletons, most of them bleached by exposure to the rain and sun, but many having hair of a colour which enabled us to recognise the remains of our own countrymen'. At Tezeen they came upon a heap of 1,500 corpses of native troops and camp-followers who had been left naked to be frozen to death. In the Khoord-Kabul pass

Captain Backhouse winced at his gunwheels crushing the skulls and other bones of his late comrades at almost every yard, for three or four miles. But Afghans had used skeletons to shore up the breastworks made of rocks and tree trunks. Retribution was a grim business.

The enemy was first met at Mamoo Khail, a village about three miles beyond Gandamack. The Afghans had flooded the fields as a defensive measure, but Pollock, moving in his customary formation of two parallel columns with his guns in the centre and his cavalry in the rear, compelled them to retreat to a fort close to the hills called Khochlee Khail. Pollock regrouped, and the Khyber veterans of the 9th Foot, together with Broadfoot's Sappers, scaled the summit. The tribesmen scattered. Mamoo Khail was destroyed before Pollock returned to Gandamack to collect further supplies and wait for news from Kandahar. Nott's signal confirming that he was on the march arrived on 6 September and Pollock broke camp the following day.

When Jugdulluk came in sight it was clear from the initial skirmishing, the rattle of jezail fire, and the standards flying from the hills that commanded the defile, that the Ghilzyes were there in strength. The fire from Abbott's light field battery and Backhouse's mountain train (a special unit he had formed, consisting of six three-pounders with its own mule transport, pack and draught) produced no more than ricochets against the steep crags, and the Afghan matchlocks outranged the aged Brown Bess muskets of most of Pollock's infantry. Amid the storm of bullets and roundshot, Pollock called forward three columns to essay the heights with the bayonet – Broadfoot with his indomitable Sappers, Taylor and the 9th, now old hands at the business, and Wilkinson with the 13th Light Infantry who had long memories of their march from Kabul. The first impetus was not lost as they clambered up the rocks to take what Pollock called the enemy's 'least assailable stronghold'. They were not very different men from those of the 44th who had perished in Elphinstone's retreat; but they were well led, and, with every success, more confident.

On 11 and 12 September, while Pollock halted in the long narrow valley of Tezeen, scouts reported that the main Afghan body lay directly ahead. Akbar Khan had chosen a strong defensive position. He knew it was his last chance and he had mustered a force later estimated at 16,000 men. In Pollock's words, 'Every place appeared covered with the enemy, and they fought really well, actually coming up to the European bayonets. I then suspected Akbar must be present, and so it turned out.' It was an exceptionally hazardous engagement, both from the enemy's heavy fire power and the nature of the country, the rocks in echelon affording continuous cover for their marksmen. But Pollock's infantry, scenting victory, eased forward with what now seemed inexorable precision, turning the flanks and crowning the heights before the 3rd Dragoons were launched through the pass. The lofty Huft Kotul crest was gained, the troops cheering loudly as they reached the summit. The Afghan force was reduced to a shambles. Akbar deserted the field and fled towards the Ghorebund valley, beyond Kabul.

There was no resistance at Khoord-Kabul, though, as a final ghastly reminder of what they had come to avenge, the advance guard found skeletons so thick on the ground that they had to be dragged to one side to allow the gun carriages to proceed. On 15 September Pollock marched unopposed along the road from Boothak to encamp on the Kabul race-course, where the complacent British had held gymkhanas during the previous occupation. The next day he took formal possession of the Bala Hissar and hoisted the British flag on the pinnacle. Kabul seemed an abandoned city. The inhabitants had either fled or locked themselves in their dwellings. Only the Kuzzilbashee chiefs — always friendly to the British — and a few others came forward to profess allegiance. Two days later the worthy Nott arrived on the outskirts of the city. He was angry that Pollock had outstripped him and felt that as they had done so much in concert they might have synchronised their arrival.

Pollock was still exercised about releasing the prisoners from Bameean, and he tells how the rescue operation was mounted. A man in full Afghan dress came to his tent, saluted in the British manner, and speaking in Pushtoo offered to lead a detachment of Kuzzilbashees to recover the *feringhees*. A moment passed before Pollock recognised his Military Secretary. It is not known what prompted Shakespear to perform this exotic charade, but he was soon on his way with 700 Kuzzilbashee horsemen and 20,000 rupees prudently provided by Pollock in case some financial inducement should be needed. Nott's behaviour was less admirable. Pollock thought that, with Akbar still at large, Nott should send a brigade to support Shakespear. This idea had already occurred to Nott's officers, but he would have none of it. He sent an evasive reply. So Pollock despatched Sale's brigade. Meanwhile Shakespear had made contact with the prisoners, and soon afterwards Sale had an emotional reunion with his family and the rest of the captives.

Pollock had neither authority nor inclination to linger in Kabul, and Nott chafed at each day spent in camp. But there was still some tidying up to be done. Amenoolah Khan, one of the instigators of the rebellion, was gathering followers in the Kohistan, and while it was unlikely that he could make a frontal attack on the combined British divisions, he might well descend to harry them on the return march. To remove this danger, and to punish the insurgents for their atrocities in the previous winter, Pollock sent a strong column under McCaskill to reduce the Afghans' cherished town of Istalif (where the rebels had lodged their families and treasure), and to destroy Charekar, the scene of an earlier British massacre. There remained the question of exacting retribution from the Afghan capital, and this in turn depended on what form of government was to be left behind. Pollock, sternly warned by Ellenborough against king-making, had been embarrassed when Soojah's son, Futteh Jung, the nominal ruler of Kabul, appeared as a fugitive in his camp at Gandamack. Pollock had to get at least a semblance of an administration set up in order to obtain supplies and prepare the way for departure. He accordingly allowed Futteh Jung to accompany him to the flag-raising at the Bala Hissar and, ostensibly, to resume his throne. It was, however, made clear that there would be no military or other support from the British, and when it became evident that Pollock was about to leave the country the craven prince, aware that he could not keep his crown by himself, pleaded to be allowed to go with him.

This left Pollock in a quandary. He consulted the Kuzzilbashee chiefs, at that time the only stable element. He found it hard to convince them that the British were no longer interested in favouring any particular interest, but he eventually agreed that

Futteh Jung's brother, Shahpoor, should be preferred, stipulating only that the British Government 'should not be supposed to have raised him to the throne'. It had been widely rumoured that the Bala Hissar would be destroyed, but the Kuzzilbashees submitted that it should be preserved to enable the new ruler to maintain at least the appearance of royal power, arguing that the Hindoos and Arabs, who had not been party to the rebellion, were all housed in the citadel and least deserved punishment. In time Pollock said he would spare the Bala Hissar (its destruction would have been difficult), but ordered the Sappers to destroy the Grand Bazaar, where Macnaghten's mutilated body had been exhibited, and two mosques, one known contemptuously as the 'Feringhee Mosque' and decorated with European trophies. For two days the Sappers were busy with their gunpowder.

Something of this kind was inevitable, but, on balance, Pollock's decision was unfortunate. His orders against looting were not observed. 'The cry went up', wrote Major Rawlinson, 'that Cabul was given up to plunder. Both camps rushed into the city, and the consequence has been the almost total destruction of all parts of the town, except the Gholam-Khana quarter and the Bala Hissar.' Pollock had later to defend himself at some length against criticism of the soldiers' behaviour. He was not the first, nor the last, commander to reflect that his troubles did not end with success in battle.

On 12 October, while the smoke was still rising from the bazaar, Pollock started his march back to India. He took with him forty-four cannon as trophies, but the perennial difficulty of lack of carriage soon caused him to destroy them. With some magnanimity, he brought back over 2,000 natives and camp-followers of Elphinstone's army who had been found, crippled by frostbite, living as beggars in Kabul. His main column met no opposition and his men scaled the heights on either side of the passes as a matter of routine. McCaskill and Nott, travelling behind, had a harder time, and Nott lost sixty-one killed and wounded on the Huft Kotul. The fortifications at Jalalabad, built and rebuilt by Sale's force, were rased to the ground. On the march, wrote one of Pollock's officers, the band played '"Away, away to the mountain's brow", and a variety of other tunes, which had a most beautiful effect on this wild scene and showed the Khyberees that we were willing to give them due notice of our whereabouts, if they had any wish to try their luck against us.' But once again, Nott and McCaskill were harassed by skirmishers. The Afghans were having the last word.

Sickness – smallpox, dysentery and fever – took a heavy toll of the weary troops while they were resting at Peshawar, but on 19 December Pollock arrived at Ferozepore to conclude his campaign. He had shown many virtues – not all of them military – determination not to advance to Jalalabad till he was ready; outstanding generalship at the forcing of the Khyber and the battles on the way to Kabul (essentially infantry engagements, fought in the main by native troops); diplomacy in his dealings with the Kuzzilbashee chiefs; compassion in his concern for the British prisoners; and above all, a perception that the wider interests of the Government required an advance to Kabul, despite the devious hesitancy of the Governor-General. Of these, the last is the most unexpected in an officer whose service had been mostly in the field.

8

At Ferozepore elaborate arrangements had been made to mark the return of the Army of Retribution. Nicolls had brought the Army of Reserve, both to stage a ceremonial welcome and to give the Sikhs a timely reminder of British might. The Governor-General, who had issued two pompous declarations justifying his own policy and criticising that of his predecessor, arrived on 9 December to supervise the erection of a comic arch and the marshalling of a line of elephants in an avenue of triumph. But, capriciously or perversely, he had willed that the principal honours should be paid to Sale and his Jalalabad garrison. Orders had been sent that they were to be the first to march over the Sutlej bridge, and Ellenborough personally welcomed them amid suitable *feux de joie* and martial music. Much less was done for Pollock when he came in some days later. The Army of Reserve was not called to present arms and there was no gun salute. Nicolls was not alone in regretting the invidious distinction.

There followed an inevitable period of formal banquets, reviews, and general junketing, but Pollock was given no special mark of favour. He was made a GCB, but compared with the barony which Keane received for the Army of the Indus's much easier march into Afghanistan, this was scarcely enough. Pollock took it philosophically. He knew that it was because of the dispute regarding the need to advance on Kabul that he got so little acknowledgment, 'as the Government did not wish to act contrary to the opinion of the Governor-General'. He was not bitter. He thought that was how it would be.

Ellenborough might have had a sense of guilt over the ambivalent orders he had given, and a bigger man would have admitted that his policy, and his reputation, had been saved by Pollock. But that is not the way with Governors-General. Serving officers had no doubt where the merit lay. Outram can serve as a spokesman when he asked Pollock's Military Secretary to convey congratulations 'for rescuing the British name from the lowest depths of infamy'.

Some acid remarks were made about Ellenborough when Parliament debated a motion of thanks to the Governor-General and the officers concerned for the conclusion of the campaign. (The proceedings were confused by references to Pollock's famous letter of 13 May 1842; it was not made public; but its existence was known.) The Marquess of Clanricarde observed that their Lordships were being asked to thank Ellenborough for successes 'achieved contrary to his opinions and orders'. Lord John Russell doubted whether any case had been made for offering the thanks of the House of Commons. Mr Hume, the Member for Montrose, Alexander Burnes's one-time patron and an old India hand, thought Ellenborough 'did not deserve any credit', and tried unsuccessfully to have the motion deferred. We have already seen what Emily Eden thought of it (chapter 3).

The references to Pollock were warm and appreciative, though Wellington confined himself to the succinct remark that 'General Pollock, marching through the Khyber according to orders, arrived at Jalalabad'. Auckland, who spoke with some embarrassment, was generous in his mention of Pollock's 'brilliant qualities of command'. Lord John Russell gave a similar encomium. Prime Minister Peel summed it up: 'I think the House will unanimously award to General Pollock the highest distinction which a military man can receive, and record their public acknowledgment to him for his gallantry and perseverance in the face of such serious difficulties.'

Pollock's reputation at home was all that he could wish it to be, but in India he got no immediate advancement. Instead, he was sent to take charge of the Dinapore division, which he could expect in the normal course of seniority. After a brief spell when he was mainly occupied in defending himself again attacks in the Indian press – the *Agra Akhbar* and the *Bombay Times* – for alleged atrocities by his troops in Afghanistan, he succeeded Nott as Envoy at Lucknow. Next year he was appointed Military Member of the Supreme Council of India. Army circles thought this was no more than his due, and Calcutta welcomed him with an address and a subscription to endow a medal to be awarded to the best cadet at the East India Company's seminary at Addiscombe. Pollock, who had not been at Addiscombe though two of his sons were, acknowledged this as 'a lasting distinction, at once delicate and far beyond my deserts'. He served for two years on the Supreme Council before ill health compelled him to come back to England in 1846.

Two features marked the rest of his life. First, a succession of (sometimes tardy) honours were conferred on him as the British public realised they had a hero in their midst. The East India Company voted him a pension of £1,000 a year and he was made a Freeman of the City. In 1861 he became one of the first Knights Grand Cross of the new Order of the Star of India, and in 1870, when at the age of eighty-four he was the senior officer in the Royal Artillery and ranked fourth in the list of generals, he was promoted to field-marshal. The next year he joined the ranks of great military men, including the Iron Duke, to be appointed Constable of the Tower of London. Finally and belatedly, he was granted a baronetcy in March 1872.

These are the trappings. The second feature of Pollock's later years is less satisfactory. The Government, as was their custom with retired warriors, made insufficient use of his experience. In 1854 he had been happy to become one of the three Crown Directors of the East India Company, but some skulduggery marked the end of his initial two-year term. The President of the Board of Control wanted to find room for Sir Henry Rawlinson and unworthily suggested that Pollock might say he would have refused if he had been offered reappointment. He mistook his man. Pollock replied with dignity. 'I do not see why any disguise should be adopted; and as I certainly should have accepted the reappointment if it had been offered to me, I think it better for the public service, and more honourable to you and myself that the truth (whatever it is) should appear.' This riposte might serve as a model for all those who are asked to play Ministers' shabby games.

In the House, D'Israeli deplored Pollock's absence from the Court of Directors, and this may have prompted the letter which Lord Stanley, the Secretary of State, wrote when the new Council for India was being formed shortly after the Mutiny. He told Pollock very graciously that he was not being invited to serve only because of his age and the onerous nature of the duties. 'The Council', he concluded, 'I feel will lose by the omission of your name, but your inclusion in it would have added nothing to, as your absence from it can take nothing from, the reputation of a career which is already historical.'

Pollock died on 6 October 1872 and was buried with full honours in Westminster Abbey. Five of the six pall-bearers belonged to the old Bengal Artillery, and it was fitting that four of them, George Lawrence, Vincent Eyre, George MacGregor and James Alexander, should have served in Afghanistan.

Pollock's is not one of the first names that come to mind in calling the roll of the most celebrated generals, but he has some historic importance, both for his recovery of British prestige when it was at a low ebb, and for his highly professional demonstration of the art of mountain warfare. The story of the Afghan war suggests that a curious inbecility overcame many of the senior officers as soon as they crossed the Indus. Pollock was not of their number. He grasped his Afghan assignment with both hands and made a success of it. As a man, he was praised for his modesty and his unassuming nature – not the most common characteristic of Indian generals. If it is surprising that there are so few warts in his portrait, his friend Sir John Kaye, the historian of the Afghan war, can be cited. 'I never in my life knew so simple-minded a man. He was perfectly transparent. There was nothing for you to find out.'

8
The Unpatronised Soldier

I

After Pollock's resourceful activities, the career of General Nott may seem less significant. His reputation depends on his defence of Kandahar and his march to join Pollock at Kabul – both, it may be supposed, secondary roles. But he merits closer scrutiny. In an age notable for hot-tempered commanders, Nott was famous for his aggressive disposition and his vituperative comments. The question is whether he was just a noisy bluster, or whether he really deserved the eulogy of J. H. Stocqueler, who edited his letters. Stocqueler went so far as to say that Nott's career was 'rendered illustrious by the practice of virtue and the assertion of mental independence'.

William Nott was born on 20 January 1783, the second son of Charles Nott, a farmer. His early days were spent in Neath and Carmarthen, where his father rented two farms. Charles Nott was ambitious; he acquired the Ivy Bush Inn as well as becoming a mail contractor; and William may have inherited some of his 'pushiness' from him. When Nott senior rode abroad to visit his properties his wife, a fragile lady, would say plaintively, 'You can leave all the children with me except William, but pray take him with you, for I cannot manage him.' Years later a Governor-General of India and more than one of his senior generals would find that they too could not control William.

In 1797 young Nott saw the local Fencibles, Militia and Yeomanry called out to meet the abortive French invasion at Fishguard. He had heard the sound of the drum; a year later he enrolled in the Carmarthen Volunteer Corps; and thereafter it had to be a military career. A Bengal cadetship was obtained for him, and in 1800 he embarked on the East India Company's *Kent*. The voyage was as eventful as the passage to India often was in these days. An accompanying ship, the *Queen*, caught fire and her passengers were crowded on board the *Kent*, which was then boarded by a French privateer. The captives were transferred to an Arab vessel, in which, weeks later, they reached Calcutta. Nott had lost everything except for the clothes he stood up in.

He was posted to the Bengal European Regiment, but soon transferred to the 20th Native Infantry (*Baillie ka Pultun* – Baillie's Regiment) and first came to notice in 1804, when he commanded a detachment of volunteers in an expedition against the pirate tribes of Sumatra, who were to be chastised for aiding and abetting the French privateers. This was the occasion when Nott first showed that he had, as the Dutch say, very long toes on which it was all too easy to tread, and as a result he ended up in front of a court martial. It is worth taking a slightly longer look at this comical episode, of which the hero-worshipping Stocqueler says that

> It may be fairly questioned if any single event in his life reflected greater brilliancy upon his character than the emanations of his lofty spirit disclosed in the defence before the court. Let it be borne in mind that he was at this time but nineteen years of age, impetuous and imperfectly educated. The sense of wrong, however, inspired the intrepid youth with eloquence suited to the occasion and reminded the hearers of the daring temper and fiery resentment of the immortal Clive.

The Sumatran expedition was commanded by Captain John Hayes of the Bombay Marine (later the Indian Navy). The Sumatrans, whom Commodore Hayes described in his official report as 'formidable, cruel and sanguinary savages', had already repulsed an earlier expedition and thus, said Hayes, been guilty of 'an act of perfidy, cruelty and treachery (which) appears to be unparalleled in the history of the world'. The Commodore had no intention of letting his report fail of its effect through understatement.

Sailing on his mission of vengeance, Hayes called in at a number of little ports known to be frequented by the French – Port Chinco, Padang, Tappanooly, Poolo Doa, Talapan, Tooso and Anabaloo. All were empty of French, so he went on to the pirates' main base, Muckee. There, having wasted some hours in fruitless parley with a procrastinating syud – 'a deceitful treacherous priest' – he opened up with his ships' guns on the enemy's shore batteries before leading a party of seamen and infantry ashore in the ships' boats. The Sumatrans fled and victory was complete within the hour, 'a rare instance of good fortune, altogether unexpected, considering the ferocious banditti we had to contend with and dislodge from very strong positions'.

Young Nott had landed with the storming party and acquitted himself well, so much so that when Hayes re-embarked his seamen he left Nott in command of the party that remained ashore. It was now that Nott got at loggerheads with Captain George Robertson, the merchant navy captain who commanded the transport *Lord Castlereagh*, in which Nott had made the voyage to Muckee. Nott and his men were safely ensconced in one of the captured gun pits when, he says, 'a rabble of sailors, lascars & c. came running into the fort, and without saying a word to me ordered my soldiers to quit their post'. Nott told his men to stand fast, being particularly incensed to find that all the rabble wanted was a comfortable place in which to drink their grog. For this and other alleged offences Robertson, whose behaviour suggests that he had himself been sampling the grog, placed Nott under close arrest – where he remained for the next four months during the long haul back to India. When the flotilla had almost reached Calcutta, Robertson ordered him to be released, but Nott insisted upon remaining under arrest till the voyage was completed and then at once demanded a court martial. A court was convened, but while Nott was under open arrest, awaiting trial, the Governor-General, the stately Wellesley, who had been given an accurate account of events at Muckee, sent him a special invitation to a Ball at Government House and despatched an ADC to tell him privately that it was His Excellency's particular wish that the young officer should attend.

Nott conducted his own defence and because then, as years later at Kandahar, he believed in attack as the best form of defence, much of his speech consisted of a furious denunciation of his accuser –

a man totally unacquainted with military duty; a man called from a merchant vessel and raised to the command of a 50-gun ship; a man who never had a commissioned officer under his command; nay, who never had the honour even to serve with one until I had the misfortune to be placed under him . . . to receive the unofficer-like orders of a man whose ignorance of military affairs rendered him incapable of judging whether an officer did or did not do his duty.

Nott now asked the court what punishment would be inflicted on Robertson, in the event of his own acquittal.

Were he endowed with these delicate feelings peculiar to British officers, I would in that case leave him exposed to the infamy which must ever attach to an individual who prefers a groundless charge. But he is void of all sense of shame and regard to veracity; he is dead to every idea of justice, lost to all feelings of humanity . . . He continued his ill-usage to the last and seemed to triumph in his cruelty; but it was the short-lived triumph of a low, illiberal mind, uninspired by sentiment, untinctured by humanity. Most assuredly, Gentlemen, he shall not escape with impunity.

Nott easily disposed of Robertson's various charges, which turned out to be ludicrous enough. An accusation of being improperly dressed, for example, amounted to no more than having changed his sodden red tunic for a white jacket after wading ashore with the storming party. His refusal to let the gang of sailors and lascars enter the gun pit was said to be in breach of Robertson's orders, to which Nott replied that he had received no orders from Robertson, who was nowhere about, 'nor did I expect to see Captain Robertson on shore, for he kept at a wary distance during the whole of the engagement with the enemy . . . and seemed to have the greatest antipathy imaginable to the smell of the enemy's powder, nor did I see him on shore until the coast was perfectly clear.'

Robertson's behaviour had become even more eccentric when the expedition had re-embarked but still lay anchored off Muckee. Nott had been summoned over to the frigate *Bombay* by Captain Hayes, but when he was rowed back to his own ship he found an officer posted on the *Castlereagh*'s gangway with instructions to prevent his coming aboard. For good measure, Robertson had posted 'two additional sentries with orders to fire at me, with evident intentions of wilfully taking away my life'. Nott returned to the *Bombay* for the night. Next morning he returned to the *Castlereagh* and was promptly placed under arrest for having quitted the ship without Robertson's knowledge, and for being absent without leave. All of which was manifest nonsense.

Having dealt with the charges, Nott swung into an eloquent peroration.

Gentlemen, into your hands I commit my honour, which is dearer to me than life. I have suffered more from the unwarrantable, nay, inhuman conduct of the prosecutor than my wounded and indignant feelings will allow me to relate before this Court. I am conscious of my own innocence and when I consider that I am to be judged by the justice and virtue of this Honourable Court, I shall make myself perfectly easy as to the event. I demand only justice, and justice I am sure I shall have.

The Court could do not other than acquit the accused on all charges, and, in conformity with Lord Wellesley's instructions, deliver a severe public rebuke to Robertson for 'a very great abuse of the power vested in him'.

The first of Nott's abiding characteristics was already there for all to see. The child is father to the man, the subaltern to the general, and throughout his career Nott, when he conceived himself slighted or unjustly treated, would react with the same indignant ferocity with which he savaged the unhappy Robertson. Not always, however, with such favourable results.

In 1805 he took a wife, who in the course of time bore him fourteen children, of whom only five survived him. This was a tranquil period, and Nott could find nothing more exciting than the office of Superintendent of Native Pensions and Paymaster of Family Pensions, at Barrackpore. He gained his captaincy in 1814; went home on furlough in 1822; and returned to India in 1825. During the following years he served with several Native Infantry regiments and achieved some notoriety for the virulence of his opinions on two subjects which exercised the minds of Indian officers, particularly in times of peace – the relative seniority of HM's and the East India Company's officers, and the abolition of full field allowance as one of the Governor-General's economy measures.

On the first of these Nott was especially outspoken. Writing in the *Bengal Hurkaru and Chronicle* in January 1834, he warned of the danger 'if the long-tried and experienced Company's officer is to be superseded and commanded by the silly and weak scions of the aristocracy, or by the men of interest, whom the whim or caprice of the Horse Guards may send across the ocean'. Four years later he was still at it, complaining about 'the advancement of favoured mediocrity, under the blighting auspices of intrigue and deadly patronage'. It was clear that Nott was not one to suffer in silence.

2

Meanwhile, Lord Auckland's plans to invade Afghanistan were taking shape. After a summer when the regimental messes hummed with rumours, the troops selected were warned to be ready for a rendezvous at Kurnaul, a few marches from the River Sutlej. There had been no major engagements in India itself since the capture of Bhurtpore twelve years earlier, and now the prospect of action – and promotion – warmed officers' hearts. Stocqueler summed it up saying that to contend at the head of the sepoys against the European cohorts of the Czar (imagined to be the real enemy), in regions beyond the Indus, was an honour so rare and unexpected, and was fraught with so much promise of distinction and advancement, that not a soldier in the whole length and breadth of India could for a moment tolerate the idea of being left behind. From the Mussoree hills, where he was convalescing, Nott wrote to the Adjutant-General, volunteering for active service.

He was rewarded with a brigade in the Bengal Division, and soon afterwards saw his name in the Army List as a major-general. His delight in his promotion was marred by the sudden death of his wife, a subject to which he frequently returns in his letters. Before the troops could march it was learned that the siege of Herat had been lifted; the size of the British force was accordingly reduced; and much of the original impetus among the officers was lost. For a time no one knew who would be going to Afghanistan. Nott thought he would be 'thrown overboard as mere lumber', but learned that he was to go with the Bengal Army. He was to have temporary command of the 1st Division while Willoughby Cotton was to take charge of the entire force, pending the arrival of Sir John Keane.

His wife's death still lay heavily on him. 'My promotion has come too late; had it been otherwise, I perhaps might have felt gratified . . .'* The Bengal Division marched uneventfully down the bank of the Indus from Ferozepore to Roree. Nott was then ordered to take part in the diversion to discipline the Sind rulers, but the Amirs capitulated before the British got within range of Hyderabad. This was a great disappointment, since there were excellent prospects of booty if the town had been taken. But Nott was philosophical about the order to return to Roree. His spirits had improved. As he wrote to his son, 'Hurrah for the Bolan Pass and Afghanistan – for poverty, a fine climate and a gallant race of people.'

He was already apprehensive about the arrival of Keane, the ill-mannered Peninsular veteran, to assume command of the Army of the Indus. 'A Queen's officer should never command in India; whatever his talents may be, he is for a thousand reasons unfit . . . Sir John Keane's appointment was from the first a dirty job . . .' His worst fears were soon realised. As soon as he reached Quetta on 6 April, Keane regrouped the infantry divisions under Cotton and Willshire. Nott was to remain at Quetta, under the pretence of commanding the Shawl province. This was too much for him to bear. He represented that he was the only major-general of the Bengal Army present, yet he was being superseded by Willshire – 'a *mere* local major-general, but a Queen's officer'. He offered to resign command of his brigade. He had heated interviews with Keane, ending, as he wrote to his son on 9 April:

'Well, your Excellency, I trust that I have left no ill impression upon your mind. I see the whole affair; I am to be sacrificed because I happen to be senior to the Queen's officers.'

'Ill impression, Sir! I will never forget your conduct as long as I live.'

'Oh! your Excellency, since that is the case, I have only to wish you a very good evening.'

Left behind at Quetta, he wrote ironically, 'What has a Company's officer to do *but* snore? What right can forty years service give *him* to command? None, as long as the Commanders-in-Chief are appointed by the Horse Guards.'

On 19 April he appealed to the Governor-General against his supersession by Willshire. He sent triplicate copies to Auckland's headquarters, but for the time being he received no reply. From

---

*Nott, *Memoirs and Correspondence*, edited by J.H. Stocqueler, 1854

now on he nursed the canker of his disappointment. He was no less punctilious in the performance of his duties, but he was bitter, and thoroughly disillusioned.

In June, Ross Bell, the Political Officer at Shikapur, asked him for an assessment of his ability to mount an attack on the delinquent Mehrab Khan at Khelat. Nott provided the information, but he suspected that Keane would reserve the glory of reducing Khelat for a Queen's officer, and so it proved. When the victorious Army of the Indus had finished its junketing in Kabul, Willshire was ordered to withdraw to India by way of Kandahar, calling at Khelat on the way in order to punish Mehrab Khan. To rub salt in his wounded pride, Nott was told to cooperate as necessary. On 14 October he wrote to the deputy Adjutant-General at Kabul agreeing that he would provide troops, but, he added, 'I conceive myself to be senior to local Major-General Willshire, and therefore can obey no orders originating with that officer, nor can I serve under him.'

At last he received a reply to his appeal. Auckland, as he was more or less bound to do, supported Keane in his decision to prefer Willshire. Maybe it was because he thought Nott was being exceptionally tiresome that he added that if he did not like it, he could resign his command and 'return to the Company's provinces'. Nott was already packing for a return to Bengal when he received a request from the Auditor-General, demanding the repayment of 9,000 rupees which he had drawn as allowances. He had no alternative but to soldier on until the sum could be repaid. He must have thought he had not a friend in the world.

3

With the approach of winter, Nott was concerned about remaining at Quetta, where forage, supplies, and even ammunition, were inadequate. Accommodation for the troops was barely basic, and two of his regiments were weakened by illness. Fortunately he was ordered to move up to Kandahar, which thereafter became his headquarters. It was the most sensible instruction he received. Nott marched on 26 October, five days before Willshire arrived at Quetta. (Willshire subsequently stormed Khelat with gallantry and success. Mehrab Khan was killed in the fighting, but his son Nusseer Khan escaped to serve as a focus of discontent.)

Kandahar lies in a plain surrounded on three sides by bare, rocky hills whose steep slopes and jagged peaks give them a sinister appearance. The open side is to the east. The country immediately round the city is fertile with meadows, orchards and grain fields, but a few miles to the east the land again becomes barren and cheerless. The town which Nott approached was built in the form of an oblong, 2,000 yards long, 1,600 yards wide, with a circuit of 4½ miles. It was surrounded by a high, narrow mud wall, and a shallow ditch, and quartered by four principal streets, meeting in the centre under a large domed building. The streets served as open sewers, and if they were not as filthy as those at Herat, they were scarcely salubrious. The fumes were especially pungent from April to June, when daytime temperatures of 112° were recorded.

Grain, as Nott was soon to find, was dear, the natives exacting exorbitant prices when they were willing to sell. Firewood was scarce, a cause of much hardship in the winter, since the British did not relish the Afghan practice of burning human excrement. It was not an attractive place, and if morale was not to crumble the troops had to be kept busy. Nott saw that they were.

He lodged part of his division in the city, together with a brigade in the cantonment about two miles outside. In between he placed the Janbaz (local Afghan) cavalry, on whom he thought it wise to keep a close watch. From Kandahar, the valley of the Turnuk extends to Khelat-i-Ghilzye, some 80 miles away, and then to Ghuznee, a further 140 miles. Both places were to be often in Nott's thoughts.

In the spring of 1840 it became clear that disaffected Ghilzye chiefs were regrouping in the Khelat-i-Ghilzye area. Nott promptly sent out a column which inflicted heavy casualties on the enemy, but this was not enough. The place had to be taken and held. From his headquarters in Kabul, Cotton told Nott to proceed. This he did with some alacrity, but, as he expected, the chiefs fled to the hills without giving battle.

Nott earned no plaudits for flogging some of the, allegedly loyal, troops of Prince Timour who had plundered native Kandaharees. His motives were admirable, but he was acting outside his jurisdiction. The affair was exaggerated and brought to the notice of Cotton who gave Nott half-hearted support, of Macnaghten who strongly disapproved, and eventually of the Governor-General who expressed his 'great regret and displeasure'. This was more of a black mark against Nott than he realised, for Auckland, in a despatch to the Secret Committee in London, said Nott had shown himself unfit 'for duties of any very delicate nature in the existing posture of affairs in Afghanistan'. With this, and other brushes with authority in mind, Auckland did not consider Nott as a possible successor to Cotton when the latter resigned his Kabul appointment in November. Instead, under pressure from the War Office in the person of Lord FitzRoy Somerset, the future Lord Raglan, he made his disastrous choice of Elphinstone. It was just what Nott had expected. As usual, the job had gone to a Queen's officer and in this case to 'the most incompetent soldier that was to be found among the officers of the requisite rank'. This assessment was completely accurate.

On the brighter side, Nott was pleased to find that, in his absence from Kandahar, Major Rawlinson had been appointed Political Agent. From the start, relations between Rawlinson, a shrewd and far-seeing officer, and the irascible Nott were good, and their correspondence shows how level-headed Nott could be when not provoked.

Meanwhile, in the south the rebels had retaken Khelat and rallied round Nusseer Khan. On 3 September Nott was ordered to make for Quetta, which was also threatened, and then advance on Khelat. In a letter written on 29 September, complaining about the shortage of troops available for the Khelat operation, Nott was at his most outspoken about the administration in Kabul.

They drink their claret, draw large salaries, go about with a numerous rabble at their heels – all well paid by John Bull (or rather by the oppressed cultivators of the land in Hindostan) – the Calcutta treasury is drained of its rupees, and *good-natured* Lord Auckland approves and confirms all. In the meantime, all goes wrong here. We are become hated by the people, and the English name and character, which two years ago stood so high and fair, has become a bye-word. Thus it is to employ men selected by intrigue and patronage! The conduct of the *one thousand and one politicals* has ruined our cause, and bared the throat of every European in this country to the sword and knife of the revengeful Affghan and the bloody Belooch, and unless several regiments be quickly sent, not a man will be left to note the fall of his comrades. Nothing but force will ever make them submit to the hated Shah Soojah, who is certainly as great a scoundrel as ever lived.

No doubt Nott carried to excess the feud between the political branch and the rest of the army. Perhaps that is why he was ignored, although he was right.

The situation in the Quetta area was far from satisfactory. Major Clibborn had failed, with the loss of most of his equipment and baggage animals, to relieve Captain Brown who was shut up in his outpost at Kahun. Nott played his part by retaking Khelat without opposition. Although the British had been justifiably incensed to come upon the mangled body of Lieutenant Loveday, the Political Agent at Khelat – and duly hanged his assassin at Quetta – Nott steadfastly preserved the inhabitants from pillaging. But, inevitably, there were rows with the Politicals.

There is an interesting sidelight on Nott's standing with his superiors in the response to his request to go to Calcutta on leave. He was told he could go, but he must not assume he would be eligible to return to his post thereafter, nor could he be guaranteed a brigade in the provinces of India. In view of this churlish reply, it is not surprising that he decided to stay at Kandahar.

4

No great hindsight is required to see that throughout 1841 signs of the coming rebellion were increasingly apparent – to all but Macnaghten and Elphinstone at Kabul. The three Political Officers, Todd at Herat, Pottinger at Charekar, and Rawlinson at Kandahar, all warned of the growing likelihood of revolt, but their reports went unheeded. Nott fully shared Rawlinson's apprehension, and differed from him only as regards the precise nature of the military measures needed to safeguard his command. In the spring of 1841 Todd, as we have seen, had to abandon his mission to Herat (chapter 4). He had told Rawlinson he expected the Heratis to instigate an attack on Kandahar. Nott thought this improbable, but he readily agreed with Rawlinson that, to meet the danger halfway, an expedition should be mounted against the fort of Ghirisk. This was done; no effective resistance was encountered, and as a small bonus the rebel chief Akter Khan made his submission.

The Kabul command might be idle, impotent, or negligent – all adjectives that occurred to Nott – but he was determined that any disorders within his jurisdiction should be promptly punished. The fort at Khelat-i-Ghilzye was being strengthened; the rebels did not like the sight of the work in progress; Rawlinson was convinced that an attack was imminent; and Nott at once despatched a punitive column under Colonel Wymer. The enemy, about 5,000 strong, were met and defeated in pitched battle. Nott's resolution had evidently been transmitted to his junior commanders.

After a series of skirmishes in the Zemindaur area it was thought prudent to send a force to deal, once and for all, with Akter Khan who had reappeared near Ghirisk and another rebel chief, Akrum Khan. Nott mustered two regiments of Native Infantry, a regiment of Janbaz cavalry, and four guns, again under Wymer. There followed a ludicrous exchange of letters between Kabul and Nott, in which he regretted being told to stay at Kandahar and not take the field. Back came the reply from Elphinstone, professing astonishment that the general had not used his discretion to take part. Nott needed no second bidding; he set off with reinforcements; and in a series of forced marches he caught up with Wymer. But once again the chiefs' forces melted away when Nott approached. He left a detachment under Captain Anderson at Durawut, but the elusive Akter Khan escaped to the Hindu Kush.

The rebellion proper started in October when the Ghilzyes closed the passes and cut the Kabul garrison's supply route. Sale, as we know, had to retire on Jalalabad instead of returning to Kabul. The significance of this was, however, lost on Macnaghten, looking forward to his return to India on promotion, and the enfeebled Elphinstone who hoped to retire at the end of October. Ironically, Auckland had now come to think of Nott as Elphinstone's successor. On 3 September he wrote to Macnaghten: 'I think highly of him as a soldier, and apparently he has not been wanting in hearty cooperation with Major

Rawlinson, but he seems to judge with a sourness and occasionally to express himself with an indiscretion much to be regretted.' Auckland, for once, had nearly got it right. Nott was eventually ordered up to Kabul, but circumstances did not allow his belated preferment. He could not get there.

Meanwhile there were rumours, but little hard information, at Kandahar. Nott was beset with anxiety. On 1 November he wrote to his daughters:

This country is in a sad state, I mean that Caubul side. Sir William Macnaghten's mistakes and weak system begin to tell most woefully; it must be changed, or we must walk out of this part of the world. Lord Auckland should long ago have placed all powers here, civil and military, in the hands of a General officer, who could have used it humanely, honourable, but when needed, roughly, and even sternly. *Half* measures will *not* do here, among an indignant, half-civilised race, who have had a hated King forced upon them. Three years ago, I told you, there never was a man so detested as the Shah, Macnaghten's '*good* King'! It would take many years to *undo* what that man, Macnaghten, has done. How could Lord Auckland allow such a person to remain in authority here, bringing into contempt everything connected with the name of Englishman? It is horrible.

Nott was right in deploring the division of powers between Macnaghten and Elphinstone, still quaintly writing letters to each other in Kabul, and his suggestion that another, plenipotentiary general (Nott) would have done better can be overlooked.

Nott still did not know exactly what was happening in Kabul. HM's 40th Foot arrived at Kandahar as a replacement, and on 2 November he used the occasion to hold a full parade of 5,000 men. Five bands played martial airs; it was, as intended, an impressive spectacle; but Nott regretted that 'we have no ladies to look on'.

On 8 November, as planned, Colonel Maclaren set off for Hindostan with the retiring native regiments, but they had done only a single day's march when news arrived that Burnes had been murdered and Kabul was up in arms. To emphasise the acute danger, a small party under Captain Woodburn was attacked and destroyed on the way from Kandahar to the capital. On 14 November Nott received orders, which had taken eleven days in transit, to recall Maclaren's brigade and despatch it to the relief of Kabul. He did this reluctantly, knowing that the passes would be snowbound and that the brigade would take an interminable time to get to its destination. Maclaren can hardly have been encouraged to be told 'the despatch of this brigade to Kabul is none of my doing. I am compelled to defer to superior authority but in my own private opinion I am sending you all to destruction.'

Nott put precautions in hand to strengthen the Kandahar defences; the local inhabitants were disarmed; troops left at Durawut and Zemindaur were recalled; Ghirisk was strengthened; and sentries everywhere were doubled. Maclaren soon returned, beaten back by frost and snow. On 9 December Nott reported direct to Auckland: 'I am concentrating at Candahar all the troops available, where they will be ready to act, according to circumstances, to march upon Caubul, when the season will admit, or to operate in any direction the Government may think necessary.' Communication with Kabul was now severed, but Nott was in good heart, as his letters show. On 21 December, 'I caution you against evil reports from this place. I am not going to be caught sleeping as my Caubul friends were . . . I am not going to sit quiet and see the throats of my officers and men cut, owing to the folly of others.' On 27 December he described chasing the mutineers from the Janbaz corps. 'Among the killed is the Chief who cut down poor Golding in his tent; his head now adorns one of the public buildings in the city.' Afghans were keeping him on the alert, he wrote on 1 January 1842, but had not yet appeared in what he would call tangible shape. 'When they *do*, we shall give them a good licking. I fancy they do not like our state of preparation. Ah! well, they are funny fellows, and so I go to tiffin.'

Nott was soon at work clearing up his area. Reports reached him that rebel Douranees were rallying to Sufter Jung, Timour's disaffected brother, in the vicinity. Nott seized the initiative and on 12 January surprised them on the Arghandeh river, five miles to the west. He had served notice that the Kabul debacle was not going to be repeated at Kandahar.

On 31 January he learned of Macnaghten's death, and was fully alive to the implications. But he remained confident; he had sufficient supplies; and he sent encouraging messages to Craigie, in charge of Khelat-i-Ghilzye, and to Palmer at Ghuznee. On 21 February he received a missive bearing the signatures of Elphinstone and Eldred Pottinger (who had taken over Macnaghten's political role) requiring the Khelat-i-Ghilzye and Kandahar garrisons to retire to India. Rawlinson and Nott had little doubt that the letter was written under coercion, as indeed it was, and therefore invalid. A similar letter to Sale at Jalalabad met with the same response.

5

A directive from Calcutta dated 6 January 1842 gave Nott and Pollock, now starting on his way to the frontier, 'a more than usual discretion' to conduct the defence or abandonment of the positions occupied by the British forces. On 25 February Nott replied. Bearing in mind the disaster that had befallen Elphinstone's army, he assumed there was no immediate intention of withdrawing from Afghanistan – as had earlier been in mind. He had the strength to hold Kandahar indefinitely 'with a little aid from Scinde'. He had five months' grain, but no more money. Were it not for the necessity of avenging the horror of Kabul, he would have thought it wise to retire towards Quetta. As it was, however, he would await instructions.

Sufter Jung bobbed up outside the walls to call on the British to quit Kandahar, but Rawlinson gave him a spirited reply. James Outram, now Political Agent in Sind, wrote to Rawlinson from Dadhar on 16 February: 'What a noble opportunity General Nott has of earning distinction! The eyes of the world are on him. Attack the enemy on every occasion, and disabuse the opinion which now obtains ground, that the Afghans are a match for us in a fair field!'

Nicolls, the Commander-in-Chief, soon made it clear that he thought it 'of the highest importance' that Nott should maintain his position 'in concentrated strength'. Nott wrote to Outram in familiar vein:

Believe me, I never for a moment contemplated retiring without positive orders from Government; and as to treating with these people, I never will, and I hope no Englishman will think of doing so. I have now got the determination of Government to hold on by Candahar; and if an army from Caubul should come down, or any other cause arise to make me too weak to keep the field, I will enter the city and defend it as long as one stone stands upon another, and then cut my way to Quettah. But I hope yet to assert the honour of Old England in this mountain land. If there was no chance of reinforcements, I would dash at the enemy daily; but now I have a card to play, and must calmly keep my eye on the ultimate object.

It is worth recalling that this letter was written while the British were still reeling from the unparalleled destruction of 16,000 troops and camp-followers at the beginning of the year. The great 'if' – and it is impossible to avoid it – is what would have happened if Nott had been able to take charge at Kabul?

Rawlinson, with Nott's full approval, next expelled over 5,000 Afghans from the city. This was recognised, both at the time and later, as a harsh measure, but the local inhabitants were known to be in touch with the rebel Douranees. Nott believed he was in for a long siege, and he could not risk the chance of wholesale treachery, such as led to the murder of Burnes.

On 7 March, leaving about 2,500 men to protect Kandahar, Nott sallied out to teach the Douranees a lesson. Two days later the enemy were sighted. Captain Charles Ford, 42nd Native Infantry, takes up the story:*

We came near them, but they retired as we advanced. We kept on following them, but could not get to close quarters with them as they moved quicker than us, and our cavalry were not of much use, as they were half starved. We marched all day and bivouacked at night, and the next day we returned to Candahar, having had some skirmishes. On our way back we heard that the fellows had got round in the night and attacked the Herat Gate held by the 2nd N.I. They had got some wood carriers to go in the evening on pretence of getting into the city to sell their wood, and on not being allowed to enter the gate, they threw down the wood saying they would take it in the morning. The officer commanding the gate, not being suspicious, and not knowing that an enemy was in the neighbourhood, allowed them to do so. About midnight hordes of the enemy attacked the gate, trying in the first instance to set fire to the wood. The alarm was thus given and our men, being on the alert, met the enemy most gallantly, and after a long fight, repulsed them with very severe loss on their side, and with very few casualties on ours. It was evident that these fellows had been only decoying the force under General Nott, so as to get as many troops away from the town as could be, thus giving them a better chance of securing the town and driving us out, but they did not succeed.

*Captain Charles Ford, 'Memoirs', private manuscript

Nott, eager to get to grips with the main body of the rebels, which he estimated at 12,000 (6,000 mounted), had for a time been outwitted, but his defensive preparations stood the test. It is of interest that Ford, a cool, objective junior officer, makes no criticism of Nott throughout his memoirs. The worthy general may have been intemperate in dealing with his superiors, but he enjoyed the total respect of those under him.

In the same month Nott learned of reverses both to the south and the north. Brigadier England had marched with reinforcements from Dadhar on 7 March. Part of his force had arrived at Quetta on the 16th, and due to a misunderstanding that Nott's troops would meet him halfway, he moved forward without waiting for the rest of his brigade. On the 28th he came under heavy fire at Haikulzai and had to return to Quetta. Nott sent him precise orders for resuming his march. Troops would set off from Kandahar on 25 April to be at the northern end of the Kojuck pass on the morning of 1 May. It was imperative that England should reach the southern end on the same day. This time the pass was successfully traversed, and Nott was glad to welcome his colleague to Kandahar.

The news from Ghuznee was bad. The garrison was without water, and at the beginning of March Colonel Palmer was tricked into surrendering, under the belief that he had been given a safe conduct. But he was deceived. Many native troops were killed and others were sold into slavery. Palmer and the other surviving officers were kept as hostages.

On 19 April Ellenborough sent Nott an explicit order to draw off the force stationed at Khelat-i-Ghilzye, evacuate Kandahar after destroying its defences, and withdraw to Quetta till the weather would allow him to retire to Sukkur. Nott replied that he would make the necessary preparations, but added acidly that, given even a single regiment of cavalry, he could have subdued the rebels round Kandahar, and that with 'a very few additional troops from Scinde to garrison this extensive and important city', he could already have been on his way to Ghuznee and Kabul. When England arrived Nott sent off to Quetta for as many camels as could be collected. (In correspondence with the Governor-General he made much of the shortage of camels and draught animals, as an excuse for not retiring.) He also despatched the admirable Wymer to combat the 5,000 Ghilzyes said to be encamped round Khelat-i-Ghilzye. He was full of confidence. 'I never saw troops in such high trim,' he wrote to his daughters on 22 May, 'full of zeal, in high spirits – cheerful laughing dogs.' (This recalls Wellington's General Picton urging his men – 'Come on you fighting rascals. Do you want to live for ever?') Wymer reached Khelat-i-Ghilzye on 26 May, but the detachment there had already effected its own deliverance. The conditions in the fortress had been exceptionally severe; the officers spent the night watches discussing 'their scanty fare, to which hunger was an excellent sauce, and the only seasoning'. The barracks and fortifications were rased, and the entire force was back in Kandahar on 9 June.

Nott continued to purge his area of the enemy. While Wymer was away he made a strong sortie against the tribesmen who had come within a mile or so of the city and drove them across the Argandeh river. He was now strengthened by England's brigade; he kept up morale with his recent successes; and till the camels he had indented for arrived he could not evacuate Kandahar. On the debit side, Ghuznee was still in Afghan hands, and Nott was looking for orders that would enable him to advance on it.

6

Pollock had joined forces with Sale at Jalalabad, but neither he nor Nott received the signal that would let them carry the war to the enemy's strongholds at Ghuznee and Kabul. Chapter 7 has shown how tortuous was the attitude of the Governor-General. On 21 June he sent a friendly letter to Nott. 'I have read with great pleasure of the constant success of your troops in the several actions in which they are engaged . . .' but eventual withdrawal from Afghanistan was still the theme.

At the beginning of July Nott was still fretting. To his daughters, to whom he confided his innermost thoughts, he wrote, 'I am ordered not to do anything. Well, our nation is disgraced. How strange that Englishmen should be so paralysed!' But Ellenborough had at last made up his mind to authorise, subject to suitable caveats, an advance on Kabul. After no less than thirteen enunciations of his wavering policy, he realised that Pollock and Nott were in a better position to advance than they had been. He may have surmised that they would be extremely fractious, to put it no higher, if they were dragged back to India without striking a 'signal and decisive' blow against the rebels. Despatches from home also left him in no doubt that British public opinion wanted to see the Kabul massacre avenged. So, on 4 July he wrote to Nott giving him the option of withdrawing direct to Quetta and Sukkur, or of going by way of Ghuznee and Kabul. It was a strange option. So far as Nott was concerned, it gave him a choice of marching less than 100 miles to Quetta, with no enemy in the way, or taking the route via Kabul, 480 miles across hostile country and through the most formidable passes.

It is impossible to decide whether Ellenborough was generous in allowing his commanders on the spot – Pollock, to whom a similar but more explicit authority had been sent, and Nott – to decide on their course of action, or whether his letters were a masterpiece of casuistry. This question has been touched on in chapter 7, but it is tempting to return to it. A contemporary (Whig) pamphlet sneered: 'The Jesuits immortalised by Pascal might be delighted with him – Talleyrand give him a fraternal embrace, and Machiavelli, as belonging to a graver and less excitable nation, bestow on him a gracious smile of approval.' It is, however, difficult not to agree with Clanricarde's statement in Parliament: 'I defy any man, if Nott had failed in his advance, to attribute any blame to Lord Ellenborough; and if no blame could attach to him in case of failure, surely no merit should accrue to him from success.' The truth might be that Ellenborough changed his mind – never easy for those in high office – and in doing so tried to save face.

In any event, neither Pollock nor Nott, who had been in touch privately, had any hesitation what to do. Ellenborough's letter reached Kandahar on 22 July. On the 28th Nott solemnly replied that, having considered his Lordship's letter, and having looked at the difficulties and advantages of such a move, he had determined to retire a portion of his army via Ghuznee and Kabul. The remainder, including the sick and wounded, would proceed towards Sukkur under Brigadier England.

7

The decision was taken. Pollock and Nott concerted plans. To his family Nott wrote on 5 August, 'At last they have untied my hands, and mark me, the grass shall not grow under my feet.' There was some embarrassment about what to do with Prince Timour, still in Kandahar and thought to be loyal, although his father Soojah had been left behind at Kabul and murdered. After some correspondence with Ellenborough, Nott decided that Timour would be an encumbrance and sent him off to India under escort.

On 7 August Nott quitted Kandahar, which he had held for three years. The enemy were not met till the approaches to Ghuznee, where the Afghan Governor, Shamsuddin, came out with a force estimated to be about 12,000 men. Nott joined battle at Goine and gave the rebels a good hiding. Flushed with success, he reported to Ellenborough that with 'one hour more daylight' he would have eliminated the Afghan infantry. On 5 September the British were once more deployed before the walls of Ghuznee. Nott sent Wymer to clear the enemy from the heights overlooking the city and brought up his 18-pounder guns – the ones which Keane had left behind at Kandahar on his march at the head of the Army of the Indus. The enemy fled. In his despatch Nott said that he had destroyed the city (an exaggeration) and citadel of Ghuznee.

Nott had been ordered to bring back from Ghuznee the gates of the Temple of Somnath, which Sultan Baber had taken from Hindostan, as the 'just trophies' of his successful march. Ellenborough was later ridiculed for the importance he attached to the gates, whose authenticity was suspect. Nott chafed at the delay in dismantling them, and Captain Ford's comment is typical of the army's reaction.

These gates were an endless trouble to us, as they were very large and heavy, and all our bullocks were in a weak state, very sulky, and would not work. Consequently the men had in many cases to pull them along, and in the passes the work was very difficult and heavy. But we got them down, and ultimately they were deposited at either Delhi or Agra, I forget which.

There was one more engagement before Nott's column reached Kabul. On 14 and 15 September a strong Afghan force under Shamsuddin, Sultan Jan and other Afghan chiefs occupied menacing positions in the hills before Beenee Badam and Mydan, but nothing could now stop Nott. His troops dislodged the Afghans and marched on. He came within sight of Kabul on 17 September – to find that Pollock had beaten him by two days.

Pollock had encountered severe opposition from Akbar Khan on his way through the passes that had witnessed the destruction of Elphinstone's army, and it would not have been realistic to expect him to wait for his fellow general in order to make a joint entry into the city. But, as Captain Ford remarked, 'It was hard upon Nott's force as we had 28 marches to make from Candahar, whereas Pollock's had only about 15 from Peshawar, and besides we had been detained before Ghuznee, and also by getting those sandalwood gates, and also the constant fights and skirmishes we had on the way.'

Now followed the disagreeable incident mentioned in chapter 7. As soon as Nott pitched camp just outside Kabul, Pollock asked him to despatch a brigade to Bameean, to reinforce Shakespear, who was on his way to make contact with Eldred Pottinger and the British prisoners. Nott ungraciously said he would so do only under protest. He argued that his troops were weary; he had many sick and wounded; he feared sending a small detachment 'will and must be followed by deep disaster'; he himself had been very unwell . . . It does not make pleasant reading. A defect in character? As a rule, Nott was most considerate of the plight of the prisoners or those under siege. On this occasion he was still sulking because Pollock had headed him into Kabul, but he should have met the request in a more generous spirit. His troops were nearer to Bameean than Sale's brigade which was sent instead. Everyone knew that Nott had committed a *bêtise*. The loyal Ford is silent on the subject.

Pollock tried to make things right between them by visiting Nott in his tent. But, many years later, he was still puzzled by Nott's behaviour. On 7 December 1870 he wrote to Low, his biographer:

Your memoir has shown clearly that General Nott did not consider the release of the prisoners as an object of any importance even when Shakespear had secured them. General Nott expressed his belief that they and Shakespear had been carried off by the enemy.

But, anxious to do justice to his old comrade, he added:

There cannot be a doubt that General Nott was from the beginning most anxious to convince the Afghans of the inferiority of their troops when opposed to British soldiers, and he did not shrink from the opportunity when he met the enemy greatly superior in strength to himself, and beat them.

[8]

Nott did not have a happy time in Kabul. He was keen to complete his march back to Hindostan; he could not understand why Pollock – much concerned with the politics of setting up a new administration – was delaying; and he complained that his rations were running short. But Pollock was the senior commander and Nott had to wait for his decision. With the troops inactive there were inevitable complaints about looting and maltreatment of Kabulees. Nott's men in particular were accused, and the general was at his most irate when asked to comment on allegations by Gholamur Mohammed Khan, which Pollock forwarded to him, perhaps with his tongue in his cheek. After denying each charge *seriatim*, Nott continued: 'What insolence in this man, whose hands are still red with the blood of our countrymen, to dictate how and when we are to replace our troops!' In Nott's opinion, 'the writer should be instantly seized and punished for sending such a grossly false and insolent statement.'

This was something of a change from his generous views on the Afghan enemy during the early days of the British invasion, when he had thought them 'very fine-looking fellows indeed . . . I like them very much.' After a friendly conversation with one of them – 'the finest-looking fellow I have ever seen, quite the gentleman' – he added: 'I really believe that the people of Afghanistan will not give up their country without fighting for it, and I know I would not were I in their situation.' One is reminded of the young Winston Churchill in a very early speech to the House of Commons: 'If I were a Boer and fighting in the field – and if I *were* a Boer I hope I *should* be fighting in the field . . .'

Nott was annoyed about the way in which retribution was to be exacted from Kabul. After much pondering, Pollock determined to spare the Bala Hissar, but to destroy the Bazaar where the body of Macnaghten had been displayed, and on 9

October the Sappers started their work of demolition. Captain Neil has recorded that Nott was 'decidedly averse' to this decision, and most strenuously urged the propriety of rasing the citadel instead. Writing to his daughters on 7 October, Nott confirmed that, had he had his way, he would have blown up the Bala Hissar and marched off. Nott had a point, if destruction there had to be. Though difficult to demolish, the citadel, as the symbol of power, would in logic have been the proper object of retribution.

General orders issued by Ellenborough on 4 October authorised medals and, even more welcome, six months' extra *batta* for all who had taken part in the exploits under Pollock and Nott. A happy touch singled out Captain Craigie, the staunch defender of Khelat-i-Ghilzye, for special mention. Nott was to be rewarded with the desirable post of Resident at the Court of Lucknow.

The victorious army turned away from Kabul and set off on the now familiar route back through the passes, with Pollock's division leading and Nott's in the rear. This in itself was a source of irritation. Captain Ford observed coldly that Nott's division had been 'up the country for three years, and Pollock's not six months'. The Afghans were still harassing the retreating columns – as they had earlier done to Keane – but Pollock got off more lightly. Nott had some stern fighting at Huft Kotal, where the imperturbable Ford was 'hit on the forehead by a spent ball, which did not trouble me much', at Jugdulluck and at Gandamack. Some historians have suggested that Nott laid himself open to attack by being less than meticulous with his march discipline. This is unlikely; it would not be Nott's way of doing things: and Ford categorically states that 'parts of the rear always crowned the heights'. But rearguards were always more likely to be harried.

By the time Nott reached the Khyber he was upset at being deprived of his fair share of carriage cattle. At Lundi Khana his bullocks were 'quite done up', and could not drag the 18-pounders over the steep part of the pass. Nott had to give the order for the carriages to be destroyed and the guns thrown over the precipice. Then, utterly fed up, he resigned his command. Ellenborough, however, saw that this was done in a moment of pique. He sent him a mollifying letter – and an invitation to dine as soon as he crossed the Sutlej.

There was something about Ferozepore that turned the heads of Governors-General. Auckland had staged a theatrical *tumasha* to mark the start of the campaign, and Ellenborough was not to be outdone. His ceremonies were, by general consent, absurdly elaborate. As we have seen, he also seemed to discriminate against Pollock and Nott, in favour of Sale. But Nott was granted the new title of 'Envoy to the King of Oude' instead of being a mere Resident, and like Pollock he was made a GCB.

The press in India (and at home) had published allegations about the conduct of the troops while retiring from Aghanistan. Pollock and McCaskill effectively rebutted these charges, but, as might be expected, Nott's was the reply that seethed with indignation.

How am I to have patience to reply to 'whether Affghans were permitted to be wantonly treated or murdered'? Is this a proper question to put to a British officer, who has ever had the honour of his country uppermost in his mind, and deeply impressed on his heart? 'Permitted', indeed! Is it supposed that I am void of religion, that I am ignorant of what is due to that God whom I have worshipped from my childhood?

He took up duty at Lucknow; he married again; and there was some talk of his assuming command in Gwalior, should circumstances so warrant. His health began to give way; a sea trip was prescribed; and leave was granted. At the end of 1843 a ball was given in his honour at Calcutta. Replying to the toast, Nott, who described himself as an 'unpatronised soldier', could not refrain from a characteristic barb. He was confident that impartial history would inform the world 'who it was that in spite of opposition, in spite of that despair, and the inaccessible panic which pervaded India, upheld the honour of Old England, and asserted the reputation of our arms.'

In the summer of 1844 he was back in England, but he was too weak to accept the many honorific invitations that came his way, and only just managed to endure a hero's welcome by the inhabitants of Neath and Carmarthen. Granted a pension by a grateful Court of Directors, made a freeman of the city, he died on 1 January 1845.

And when they buried him the little port
Had seldom seen a costlier funeral.

Change 'port' to 'town' and what Tennyson wrote of Enoch Arden could be said of Nott's funeral at Carmarthen. The procession was led by the mayor and corporation, 'three abreast, with satin hatbands and scarfs', and behind them plodded 'Inhabitants', also three abreast. Then came twenty-six carriages, of which the last three, containing members of the family and 'the domestics of the late GENERAL NOTT' followed the hearse. Behind the last of the carriages marched veterans of the Afghan War, their Ghuznee medal ribbons covered with crepe. Bringing up the rear, appropriately enough for a maverick like Nott, were the Order of Odd Fellows and the Ivorites, whoever they may have been.

Old soldiers of the 41st lowered the coffin into the grave, cast earth upon it, and turned away in tears. A public subscription was at once opened to erect a memorial worthy of the hero. The Queen contributed £200, the East India Company and Lord Ellenborough each gave £100, and Auckland managed £30. Several houses near the Town Hall of Carmarthen were demolished to provide a proper setting in what is still called 'Nott Square', and a statue was cast from the bronze of guns captured at Gwalior. The plinth bears the simple inscription:

NOTT
BORN 20TH JANUARY 1782
DIED 1ST JANUARY 1845

'The most elaborate epitaph', says Stocqueler, 'could not have better have told the story of a life rendered brilliant by military skill, undeviating virtue and exalted patriotism.'

What Lord Keane of Cappoquin and Ghuznee thought about it all is not recorded.

Nott is far from easy to assess. (It is too facile to say he was Pollock's *alter ego*.) The *Quarterly Review* observed that 'there is a scorching vehemence in his language whenever his bile had been stirred.'* He was oversensitive about his status, and he was a very prickly thorn in the flesh of his superiors. But his junior officers

Quarterly Review, October 1846

admired him and gave many proofs of their genuine respect. There was no question of his old comrades giving three hearty British cheers on his death, as happened with another Afghan veteran – Brigadier Shelton. He got on well with Rawlinson, one of the most thoughtful officers on the Afghan scene, and he saw at an early stage the folly of the expedition across the Indus and the ineptitude of those in charge at Kabul. Certainly his defence of Kandahar was crucial, and if he had failed it would have been hard, perhaps even impossible, to reestablish the reputation of the Raj in Afghanistan.

One of his most endearing qualities was his love for his Indian troops. 'I and my *beautiful* troops are in high spirits,' he had written to Ellenborough when he set out to march from Kandahar to Kabul, and any suggestion that Elphinstone's debacle was due to the sepoys' shortcomings roused him to a wrath reminiscent of his assault on Captain Robertson nearly forty years before.

These are the men whom it has become the fashion to reflect upon, that they cannot face the Afghans! Even the Press whine forth 'the sepoys cannot cope with the Afghans. They cannot bear the cold and we want more Europeans.' *We want better officers!* I have it in my power to *prove* that the Bengal sepoys *did* bear the cold better than Europeans, that there was a greater proportion of deaths from cold among Europeans than among the sepoys, although the sepoys stood sentry, day and night, in frost and snow, while the European was snug in his barrack! . . . Not stand Afghans, indeed! One thousand sepoys, properly managed, will always beat ten thousand Afghans.

To such a one, however touchy he may have been, much may be forgiven.

He was the epitome of the general who retains all the instincts of a regimental officer. That was why he was so good in the field. He was no diplomat like Pollock, and, as he said in his report to the Government of India on his march to Khelat in 1841, 'As a military man, I always confine myself to my military duties.' In this he resembles another great Indian soldier, Field-Marshal Auchinleck. Both had lonely careers; to both recognition of their true worth came late; and both would want to be remembered in the affection of their sepoys.

9
'Our Lord Palmerston'

I

As the Chief Secretary to the Government of India, William Macnaghten was the main author of the plan to replace Dost Mahomed by Shah Soojah, the chief draftsman of the notorious Simla Manifesto by which the Calcutta Government strove to justify its policy to a sceptical audience. Then, as senior Political Officer, Envoy and Plenipotentiary at Soojah's court, he accompanied the Army of the Indus to Afghanistan to implement that policy. When everything went wrong he did his best to retrieve by diplomacy what his army commanders, the wretched Elphinstone and the churlish Shelton, proved incapable of achieving by military exertion, and in consequence was brutally murdered by the Afghans. Because of his key role, because there has always been some doubt about the exact circumstances of his death, and to some extent, because of his colourful Ulster ancestry, he merits a section to himself.

The Clan MacNaghtan, as the name was originally spelt, was an Argyllshire family of some distinction, one ancestor having reputedly fallen at Bannockburn and another at Flodden. In 1580 or thereabouts a Macnaghten (we will use the modern spelling) moved from Scotland to Ulster as land agent for the thousands of Ulster acres belonging to his Antrim kinsman, Sorley Boy Macdonnell. Before long the Macnaghtens were established on their own Ulster estates in the county, Benvarden, Beardiville and finally Dundarave, near Bushmills, which takes its name from the Macnaghtens' ancestral castle in Argyllshire and which is still the family seat today.

The first of our William Macnaghten's ancestors who calls for comment is Edmund who, in 1688, as a small boy, was carried by his mother to take shelter behind the famous walls of Derry from James 11's invading Jacobite army. In a nineteenth-century print of *The Relief of Derry* you can see him on the ramparts, still in his mother's arms, watching the Mountjoy coming up the Foyle, and sufficiently identified in the key as 'the child Macnaghten'. The child not only survived the siege but lived to the age of a hundred, by which time he had become a repulsive old man who never cut either his finger nails or his hair. For this reason, or maybe from the name of his house, Beardiville, he was known in the neighbourhood as 'Beardy'.

Beardy's nephew John was a colourful character the bizarre manner of whose death has earned him a place in the *Dictionary of National Biography*. He was a man of great charm and William Hickey, who met him in India, describes him as one of the handsomest men he ever saw, 'notwithstanding that there was a fierceness in his manner that astonished those not intimately connected with him'. He had 'a handsome person and insinuating address', but his passion for gambling kept him perpetually on the verge of bankruptcy. He consoled himself with the thought that he was heir presumptive to his uncle Edmund's ample estates and that it could not be long before he entered upon his inheritance, since old Beardy was now a childless widower of eighty. Beardy outsmarted him. Describing himself as 'revolted by the infamous career of his nephew', he remarried and proceeded to beget two sons.

John, undaunted, now decided to retrieve his fortunes by marrying an heiress and there was one ready to hand in the person of the fifteen-year-old Mary Anne Knox of Prehen, near Derry, who had a fortune in her own right of £5,000. Mary Anne, no doubt dazzled by John's charm and good looks and perhaps romantically hoping to reform the handsome rake, happily agreed and they went through a bogus form of marriage, after which she returned to her father's home. Andrew Knox knew nothing of what had happened until John Macnaghten impudently claimed that the charade amounted to an enforceable marriage contract. This was instantly repudiated by Knox. There followed a duel and a lawsuit, in which the Prerogative Court at Armagh set aside the alleged marriage contract and mulcted John in £500 damages.

Mary Anne continued to live with her father until one night John turned up outside Prehen, obviously in his cups, loudly bawling that he wanted his 'wife'. To discourage the unwelcome visitor Andrew Knox let fly with a blunderbuss from an upper window, but missed. Then, as John was loudly proclaiming his intention of abducting Mary Anne, he decided to remove his daughter to Dublin for greater safety. Macnaghten got wind of the plan and when the Knox post-chaise with an armed escort approached Strabane he was waiting behind the trees with a faithful but dim-witted henchman called Dunlop. They rode out like a pair of highwaymen to intercept the coach. There was a spirited chase along the Strabane road and the single-minded Knox again pooped off with his blunderbuss and again missed. Further shots were exchanged and Macnaghten was wounded. Mad with pain and rage, he rode up alongside the coach and fired his pistol through the window at Andrew Knox but missed. A second reckless shot mortally wounded poor little Mary Anne, who died in agony a few hours later.

Macnaghten and Dunlop were soon arrested and brought to trial at the Assizes, where, although Macnaghten tried to take all the blame on himself and pleaded for Dunlop's life, both were condemned to death. Public sympathy was now solidly behind Macnaghten, and no one was willing to help in putting up a gallows until an uncle of Mary Anne's happily agreed to do so. It was erected on the plain between Strabane and Lifford and a large crowd of sympathetic spectators assembled to witness the execution, with a strong body of troops posted round the scaffold to prevent a rescue. Macnaghten was the first to be turned off. In the hopes of a quick death he climbed to the top of the ladder and flung himself off, intending to break his neck, but it was the rope that broke and he fell to the ground half-stunned. His wellwishers broke through the cordon of soldiers, picked him up, dusted him down and urged him to escape. He thrust them impatiently aside and climbed back on to the scaffold, demanding Dunlop's rope and telling the sheriff to proceed. 'I have no intention', he said, 'of being known as Half Hanged Macnaghten.' At the second attempt the execution was successful and ever since, inevitably, he has been known as Half Hanged Macnaghten.

Old Beardy's second son, Francis, was born in 1762 and, although first cousin of Half-Hanged John, always referred to him as an uncle, not having been born until after the latter's death. In 1787 he married Letitia Dunkin, whom William Hickey describes as 'gentleness personified and altogether one of the most delightful women I ever knew'. Her husband showed some of the traits of his half-hanged cousin. Hickey thought him 'a fine high- spirited honourable young man; by nature of a violent temper but he possessed sufficient resolution not only to curb but in great measure to correct the infirmity, rarely allowing any person except such intimates as myself to see him impetuous or irascible'.

In 1788 Francis was called to the Bar in England and three years later he sailed for India, accompanied by Letitia, to practise law in Calcutta, where his father-in-law, Sir William Dunkin, was a powerful figure. His practice flourished and, having been appointed High Sheriff of Calcutta, in 1809 he became a judge of the Madras Supreme Court of Judicature, a post which carried a knighthood. (Years later, near the end of his life, this became a baronetcy.) Presently he moved to the Supreme Court of Bengal in Calcutta where he remained until his final retirement in 1825 to Ulster. Soon, afterwards he inherited the family property at Beardiville on the death of his elder brother, Edmund, and he had already been left an estate in County Armagh by his cousin Caroline Workman, whose surname he added to his own. With these acquisitions and the money he had made in India he was now a man of some wealth – and he needed to be, for Letitia had borne him seventeen children, of whom only one died young. His second son was William Hay Macnaghten who was to meet his end in Kabul at the age of forty-eight.

William was born in Calcutta in 1793 and educated at Charterhouse but not for long, for at the age of sixteen he arrived in India as a cavalry cadet in the Company's Madras army. His ability and industry, above all his gift of mastering Eastern languages (the parallel with Burnes is obvious), soon marked him out for higher things and in 1814 he was transferred to the Bengal Civil Service. On a course at Fort William College he won all the prizes, together with a public tribute from the then Governor-General, Lord Hastings, that 'there was not a language taught in the College in which he had not earned the highest distinction which the Government or the College could bestow'.

Thereafter his career proceeded smoothly upwards with almost effortless superiority. After one or two appointments on the legal side he was given charge of the Secretariat's Secret and Political Department and soon after Auckland's arrival as Governor-General he reached the heights and became Chief Secretary to the Government of India. 'A very great man in India, I can tell you', wrote Macaulay, who considered him one of the few people in Calcutta whose conversation was worth listening to. His success was fully deserved. 'There is no doubt of his personal high character and his brilliant attainments', says the *Dictionary of National Biography*; 'he was a most accomplished Orientalist and possessed an almost unique knowledge of the habits and modes of thought of the various native races of India ... an admirable secretary, unwearying and facile, and an assiduous official.' Emily Eden called him '*Our* Lord Palmerston', perhaps sarcastically but possibly in genuine admiration. She describes him as 'a dry sensible man who wears an enormous pair of blue spectacles and speaks Persian, Arabic and Hindustani rather more fluently than he does English'. James Atkinson's drawing in the National Portrait Gallery shows him in a chimney-pot hat, a sharp nose, a heavy moustache, the famous spectacles and a not very impressive chin.

The major problem that confronted the newly appointed Governor-General and the still more newly appointed Chief Secretary was that Directive from the Secret Committee in London which enjoined them to take steps to counter the spread of Russian influence in Afghanistan. We have already heard the reasons which led Macnaghten to urge upon Auckland the most hazardous and certainly the most expensive of the courses open to him, because it would mean war: the occupation of Afghanistan, the removal of Dost Mahomed and the restoration of Soojah. The debate showed Macnaghten's besetting weakness, a resentment of opposition, an obstinate refusal to listen to advice and a determination to see things as he wanted them to be rather than as they really were. The warnings of such old hands as Sir Charles Metcalfe and Mountstuart Elphinstone (a distant kinsman of the general – but a very different character) were ignored. The decision was taken, the Army of the Indus trudged off towards the Bolan Pass and with it went Macnaghten as the senior Political Officer, Envoy and Plenipotentiary at the Court of Shah Soojah. He was given more authority than seemed proper to Sir Henry Fane, Commander-in-Chief of the Army in India, who refused command of the Army of the Indus because, as he explained to Auckland, 'your instructions to Sir William Macnaghten are such as an officer of my rank could hardly submit to serve under'.

As we know, the Army of the Indus duly if ponderously accomplished its task and Soojah was restored to the throne. But, as the Duke of Wellington had laconically forecast, the real difficulties began when the military successes ended. Mountstuart Elphinstone had warned that

> no doubt you can take Candahar and set up Soojah, but for maintaining him in a poor, cold, strong and remote country among a turbulent people like the Afghans, I own it seems to me to be hopeless. If you succeed, I fear you will weaken the position against Russia. The Afghans were neutral and would have received your aid against invaders with gratitude. They will now be disaffected and glad to join any invader to drive you out. I never knew a close alliance between a civilised and an uncivilised state that did not end in mutual hatred in three years.

Macnaghten cared for none of this but reluctantly accepted that an army of occupation must be left in Afghanistan to keep Soojah in place. So, while Keane and the bulk of the Army of the Indus returned to India, a division under Nott was left at Kandahar and a 'British Kabul Force' of two brigades at Kabul, under Willoughby Cotton, who now became Commander-in-Chief for all Afghanistan. But where was this Kabul Force to be housed when winter set in? The answer was staring them in the face – the mighty citadel of the Bala Hissar itself, which had ample accommodation and which a thousand trained soldiers could have held against all Afghanistan indefinitely. Steps were already in hand to adapt it to the garrison's needs when Soojah set up a wail of protest against this affront to his prestige. Macnaghten now made one of his great mistakes, one that would have fateful consequences, and gave way to Soojah's protest. Instead of the almost impregnable Bala Hissar the British built those indefensible cantonments on the plain. Macnaghten, with his entourage of political officers, took up residence in 'the

Mission Compound', which was at the northern end of the cantonment and 'rendered the whole face of the cantonment to which it was annexed nugatory for purposes of defence'. Here he was presently joined by his wife, and other British officers' wives arrived in Kabul, as did the wives and children of the thousands of native servants who had been brought from India to minister to the needs of the sahibs and their mems.

The Macnaghtens had been married since 1823 and the marriage, though not blessed with children, seems to have been a reasonably happy one, although Macnaghten's choice seems rather surprising. His wife was Frances, daughter of John Martyn, and Emily Eden, who disliked her, delicately described her as being 'without exquisite taste or tact'; in short, she was common and vulgar, without many aitches to her name, and during her Afghan captivity she behaved with selfish arrogance. Yet she must have had something, for in the course of a long life she found three husbands. When she married Macnaghten she was already the widow of an army colonel called M'Clintock, and if it be true that he was a veterinary officer this would have been a further black mark in Emily Eden's eyes, for at that time the Veterinary Corps were quite unfairly looked down upon. After Macnaghten's death his widow married the second Marquess of Headfort. When she died in 1878 she left her valuable collection of jewels to whoever should be the holder of the Macnaghten baronetcy in 1935 (Francis's baronetcy, not William's, which died with him). Sure enough, in 1935 the Revenue, faint but pursuing, demanded payment of estate duty.

2

We return to Kabul where, as 1839 drew to a close, Macnaghten faced a multitude of problems. 'I am much fatigued', he wrote to Auckland, 'having been severely worked the whole day', and in a phrase which suggests that he was not much of a delegator, 'I have about fifty chits to answer every half hour.' Dost Mahomed was still at large and up to God knew what mischief out in the wilds and the position of Soojah and his British protectors was far from secure. The Envoy warned Auckland that the whole country from Kabul to the Oxus was up in favour of the Dost; the Kohistan, the mountainous region fifty miles north of the capital, was seething with revolt, and Kabul itself seemed to be on the verge of insurrection. He felt compelled 'to apprise your Lordship that affairs in this quarter have the worst possible appearance', quoting Willoughby Cotton who had advised him that 'the time has come for you and I to tell Lord Auckland, *totidem verbis,* that circumstances have proved incontestably that there is no Afghan army [i.e. an army loyal to Soojah], and that unless the Bengal troops are instantly strengthened we cannot hold the country'.

The picture changed miraculously for the better with the unexpected surrender of Dost Mahomed after his victory at Purwundurrah. Macnaghten treated the Dost with a chivalrous generosity which completely won the latter's heart and his mood became one of euphoric optimism, which persisted until the final disaster overwhelmed him. Again we see that streak of obstinacy, that purblind determination to see things as he wanted them to be, that resentment of opposition and criticism. The warnings of such officers as Eldred Pottinger, Sturt and Rawlinson were disregarded and they were pompously rebuked for croaking. Cotton too had joined the ranks of the optimists and when he handed over the Afghan command to Elphinstone in the spring of 1841 he fatuously assured his successor that 'you will have nothing to do here. *All is peace.*'

Macnaghten was now under great pressure from Calcutta to reduce the costs of the occupation, running at about a million and a quarter pounds a year, which Macnaghten agreed was 'certainly an awful outlay' but which could, he thought, be substantially reduced. Only two months earlier he had been asking Auckland to send him five more regiments, two of them to be European. Now, 'the whole country is as quiet as one of our Indian chiefships – and more so.' No need to keep so many troops in Afghanistan. 'Barring Herat, I am quite certain that the Shah's force would be ample, with the addition of one European regiment at Caubul and another at Candahar, to keep the entire country in order.' He got Elphinstone to agree that the Kabul garrison could be halved and that one of its two brigades, Sale's, should return to India. At the same time, he wrote, 'I am making great reductions in our political expenditure.' He proceeded to halve the annual subsidy of about £8,000 which the British had been paying to the Eastern Ghilzye tribes to protect their lines of communication back through the mountain passes to India. The Ghilzyes had scrupulously kept their bargain, and Havelock said that 'the transmission of letters to our own provinces was as regular as between Calcutta and any station in Bengal'. The Ghilzyes, incensed by what they understandably regarded as a British breach of faith, at once retaliated by beating up the next convoy of supplies coming up to Kabul and blocked the passes.

To Macnaghten this was 'very provoking to me at this juncture', as he was on the point of returning to India. His exile in Afghanistan was about to be rewarded by one of the juiciest plums in the Company's gift, the Governorship of the Bombay Presidency. And after that, what? Perhaps the Governor-Generalship itself. He would still be young enough. So he made light of the Ghilzyes' disturbance, airily dismissing them as 'kicking up a row about some deductions that have been made from their pay' and adding that 'the rascals will be well trounced for their pains' by Sale's brigade as it passed through their country on its way back to India. Then, when the passes were clear, the Macnaghtens and Lady Sale would follow, together with the decrepit Elphinstone whose urgent and genuine plea of ill health had at last been heeded by Auckland, and Nott had been ordered up from Kandahar to take over the command. Alas, the order came just too late and before Nott could move, his road to Kabul was blocked. The rising in the capital found Elphinstone still in the saddle, although only metaphorically so. On the morning of Burnes's murder the gout-ridden general mounted his horse to show willing, but the animal threw him and rolled on him.

Macnaghten's eyes were now fully opened to the futility of the generals with whom he had been supplied. Elphinstone was a dithering poltroon, seeking counsel from all and sundry and taking the advice of the last person who spoke to him. Shelton, who had succeeded Sale as second in command, was personally as brave as a bulldog but a bad-tempered thug who had already written off the British cause as hopeless and whose one thought was to get the force back to India as quickly as possible. He despised Elphinstone, not without justification, and treated him with an open insolence which the general meekly tolerated, attending Elphinstone's meetings, misleadingly called 'Councils of War', rolled up on the floor in his sleeping bag, from which requests for his opinions were answered by loud snores. His contempt for Elphinstone was equalled by his cordial dislike of Macnaghten, whom he criticised viciously. On one occasion the exasperated Mackenzie rounded on the Council of War to tell them that they were behaving like a pack of troublesome schoolboys and that this constant carping at the Envoy behind his back was disgraceful. Shelton was unabashed. 'Damn it, Mackenzie,' he snarled; 'I *will* sneer at him! I *like* to sneer at him!'

Within three days of the unavenged murder of Burnes, Elphinstone, with a garrison of 5,000 trained troops intact behind him in the cantonment and with ample supplies of food and ammunition, was urging the Envoy to consider making terms with the insurgents, while Shelton was proclaiming to all and sundry that the only hope of safety lay in immediate retreat to India. In consequence, says Eyre, 'the number of *croakers* in garrison became perfectly frightful, lugubrious looks and dismal prophecies being encountered everywhere.' Macnaghten, having failed to persuade Sale to bring his brigade back to Kabul, was reduced to writing to the latter's Political Officer, Macgregor, in despair that 'our troops are behaving like a pack of despicable cowards and there is no spirit or enterprise left among us'.

Some of the younger and bolder officers, men such as Sturt and Broadfoot, were urging that the indefensible cantonments should be abandoned and the whole force withdrawn to the Bala Hissar, there to hold out until reinforcements arrived from India. Soojah himself, who had once complained that a British garrison in the Bala Hissar would be damaging to his prestige, was now strongly in favour of this course, which was supported by Macnaghten. 'Though certainly attended by risk, it would be by far the most safe and honourable which we could adopt.' It would be strange, he thought, if with four or five regiments under command the British could not obtain fuel and provisions; they would be in a position to overawe the city and to encourage the Kuzzilbashees and other wellwishers to rally to their support.

Elphinstone, the eternal croaker, would have none of it, protesting that to convey the ammunition, sick and wounded into the citadel would be an operation of the greatest difficulty, particularly in view of 'the harassed and dispirited state of our troops'. Shelton, for once in agreement with his general, loudly asserted that a retreat to the Bala Hissar would certainly be contested and was out of the question. Thereupon Macnaghten, as he was fully entitled to do, formally requested Elphinstone to state in writing whether from a military point of view it was any longer feasible to maintain the British position in Afghanistan. In reply he was given a long catalogue of difficulties and dangers which culminated in the statement that 'it is not any longer feasible to maintain our position in this country' and urging him to negotiate for terms for a retreat. Reluctantly he set himself to seeing whether by diplomacy he could rescue anything from the shipwreck of his hopes for his Afghan policy; plainly his generals were incapable of doing so by military means.

The first round of negotiations soon broke down. The Afghans would offer no concessions while Macnaghten had no intention of abandoning Soojah, and to do so, he said, would be 'an unparalleled political atrocity . . . a cheat of the first magnitude'. He firmly rejected the proffered terms, saying that 'death was preferable to dishonour – that we put our trust in the God of battles and in His name bade them come on.' 'We shall meet, then, on the field of battle,' said a Barukzye chief. 'At all events', replied Macnaghten rather strangely, 'we shall meet at the day of judgement.'

The brief truce ended, hostilities were resumed and matters went from bad to worse. The garrison were on starvation rations and camels and surplus ponies were being slaughtered for human consumption. Snow fell daily and the sepoys, forbidden to light fires to thaw out when they came in from their tour of duty on the freezing battlements (although there was plenty of firewood in stock), were dying right and left of pneumonia. On 8 December Macnaghten again asked Elphinstone to state in writing 'whether or no I am right in considering it as your opinion that any further attempt to hold out against the enemy would merely have the effect of sacrificing both his Majesty and ourselves, and that the only alternative left is to negotiate for our safe retreat out of the country on the most favourable terms possible'. Without hesitation, almost eagerly, Elphinstone replied that 'the present situation of the troops here is such, from the want of provisions and the impractability of procuring more that no time ought to be lost in entering into negotiations for a safe retreat from the country.'

He disclaimed responsibility for the possible consequences to Soojah. 'As regards the King, I must be excused from entering upon that point of your letter ... I can only repeat that you should lose no time in entering into negotiations.' Nor was his the only signature upon this defeatist communication. 'I concur in the above opinions,' wrote Shelton. 'I also concur,' added Colonel Chambers, the senior cavalry officer. Brigadier Anquetil, who as commander of Soojah's own levies may have felt some qualms about the Shah's fate, added a qualification: '*In a military point of view* I concur in the above.'

Macnaghten was thus compelled to reopen negotiations, and now found himself confronted by an opponent more formidable and resolute than any with whom he had so far had to deal. Akbar Khan, the Dost's son, had returned from the wilds to a rapturous welcome in Kabul and had taken charge of matters with a firm hand. On 11 December, on the banks of the Kabul river, the Envoy met him and other Barukzye chiefs to whom he read out a draft treaty, written in Persian. It amounted to complete capitulation. The British Kabul Force would return to India, to be followed by the garrisons of Ghuznee, Jalalabad and Kandahar, and as soon as they had safely reached Peshawar Dost Mahomed would be allowed to return to Afghanistan. Soojah could choose between remaining in Kabul or accompanying the British, and in either event would receive a pension. There must be a general amnesty. (To this Akbar angrily objected but he was overruled by his elders.) There was always to be friendship between the British and Afghan nations. Finally, and of urgent importance, once the treaty had been agreed provisions would be supplied to the cantonments and the British would pay for them.

After about two hours of argument, conducted 'with as much calmness as could have been expected', the Afghans accepted the terms in principle. It was agreed that the British would leave Kabul within three days and that provisions would be supplied immediately. Playing the weakest of hands, it was the best that Macnaghten could do, and in an unfinished report found among his papers after his death he attempted to justify the course that he had reluctantly been forced to follow:

The whole country had risen in rebellion; our communications on all sides were cut off. We had been fighting forty days against very superior numbers, under most disadvantageous circumstances, with a deplorable loss of valuable lives, and in a day or two we must have perished from hunger, to say nothing of the advanced season of the year and the extreme cold, from the effects of which our native troops were suffering severely. I had been repeatedly apprised by the military authorities that nothing could be done with our troops; and I regret to add that desertions to the enemy were becoming of frequent occurrence... The terms I secured were the best obtainable, and the destruction of fifteen thousand human beings would little have benefited our country, whilst our government would have been almost compelled to avenge them at whatever cost.

In the event this is exactly what happened. Fifteen thousand human beings did indeed perish and Pollock's Army of Retribution had to be sent to avenge them.

Macnaghten ended optimistically, 'We shall part with the Afghans as friends, and I feel satisfied that any government which may be established hereafter will always be disposed to cultivate a good understanding with us.' And ultimately this too proved to be true. After Dost Mahomed returned to his throne, apart from a brief and unfortunate intervention in the Second Sikh War he remained a good friend to the British and refused to listen to those who urged him to go to the aid of the mutineers in 1857.

In December, 1841, however, instead of friendship there was deep distrust. The Afghan leaders, probably suspecting that the Kabul force would never leave until they were actually starving, withheld the bulk of the promised supplies and such small amounts as were sent were intercepted outside the cantonments by the Ghazis, whom Paymaster Captain Johnson described as 'the most barefaced impertinent rascals under the sun... They acknowledge no chief but act independently – they taunt and insult the whole of us. People from the town, bringing in grain or bran, are often plundered and beaten. Although our cattle and men are starving, no measures are taken by our military authorities to check all this.' The chiefs professed that they were unable to control the Ghazis and refused to interfere.

Macnaghten decided that this breach of faith by the Afghan leaders justified him in trying to outsmart them by going back on the word he had given at the conclusion of the treaty negotiations.

He was unfitted for such a dangerous game of intrigue and, as George Broadfoot said when he heard of the Envoy's murder, 'poor Macnaghten should never have left the secretary's office. He was ignorant of men, even to simplicity.' His aim was to set the Afghan leaders at loggerheads by playing off one against another, normally an easy task but now, as he complained to Macgregor, 'it is perfectly wonderful how they hang together'. In trying by bribes and promises to bring the Ghilzyes and Kuzzilbashees out in favour of Soojah and the British, while ostensibly continuing to treat with Akbar and his Barukzyes, he used as his chief go-between Mohun Lal, the late Alexander Burnes's moonshee, or secretary. Mohun Lal, himself no mean hand at intrigue, saw plainly enough the risk that Macnaghten was running and 'begged him to take very great care of himself, and do not go so often to meet Mahomed Akbar out of the cantonments, as he is the man that nobody can trust his word upon oath'. The warning was echoed by Hassan Khan, the loyal *jemadar* of Mackenzie's *jezailchis*, who 'repeatedly warned Sir William of the likelihood of a fatal termination of his hazardous interviews with the Afghan chiefs'. He argued that surely he was a better judge of the intentions of his own countrymen than Sir William could be, and that among them no dishonour was attached to what we call treachery. Macnaghten, as usual, ignored the warnings, telling Mohun Lal that 'if any portion of the Afghans wish our troops to remain in the country I shall think myself at liberty to break the engagement which I have made to go away, which engagement was made believing it to be in accordance with the wishes of the Afghan nation.'

Then came what seemed like a sudden ray of hope. On 22 December Captain Skinner, the Commissariat Officer, rode into the cantonments to dine with Macnaghten. Skinner had been trapped in Kabul at the start of the rising where he had since been detained partly as Akbar's prisoner and partly as Akbar's honoured guest. Now he presented himself to the Envoy, 'charged with a message of the most portentous nature' and accompanied by two Afghans, one of them Akbar's cousin, Sultan Jan. After remarking with a nervous laugh that he felt 'as if laden with combustibles', Skinner revealed the portentous message. Akbar, unbeknown to the other Barukzye chiefs, was now proposing a private deal with Macnaghten very different from the terms already agreed. Soojah could remain on his throne provided that Akbar became vizier and received a personal reward from the British, a lump sum of thirty lakhs of rupees and a life pension of four lakhs annually. The British might save their faces by remaining in the country for another eight months or so and then leave as if of their own free will. The Eastern Ghilzyes, said Skinner, were willing to cooperate and the bargain was to be concluded next day at a meeting outside the cantonments to which the Envoy must bring a substantial body of troops who would seize the key point of Mahmood Khan's fort and arrest old Amenoolah Khan, their inveterate enemy and a ringleader in the murder of Burnes. Sultan Jan hinted that for an extra payment the Envoy might be presented with Amenoolah's head as a token of good faith but from this suggestion Macnaghten recoiled with horror. The rest of Akbar's proposals he accepted and signed a paper in Persian to that effect.

It has always been believed that Akbar's new proposals were not serious and that it was all 'a plot' as Mackenzie said at the time; that Akbar had no intention of allowing Soojah to remain on the throne, nor to allow the British to remain for another eight months, nor yet to sacrifice Amenoolah; it is supposed that he had got wind of Mohun Lal's machinations, as he may well have done, and had devised the Skinner proposals as a test of Macnaghten's good faith. If the Envoy showed himself willing to break the promise which he had given to the assembled chiefs a day or two earlier it would prove that he was not to be trusted and Akbar would know how to act. By accepting Akbar's bogus proposals Macnaghten had damned himself. It may be so, but this explanation overlooks one significant factor, which will be mentioned shortly and which suggests a quite different explanation.

On the morning of 23 December Macnaghten told Elphinstone of the new developments and the part that the troops were to play. When the general asked about the attitude of the other Barukzye chiefs, they were not in 'the plot' said Macnaghten impatiently. When the general asked anxiously whether he did not fear treachery, 'None at all,' he snapped; 'I wish you to have two regiments and two guns got ready as speedily and quietly as possible for the capture of Mahmood Khan's fort; the rest you may leave to me.' Elphinstone continued to express doubts and

Macnaghten, his spirit still undaunted, said 'Very well; if you will at once march out the troops and meet the enemy, I will accompany you and I am sure we shall beat them.' 'Macnaghten, I can't,' wailed the general; 'the troops are not to be depended on.' So an hour later the Envoy rode out of the cantonments to his rendezvous with Akbar.

Shelton was to have accompanied him with the two regiments that were to seize the fort and arrest Amenoolah but, true to form, neither he nor his troops were ready. Impatiently Macnaghten went to the meeting accompanied only by his three aides, Lawrence, Mackenzie and Trevor, and a few chaprassis from this Mission guard. He commented bitterly to Lawrence that this slackness on the part of the military was all of a piece with every arrangement that had been left to them since the start of the insurrection. He told Lawrence that there was a risk of treachery,

but what can I do? The General has declared his inability to fight, we have no prospect of aid from any quarter, the enemy are only playing with us, not one article of the treaty have they fulfilled and I have no confidence whatever in them. The life I have led for the last six months you, Lawrence, know well; and rather than be disgraced and live it over again I would risk a hundred deaths; success will save our honour and more than make up for all risks.

There is no need to repeat the details of Macnaghten's murder, of which we have already heard from Mackenzie's eyewitness account. It ended with the Envoy dead, his head and limbs brutally cut off and paraded in triumph. (The remains were later recovered by Pollock's Army of Retribution and taken back to Calcutta for proper burial.) Mackenzie has told us how the Envoy's severed hand was bobbed up and down derisively on a pole outside the window of the fort in which he and Lawrence had been confined for their own safety. There is a Macnaghten family tradition that Lady Macnaghten's first intimation that she was a widow was when the hand was brutally thrown into her tent and that she recognised it by the ring on its finger. (The ring survived until about 1938, when it seems to have been lost.) But Lady Sale specifically tells us that it was she who had to break the news of their husbands' deaths to Lady Macnaghten and Mrs Trevor.

Uncertainty remains about who actually killed Macnaghten. The general belief, which seems to be correct, is that he was shot by Akbar himself, using a pistol presented to him as a gift of honour by Macnaghten a day or two earlier. But Akbar always protested his innocence and blamed the uncontrollable Ghazis, and on one occasion, according to both Mackenzie and Skinner, he wept for two hours to prove his innocence. Later, when Lady Macnaghten was his captive, he assured her that he would give his right arm if the deed he so much regretted could be undone. Mackenzie thought that he spoke 'in grave mockery' but Lady Sale, who says that the widow 'sate in silent sorrow before him', seems to have thought that his regrets were genuine. She also agreed with the general view that in the first instance Akbar never intended to kill the Envoy but only to kidnap him.

A report from Akbar's cousin (presumably Sultan Jan again) to an uncle at Kandahar seems to put the matter beyond doubt:—

The Sirdar at last said to the Envoy: 'Come, I must take you to the Nawab's.' The Envoy was alarmed and rose up. Akbar seized him by the hands, saying 'I cannot allow you to return to cantonments.' The Sirdar wished to carry him off alive but was unable; he then drew a double-barrelled pistol from his belt and discharged both barrels at the Envoy, after which he struck him two or three blows with his sword and the Envoy was thus killed on the spot.

One highly relevant factor seems to have been universally overlooked by those who have debated the circumstances of Macnaghten's death. Akbar's proposal, as explained to Macnaghten on his behalf by Skinner, had stipulated that the Envoy must be accompanied to the meeting by a strong body of troops, who were to seize the fort and arrest Amenoolah. Now, it is surely inconceivable, or at least most unlikely, that, kill or kidnap, Akbar would have dared to act as he did, and resort to violence if confronted by two British regiments. But how could he have foreseen that Shelton and his troops would be late on parade and fail to turn up? The inference is that Akbar must have acted on an audacious change of plan, improvised on the spur of the moment when he found that the Envoy had come without the troops that Akbar was expecting him to bring with him. It is even possible that had Shelton and his two regiments been there,

Akbar would have gone ahead with the proposals put forward by Skinner. He had much to gain by them. As Vizier he would have all power concentrated in his hands, plus a handsome subvention in rupees; there would have been no threat of an avenging British army coming from India; and Soojah could always be replaced at a later date. All this must remain speculation.

3

On his way to that last fatal meeting in the snow Macnaghten had told Lawrence that he would prefer death to dishonour and, in effect, he got both. Of the death we have already heard. Ever since he has been considered the man most to blame for the policy which led to the disaster of the First Afghan War. This is true, and he persisted with that policy in disregard of the warnings of older and wiser men. So too, in Afghanistan, he obstinately ignored warnings of impending trouble and insisted that all was peaceful when rebellion was just around the corner. Strategically the British plans at the outset did not appear all that unsound, and it is to be remembered that twice, once under Keane and again under Pollock, the British successfully invaded Afghanistan from India, a feat rarely achieved in history. But they could never have made good their footing permanently. They had failed to realise that never, never will the Afghans, 'the Spaniards of Asia', as someone called them, be reconciled to the interference and domination of a foreign power. The Russians have recently learnt the same lesson.

Macnaghten's responsibility for a misguided policy that was doomed to end in failure and withdrawal from Afghanistan is heavy. But it is not his fault that the withdrawal, when it came, took the form of a disgraceful capitulation, a shameful and chaotic retreat, and the appalling massacre of a British army. For this responsibility rests firmly on the shoulders of the generals. It was Macnaghten's misfortune, not his fault, that the moment of crisis found him saddled with such an incompetent as Elphinstone. Had Nott been in command at Kabul on the day of Burnes's murder, as he so very nearly was, the revolt would have been crushed within forty-eight hours, as the Afghans fully expected it to be. No doubt the British would have had to leave the country in the end, but under Nott, or even under 'stupid unteachable old Sale' (Sir John Fortescue's unkind description of Fighting Bob), it would have been a fighting retreat and an orderly withdrawal instead of a shambles that ended in one of the worst disasters in British military history. But the stars in their courses ordained that by a maddening mischance, a mere matter of days, it was not Nott but the useless Elphinstone who was in command at the crucial moment.

From the start of the insurrection until his death Macnaghten behaved with courage and resolution, in shining contrast to his generals. There is no reason to disagree with the verdict of the *Dictionary of National Biography*:

His courage and steadfastness during the last seven weeks of his life are beyond praise; and if acceptance of Akbar Khan's offer must be censured, it is to be recollected that he was worn out with weeks of harassing anxiety and surrounded by almost helpless colleagues; that he thought the chiefs utterly untrustworthy – as in fact they were; that there was no time to be lost in seizing any opportunity that offered of saving the troops, the women and the children, then besieged in the cantonments. His statesmanship has been judged solely by his Afghan policy, which undoubtedly was a failure, and by his reports of the state of Afghanistan, which events signally falsified. The task which was set him, that of governing the Afghan people without direct authority over them, and of preserving the seeming independence of Shah Soojah while leaving him only a power for mischief was in itself a hopeless one.

Against the strictures of Nott and the sneers of Shelton we may set the views of younger officers who worked more closely with Macnaghten and knew him better, men whose later achievements entitle their opinions to respect. They regarded him with admiration and affection, almost with love. Colin Mackenzie was 'convinced of his worth, both as a public servant and private gentleman' and George Lawrence never forgot 'the man I loved and revered as a father' and described his 'beloved and ever-to-be lamented chief' as 'above all an upright, high-minded, chivalrous gentleman, a fitting representative of the British Government from his brilliant talents, entire devotion to the honour and interest of his country and his undaunted personal courage'.

Finally, there is the resounding tribute from Sir John Kaye: 'There was but one civilian at Caubul, and he was the truest soldier in the camp.'

Sources

MANUSCRIPT SOURCES

Nicolls papers, vols. 39 and 40; papers connected with Sale's Brigade, HM 34–5, India Office Library.
Ellenborough papers PRO 30.12, Public Record Office.
Auckland papers 37690–37708, British Museum.
Broughton papers 36473, British Museum.
Captain C.W. Ford, 'Memoirs', privately owned.

OFFICIAL RECORDS

Correspondence relating to the Affairs of Persia and Affghanistan, Parliamentary Papers (PP) 1839 XL; 1840 XXXVII; 1842 XLV; 1843 XXXVII; 1859 (Session 2) XXV.
Indian Papers Collections 1–7, included in PP 1839.
India Office Records, Board's Drafts of Secret Letters and Despatches (IOR/BD); Bengal Secret Letters (IOR/SL).
Hansard.

PUBLICATIONS

Henry Pottinger, *Travels in Beloochistan and Sinde*, 1816.
Alexander Burnes, *Travels into Bokhara*, etc., 1834 (Oxford University Press edition in three vols., 1973).
Henry Havelock, *Narrative of the War in Afghanistan*, 1840.
James Outram, *Rough Notes of the Campaign in Sinde and Afghanistan*, 1840.
W.G. Osborne, *The Court and Camp of Runjeet Singh*, 1840 (OUP edition, 1973).
G.T. Vigne, *Personal Narrative of a Visit to Ghuzni, Kabul*, etc., 1840.
Alexander Burnes, *Cabool, being a personal narrative*, 1842.
Lady Sale, *Journal of the Disasters in Afghanistan*, 1843 (new edition, edited by Sir Patrick Macrory, 1969).
William Dennie, *Personal Narrative of the Campaigns in Afghanistan*, 1843.
J.H. Stocqueler, *Memorials of Afghanistan*, 1843.
Vincent Eyre, *The Military Operations at Caubul*, 1843.

India and Lord Ellenborough, unsigned pamphlet, 1844, Cambridge University Library.
G.R. Gleig, *With Sale's Brigade in Afghanistan*, 1846.
Mohun Lal, *Life of Dost Mahomed*, 1846.
Sir J.W. Kaye, *History of the War in Afghanistan*, 1851 (revised edition in three vols., 1874).
E. Buckle, *Memoirs of the Bengal Artillery*, 1852.
Sir William Nott, *Memoirs and Correspondence*, edited by J.H. Stocqueler, 1854.
Emily Eden, *Up the Country*, 1866.
J.C. Marshman, *Memoirs of Sir Henry Havelock*, 1867.
Emily Eden, *Letters from India*, 1872.
Sir George Pollock, *Life and Correspondence*, edited by C.R. Low, 1873.
Sir Henry Marion Durand, *The First Afghan War and Its Causes*, 1879.
Augustus Abbott, *The Afghan War 1838–42*, edited by C.R. Low, 1879.
Sir J.W. Kaye, *Lives of the Indian Officers*, 1880 (new edition in two vols., 1889).
The Journal of the Asiatic Society of Bengal, 1844.
Colin Mackenzie, *Storms and Sunshine of a Soldier's Life*, 1884.
William Broadfoot, *The career of Major George Broadfoot*, 1888.
Lionel Trotter, *The Earl of Auckland*, 1890.
R. Sale-Hill, 'Major-General Sir Robert Sale', *Illustrated Naval and Military Magazine*, January 1890.
H.M. Vibart, *Addiscombe: Its Heroes and Men of Note*, 1894.
Emily Eden, *Letters*, edited by Violet Dickinson, 1919.
Sir John Fortescue, *History of the British Army*, vol xii, 1927.
W.K. Fraser-Tytler, *Afghanistan, a study*, 1950.
Angus I. Macnaghten, *The Chiefs of the Clan Macnaghten and Their Descendants*, 1951.
Alfred De Vigny, *Servitude et Grandeur Militaires*, 1835, translated as *The Military Necessity* by H. Hare, 1953.
Sir Patrick Macrory, *Signal Catastrophe*, 1966.
J.A. Norris, *The First Afghan War*, 1967.
J.G. Elliott, *The Frontier*, 1968.
James Lunt, *Bokhara Burnes*, 1969.
Louis Dupree, *Afghanistan*, 1973.
Honoria Lawrence, *The Journals of Honoria Lawrence*, 1980.
Sir John Colville, *The Portrait of a General*, 1980.
G. de Gaury and H.V.F. Winstone, *The Road to Kabul*, 1981.
George Pottinger, *The Afghan Connection*, 1983.
Raleigh Trevelyan, *The Golden Oriole*, 1987.

Index

(Titles and ranks are the highest eventually reached)

Abbott, Maj-Gen Augustus, 171, 179–80
Abbott, Gen Sir James, 83, 95
Abdoolah Khan, 58–9
A'Court, William, Baron Heytesbury, 40
Addiscombe, East India Company seminary, 82, 186
Akbar Khan: commands rebel forces, 127, 255; negotiates with Macnaghten, 109, 225–8; murders Macnaghten, 109–11, 230; negotiates with Pottinger, 113; activities on British retreat, 113, 145; takes British hostages, 113, 145; sends Mackenzie as emissary to Pollock, 114–15; defeated by Sale, 148, 171; sends hostages to Bameean, 179; defeated by Pollock, 181; other mentions, 15, 43, 80, 90, 100, 116, 127, 131, 150, 161, 163, 175, 178, 232
Akter Khan, 199
Akrum Khan, 199
Ali Musjid, fort, 162, 169
Alipore jail, 70
Amenoolah Khan, 58, 182, 228, 231
Amherst, Earl: see Pitt, William
Anderson, Maj, 168
Anquetil, Brig Thomas, 56, 145, 225
Argandeh, 54, 205
Army of the Indus, 11, 53, 78, 91, 93, 219
Army of Retribution, 12, 114, 149, 151, 155, 162
Army of the Reserve, 184
Astley's Circus, 7, 121
Auckland, Earl of: see Eden, George
Avitabile, Gen Paolo de Bartolomeo, 43, 105–6, 117, 163, 167

Backhouse, Capt, 180
Bahawalpur, Nawab of, 23, 52
Bameean, 31, 54, 56, 116, 179, 208
Barukzye tribe, 13, 77, 224–5, 227

Beaconsfield, Earl of: see D'Israeli, Benjamin
Begramee, 113, 141
Bell, Ross, 195
Bentinck, Lord William Cavendish, 12, 25–6, 37, 42
Bethune, Maj-Gen Sir Henry Lindesay, 85
Bhurtpore, siege of, 157
Brown, Captain, 79, 198
Broadfoot, Maj George, 102, 104, 107–8, 115, 129, 136, 146–8, 163, 165, 171, 180, 223, 227
Broadfoot, Lt James, 126
Bryce, Dr Alexander, 144
Brydon, Dr William, 131, 147, 161
Budeeabad, 113, 149
Burmese War, 159–60
Bukkur, fortress, 23, 43, 51
Burnes, Sir Alexander: ancestry and early career, 17; sails to India, 18; promoted Adjutant, 18; transfers to Political Branch, 19; abortive Indus expedition, 19; mission to Runjeet Singh, 21–5; 'Account' published, 25; mission to Bokhara, 25; reunion with Runjeet Singh, 26; meets Dost Mahomed, 13, 28; offered command of Dost's army, 29; reaches Bokhara, 32; journeys to Meshed, 35; meets Shah of Persia at Tehrean, 37; acclaimed on return to England, 38; *Travels to Bokhara* published, 38–9; visits native Montrose, 38; expedition to Indus, 41; reaches Kabul again, 43; meets Vickovich, 45; recommends support for Dost Mahomed, 44, 46, 49; *Cabool* published, 46; advice on Afghan question, 48–9; knighted and assigned to Army of Indus, 52; negotiates with Mehrab Khan, 53; entry to Kabul with Army, 54; resident at Kabul, 56; at battle of Bameean, 56; at Purwundurrah, 127; assassination, 8,

[235]

59, 80; character, 59–60; other mentions, 20, 54, 90, 94, 107, 161, 232
Burnes, Charles, 59

Campbell, Gen Sir Archibald, 159–60
Cawnpore, 65, 69–70
Chads, Admiral Sir Henry Ducie, 103
Chambers, Col, 225
Charekar, 15, 56, 106, 108, 116, 182
Churchill, Winston, 209
Clark, Lt, 79
Clerk, Sir George Russell, 161, 175
Clibborn, Maj Thomas, 198
Cochrane, Sir John, 101
Cochrane, Mary, 101
Codrington, Lt Christopher, 102, 117
Colvin, John Russell, 12, 48, 59
Conolly, Capt Arthur, 29, 33
Conolly, Lt Edward, 126
Cotton, Gen Sir Willoughby, 51, 55, 72, 193, 219, 221
Craigie, Capt, 200, 210
Crispin, Lt, 126
Cumming, Lt James, 172

Dadhar, 202, 204
Deane, Sgt, 144
Deirg, siege of, 157
Dennie, Col William Henry, 94, 124–5, 129, 145, 148, 171
D'Israeli, Benjamin, Earl of Beaconsfield, 7, 187
Dost Mahomed Khan: hatred of Sikhs, 27, 29, 41, 43; negotiates with Burnes, 29, 46; escapes Army of the Indus, 54, 78, 125; at Purwundurrah, 56; surrenders to Macnaghten, 56, 79; exile, 56–7, 76–7; other mentions, 13, 46–7, 103, 132, 218, 221, 226
Douranee tribe, 96, 126, 201, 203
Dunkin, Letitia, 217
Dunkin, Sir William, 217
Durand, Maj-Gen Sir Henry Marion, 99, 136
Durawat area, 199, 201

East India Company, 16, 17, 38, 40, 42, 82, 186–7, 218
Eden, Hon Emily: Greville's assessment, 62; views on Auckland, 61, 79; ancestry and early career, 62; *Letters from India*, 62–3; *Up the Country* and other works, 63, 69, 91; dislike of India, 63; sails on *Jupiter*, 64; arrives at Calcutta, 64; discontent with life in India, 65; disenchantment with official balls, 69; reaction to famine, and prisoners, 70; life at Simla, 70–1, 78, 91; views on military commanders, 72–3; views on Macnaghten, 73, 218; views on Lady Macnaghten, 220; at Ferozepore durbar, 74; views on Runjeet Singh, 74–5; reaction to Afghan War, 77–80, 126; final letter from India, 80–1; other mentions, 76, 185
Eden, Hon Fanny: tiger shooting, 66; extracts from letters, 66–7
Eden, George, Earl of Auckland: offered Governor-Generalship, 63; arrives at Calcutta, 41; lengthy tour of country, 47–8; policy towards Afghanistan, 42, 46, 48; tripartite treaty, 48, 71; Simla Manifesto, 12; relations with Burnes, 46; poor choice of Generals, 73, 197; orders detachment to Karrack, 77, 90; anger at Todd leaving Herat, 98; distress at Kabul disaster, 162; efforts to release hostages, 12, 81, 172; orders to Pollock, 162, 172; praises Pollock in Parliament, 185; criticised by Nott, 200; other mentions, 11, 46, 61, 66, 195, 197, 199–200, 221
Ellenborough, Earl of: *see* Edward Law
Ellis, Sir Henry, 42, 84–5
Elphinstone, Maj-Gen William George Keith, 15, 55, 80, 107, 112–13, 128, 133, 138, 145, 149, 223, 228
Elphinstone, Mountstuart, 39, 218–9
England, Gen Sir Richard, 172, 204, 206
Eyre, Maj-Gen Sir Vincent, 138, 149, 155, 187
Eyre, Lady, 116, 150

Fane, Gen Sir Henry, 52, 72, 219
Ferozepore: Auckland's durbar, 14, 51, 72, 74–5; Ellenborough's reception, 16, 117, 152, 184, 211
Fitzgerald, William Vesey, Baron Fitzgerald and Vesey, 40
fforde, Maj Charles W. de L., 9
Ford, Capt Charles Wilbraham, 9, 203–4, 207, 210
Fraser, Capt, 126
Futteh Jung, 182
Futtehabad, 178

[236]

Gandamack, 28, 47, 114, 135–6, 179, 210
Gerard, James Gilbert, 26–7, 32, 35–6
Ghilzye tribe, 15, 27, 55, 58, 80, 107, 128, 145, 161, 180, 222, 227
Ghirisk, fort, 97, 199
Gholamur Mohammed Khan, 209
Gholaub Singh, 167, 169–70
Ghuznee, 15, 53, 78, 93, 172, 196, 200, 204, 207
Grant, Capt William, 141
Greville, Charles Cavendish Fulke, 61–2, 73

Haikulzai, 204
Hassan Khan, 227
Havelock, Maj-Gen Sir Henry, Bt, 100, 136, 147–8, 155
Haughton, Lieut-Gen John Colpoys, 108
Hayes, Capt John, 189–91
Herat: threat to, 77, 86; siege of, 77–8, 87–8, 193; Todd's mission, 94–7; other mentions, 13, 44, 94
Heytesbury, Lord: *see* William A'Court
Hislop, Gen Sir Thomas, Bt, 101
Hobhouse, John Cam, Baron Broughton de Gyfford, 39, 52
Huft Kotal, 181, 183, 210
Huish, Maj, 168
Hume, Joseph, M.P., 17, 38, 185
Hyderabad, 21, 22, 43, 48, 194

Istalif, 116, 182

Jalalabad, 11–2, 15, 56, 80, 90, 100, 106, 113, 133, 145, 149, 161, 178, 183
James, Mrs, (Lola Montez), 69
Johnson, Capt, 116, 130, 141–2, 226
Jubbar Khan, Nawab, 30
Jugdulluk, 28, 90, 113, 144, 210
Jumrood, 43

Kabul, *passim*, including: Bala Hissar citadel, 14, 43, 54, 78, 90, 133, 181–2, 209–10, 219, 223–4; British occupation, 14, 78; social life of garrison, 14, 54; British retreat, 112, 140, 161; reoccupation by Pollock, 15–6, 181; other mentions, 8, 11, 28–30, 43, 48, 161, 183, 219
Kahun, 79, 198
Kamran, Shah, 13, 44, 86–7, 89, 94–7

Kandahar, 11, 15, 44, 48, 52–3, 78, 89, 93–4, 115, 161, 172, 195–6
Karrack, 77, 90
Kaye, Sir John William, 7, 8, 99, 187, 232
Keane, Lt-Gen John, Baron Keane, 51, 78, 89, 92–3, 124–5, 193–4, 231
Kershaw, Capt, 125
Khairpur, Amir of, 23, 43, 53
Khelat, 53, 79, 195, 197, 213
Khelat-i-Ghilzye, 15, 161, 173, 196, 202, 210
Khiva, 35, 95
Khoord-Kabul pass, 105, 107, 113, 141, 179–80, 181
Khyber pass, 15, 27, 155, 162, 167, 175
Khyberee tribe, 27, 162, 167, 184
Knox, Andrew, 215–16
Knox, Mary Anne, 215–16
Kohun Dil Khan, 44
Kurnaul, 65, 69, 83, 193
Kuzzilbashee tribe, 116, 151, 181–2, 223, 227

Lake, Gen Gerard, Viscount Lake, 157
Law, Edward, Earl of Ellenborough: replaces Auckland, 80, 99; first orders to Pollock, 166; policy after Jalalabad relieved, 172; confused orders to Pollock, 12, 172–3; changes mind on hostages, 177–8; new orders to Pollock and Nott, 15, 177, 205–6; reception at Ferozepore, 16, 117, 184; self-justifying declaration, 184; criticism in Parliament, 61, 184; other mentions, 23, 40, 171, 176, 210, 213
Lawrence, Gen Sir George St Patrick, 108, 110–11, 126, 129, 135, 145, 148, 155, 187, 229, 231, 232
Lawrence, Brig-Gen Sir Henry Montogomery, 163
Lawrence, Honoria, 83, 93
Leckie, Ensign, 22
Leech, Lt Robert, 42, 44
Login, Asst Surgeon John, 95–6
Lord, Percival Baron, 42–3, 47, 126
Loveday, Lt, 198
Ludhiana, 13, 25, 49, 76, 104, 118
Lumley, Maj-Gen, 162
Lundi Khana, 170, 210

MacCaskill, Maj-Gen, 116, 162–3, 168, 182–3, 211

[237]

MacGregor, George, 129, 165–6, 176, 187, 223
Mackenzie, Lieut-Gen Colin: ancestry and early days, 101; cadet, Madras Army, 101; action in Straits of Malacca, 103; en route for Kabul, 103; views on Dost Mahomed, 105; meets Avitabile, 105; Political Assistant, Peshawar, 106; action at Khoord-Kabul, 107, 129; fighting at Kabul, 107; offers to relieve Charekar, 108; wounded at Beymaroo, 109; witnesses murder of Macnaghten, 110, 229; made hostage, 113, 145; sent as emissary by Akbar Khan, 114; returns to captivity at Tezeen, 116; second mission to Pollock, 115; released with other hostages, 116; at reduction of Istalif, 116; leave in England, 117; posted to Ludhiana, 118; Agent at Murshadabad, 118; promoted Lieut-General, 119; character and assessment, 119–20; other mentions, 8, 28, 30, 81, 123, 151, 223, 232
Mackenzie, Kenneth, 101
Mackeson, Col Frederick, 49, 106, 170, 176
Maclaren, Brig, 200–1
Macnaghten, Edmund 'Beardy', 214–15, 216
Macnaghten, Francis, 217
Macnaghten, John 'Half Hanged', 215–16
Macnaghten, Lady, 74, 220, 230
Macnaghten, Sir William Hay: early career, 217; 'Our Lord Palmerston', 218; negotiates tripartite treaty, 47–8; with Army of the Indus, 14, 51, 53; entry to Kabul, 54; disagreement with military commanders, 55, 222; accompanies Soojah to Jalalabad, 56, 106; temporary apprehension about Kabul, 221; unreal optimism at Kabul, 56, 221; ignores reports from Political Officers, 56, 221; confirmed as Governor-designate of Bombay, 57, 107, 222; negotiates with Afghan chiefs, 109, 224–6; justifies his conduct, 226; assassination, 110–11, 230; alternative theory on assassination, 230–1; character and assessment, 231–3; other mentions, 12, 44, 70, 73, 97–8, 183
McNeill, Sir John, 47–8, 77, 86–8

Mahomed Ali, 22, 26
Mahomed Shah, Persian King, 37, 84, 86
Mahomed, Sultan, governor of Peshawar, 27, 45
Mainwaring, Col (Jung-i-Bahadur), 152
Mainwaring, Ethel, 154
Mainwaring, Mrs, 150, 153
Malcolm, Sir John, 19, 21
Mamoo Khail, 180
Masson, Charles, 45–6, 49
Meerut, 65, 83, 153
Mehrab Khan, 53, 79, 195
Mein, Lt George, 144
Metcalfe, Charles Theophilus, Baron Metcalfe, 19, 64, 218
Mohun Lal, 26, 36, 58, 227
Monteith, Col Thomas, 171, 175
Montez, Lola: see Mrs James
Moorad Beg, 30–1, 47
Moorcroft, William, 31–2, 47
Moseley, Lt-Col, 168

Nasrullah Bahadur Khan, 33
Nepalese War, 158, 170
Nicolls, Lt-Gen Sir Jasper, 158, 161, 165, 172, 178, 184
Nott, Charles, 188
Nott, Maj-Gen Sir William: ancestry and early career, 188; Bengal cadetship, 188; Sumatran expedition, 189; court-martialled and acquitted, 190–2; Barrackpore appointment, 192; service with native regiments, 192; Major-General, Bengal Division, 193; with Army of the Indus, 194; detained at Quetta, 14, 194, appeals against supersession, 194; posted to Kandahar, 195; success at Khelat-i-Ghilzye, 196–9; Auckland's disapproval, 197; sorties against rebels, 198–9; views on Macnaghten, 200; strengthens Kandahar defences, 201; ignores order to withdraw, 174; sorties against Douranees, 201, 203; reinforced by England's force, 174, 204–6; evasive replies to Ellenborough, 202, 204; Khelat-i-Ghilzye relieved, 174, 177, 205; option to retire via Kabul, 177, 206; captures Ghuznee, 207; removes gates of Somnath, 207; reaches Kabul, 181, 208; declines to rescue hostages, 151, 182, 208; return march to Ferozepore, 183, 210;

[238]

'Envoy to King of Oude', 211; honoured at Calcutta, 211; funeral and statue at Carmathen, 212; character and assessment, 213; other mentions, 8, 115, 128, 172, 232
Nusser Khan, 196–7

Ochterlony, Maj-Gen Sir David, Bt, 158
Oliver, Lt-Col Thomas, 132–3, 137
Osborne, Lt W. G., 64, 75
Outram, Lieut-Gen Sir James, Bt, 92–3, 94, 155, 202

Palmer, Lt Col Thomas, 161, 172, 200, 204
Palmerston, Viscount: *see* Henry John Temple
Peel, Sir Robert, Bt, 125, 176, 185–6
Peshawar, 11, 13, 27, 41, 43, 45, 47, 117, 161
Pitt, William Earl Amherst, 21
Pollock, Field-Marshal Sir George, Bt.: ancestry and early career, 155; joins Bengal artillery, 155; Mahratta War and Bhurtpore, 156–8; Nepalese campaign, 158; Burmese War, 159–60; promoted major-general, 161; Commander, Army of Retribution, 12, 162–3; reorganises force, 164–5; orders from Ellenborough, 166; through Khyber pass to Jalalabad, 155, 167–70; receives Mackenzie as emissary, 100, 115; confused orders from Ellenborough, 173, 176; evasive reply, after consulting Nott, 174–5; obtains option to proceed via Kabul, 15, 177; advance through Gandamack to Jugdulluk, 179–80; defeats Akbar Khan at Tezeen, 180; reoccupies Kabul, 180; disagreement with Nott, 181; sends troops to rescue hostages, 116, 208; reduction of Istalif, 116; destruction of Grand Bazaar, 117, 183, 209–10; return to Ferozepore, 117, 183; appointed to Dinapore Division, 186; later honours, 186; Crown Director, East India Company, 186–7; death, 187; other mentions, 8, 184, 231
Pottinger, Maj Eldred: at siege of Herat, 13, 77, 87–8; despatches from Herat, 56, 94; leaves Herat on Todd's arrival, 95; seeks help at Charekar, 56, 108; escapes from Charekar, 108; negotiates with Akbar Khan, 15, 112–13; made hostage, 113, 145; rescued with other hostages, 116; other mentions, 116–17, 202, 221
Pottinger, Sir Henry, Bt, 19, 22, 41, 48, 51
Purwundurrah, 56, 79, 104, 125

Quetta, 14, 48, 93, 194–5, 197, 202, 206

Ramsay, Maj-Gen Hon John, 72
Rawlinson, Sir Henry Creswicke, Bt, 56, 84, 183, 186, 197, 200, 202, 213, 221
Riley, Conductor, 151
Riley, Mrs, 151
Roberts, General Sir Abraham, 56
Robertson, Captain George, 190–2, 213
Roree, 51, 194
Runjeet Singh: seizure of Peshawar, 13; tripartite treaty, 13, 47; other mentions, 23–4, 43, 74–5, 76
Russell, Lord John, Earl Russell, 185

Sale, Emily: *see* Mrs Sturt
Sale, Florentia, Lady: at Agra, 123; joins husband at Kabul, 127; daughter marries Lt Sturt, 127; *Kabul Diary* published, 1843, 130; reflections on the war, 130–4; writes to Emily Eden, 80; watches Beymaroo battle, 137; starvation in camp, 139; orders for retreat, 140; march through Khoord-Kabul, 143; taken hostage, 145; reaches Budeeabad, 149; rescued by Shakespear and husband, 116, 151; returns to England, 152; death in South Africa, 153; other mentions, 8, 179, 220
Sale, Gen Sir Robert Henry: early career, 122; India with 13th Foot, 122–3; Burmese War, 122; posted to Agra, 123; Brigade in Army of the Indus, 124; knighted for attack on Ghuznee, 125; at Purwundurrah, 56, 125–7; action against Ghilzyes, 15, 107, 129; declines order to return to Kabul, 135–7, 161; at Jalalabad, 15, 80, 113, 178; sortie against Akbar Khan, 113, 148, 171; relieved by Pollock, 110, 149, 155, 170–1; reunited with wife, 116, 151–2; parade at Ferozepore, 151; acclaimed in England, 152; in India, killed at Moodki, 152;

[239]

assessment, 152–3; other mentions, 8, 153–4, 164–5, 182, 208, 232
Sanders, Capt, 95
Shahpoor, son of Soojah, 183
Shakespear, Brig-Gen Sir Richmond Campbell, 95, 116, 151, 181, 208
Shamsuddin, governor of Ghuznee, 207
Shelton, Brig John, 55, 80, 104–5, 108, 113, 117, 133–4, 138, 213, 222–3, 230
Shikarpur, 51, 91, 195
Shinwaree district, 175
Simla, 25, 47–8, 51, 69–70, 78, 88, 91
Simla Manifesto, 12
Simonich, Count, 45
Sind, Amirs of, 21, 43, 48, 51, 53, 194
Skinner, Capt James (Skinner's Horse), 72
Skinner, Capt James ('Gentleman Jim'), 227–8, 230–1
Somerset, Lord FitzRoy James Henry, Baron Raglan, 197
Somnath, gates of, 207
Soojah-ool-Moolk, Shah, 13, 25, 48–9, 51, 55–6, 92, 106, 163, 219, 225
Stanley, Edward George, Earl of Derby, 187
Stocqueler, 188
Sturt, Lt, 127–8, 133, 140–1, 143–4, 145, 221, 223
Sturt, Mrs (née Emily Sale), 127, 141, 143–4, 145, 150, 152–3
Stoddart, Lt-Col Charles, 29, 33, 86
Suddoyze tribe, 13
Sufter Jung, 202
Sukkur, 204, 206
Sultan Jan, 207, 230

Taj Mahomed, 58, 140
Taylor, Lt-Col, 168, 180
Temple, Henry John, Viscount Palmerston, 7, 13, 86
Tezeen, 107, 113, 115, 149, 155, 179
Thain, Maj William, 144
Thomson, Lt-Col George, 124
Timour, Prince, 196, 207

Todd, Maj Elliott D'Arcy: early career, 82; Persian assignment, 83; Legation secretary, Teheran, 86; at siege of Herat, 86; mediates with Shah Kamran, 87; journey to Simla, 88; reflections on Herat and Ghuznee, 88–9; assistant to Macnaghten, 91; en route to Kabul, 91–4; sent on mission to Herat, 94; difficulties with Yar Mahomed, 94–7; closes Herat mission, 97; dismissed from Political service, 9, 98; unsuccessful appeal, 99; killed at Ferozshuhur, 99; other mention, 9
Torrens, Henry Whitelock, 12, 48, 70
Trevor, Capt Robert, 108, 110
Trevor, Mrs, 149
Troup, Capt, 109, 116, 142, 178, 229

Vickovich, Capt, 45–6

Wade, Col Sir Claude Martine, 24, 49, 74
Wade, Maj Hamlet, 121
Wade, Sgt, 151
Waghorn, Lt Thomas, 65
Waller, Mrs, 150
Wellesley, Arthur, Duke of Wellington, 177, 185, 219
Wellesley, Richard Colley, Marquess Wellesley, 190
Wellington, Duke of: see Arthur Wellesley
Wild, Brig, 161–2, 168–9
William IV, King, 38–9
Williams, Maj-Gen Sir Edmund, 162
Willshire, Gen Sir Thomas, Bt., 79, 194–5
Wood, Lt John, 42
Woodburn, Capt, 200
Wolff, Joseph, 28–9
Wymer, Col, 174, 199, 205

Yar Mahomed Khan, 36, 44, 94–8

Zemaun, Shah, 25, 104
Zemindaur area, 199, 201
Zurmat, 106